SEVEN WAYS

OF LOOKING AT

POINTLESS SUFFERING

SEVEN WAYS

OF LOOKING AT

POINTLESS SUFFERING

*What Philosophy Can Tell Us about
the Hardest Mystery of All*

SCOTT SAMUELSON

The University of Chicago Press
Chicago and London

The University of Chicago Press, Chicago 60637
The University of Chicago Press, Ltd., London
© 2018 by The University of Chicago
All rights reserved. No part of this book may be used or reproduced in any manner whatsoever without written permission, except in the case of brief quotations in critical articles and reviews. For more information, contact the University of Chicago Press, 1427 E. 60th St., Chicago, IL 60637.
Published 2018
Printed in the United States of America

27 26 25 24 23 22 21 20 19 18   1 2 3 4 5

ISBN-13: 978-0-226-40708-1 (cloth)
ISBN-13: 978-0-226-40711-1 (e-book)
DOI: https://doi.org/10.7208/chicago/9780226407111.001.0001

Library of Congress Cataloging-in-Publication Data

Names: Samuelson, Scott, author.
Title: Seven ways of looking at pointless suffering : what philosophy can tell us about the hardest mystery of all / Scott Samuelson.
Description: Chicago ; London : The University of Chicago Press, 2018. | Includes bibliographical references and index.
Identifiers: LCCN 2017038262 | ISBN 9780226407081 (cloth : alk. paper) | ISBN 9780226407111 (e-book)
Subjects: LCSH: Suffering. | Pain. | Suffering—Religious aspects.
Classification: LCC BF789.S8 S265 2018 | DDC 204/.42—dc23
LC record available at https://lccn.loc.gov/2017038262

♾ This paper meets the requirements of ANSI/NISO Z39.48-1992 (Permanence of Paper).

It began to seem that one would have to hold in the mind forever two ideas which seemed to be in opposition. The first idea was acceptance, the acceptance, totally without rancor, of life as it is, and men as they are: in the light of this idea, it goes without saying that injustice is a commonplace. But this did not mean that one could be complacent, for the second idea was of equal power: that one must never, in one's own life, accept these injustices as commonplace but must fight them with all one's strength. This fight begins, however, in the heart and it now had been laid to my charge to keep my own heart free of hatred and despair.

JAMES BALDWIN

CONTENTS

THE PARADOX OF

POINTLESS SUFFERING

Man from *his* vantage point can see Reality only in contradictions. And the more faithful he is to his perception of the contradiction, the more he is open to what there is for him to know.

ALFRED KAZIN

I think of my pal Matt Kaufman, a curly-blond fifth-grader, full of possibility and mischief, who was popping wheelies on the edge of town when a high-schooler came whizzing over the hill in a car. On impact Matt's body vaulted through the air, landed on the nearby playground, and ballooned to what seemed like twice its original size. Since school had just been let out, a young audience witnessed the scene and waited beside his immobile bleeding body for the med-evac. He died on the way to the hospital. I was in fourth grade at the time. My mom confirmed my friend's death as I was playing anxiously on the stairs with my action figures. I felt the question "Why?" creep through my whole body. My toys fell and lay in awkward poses on the steps.

The suffering of children sharply illustrates the gap between how the world is and how we think it should be. You need the imaginative gymnastics of past lives or inherited sin to see anything remotely like justice in most of it. Just think: somewhere right now there are children cringing at the screams of their parents, children begging for food, children walking in fear to school, children coughing up blood, children being born with painful deformities, children dying. Somewhere right now another Matt Kaufman is writhing in pain. According to the National Center for Victims of Crime, one in five girls and one in twenty boys are the victims of sexual abuse: so it's too painful to continue to imagine what children are going through somewhere right now.

Fleeing to the adult world isn't much help. Every minute some of us are being raped. Every minute some of us are dying before we had time to bring to fruition our potential. Every second, every fraction of a second, we're enduring pains that we did not choose and that serve no apparent purpose: madness, injustice, loneliness, grief, terrorism, torture, tyranny, boredom, depression, humiliation, oppression, despair, unrequited love, and—for that matter—requited love. In *The Anatomy of Melancholy* Robert Burton observes,

> I can show no state of life to give content. The like you may say of all ages: children live in a perpetual slavery, still under that tyrannical government of masters: young men, and of riper years, subject to labour, and a thousand cares of the world . . . the old are full of aches in their bones, cramps and convulsions, *silicernia* [a funeral feast], dull of hearing, weak-sighted, hoary, wrinkled, harsh, so much altered as that they cannot know their own face in a glass, a burden to themselves and others; after seventy years, "all is sorrow" (as David hath it), they do not live, but linger.[1]

As Burton's four-century-old book reminds us, pointless suffering was hardly invented yesterday. Our ancestors, on top of the usual miseries, from which they were anything but immune, had to cope with such horrors as lynching, the plague, Hiroshima, the Thirty Years' War, beheading, the Middle Passage, and Treblinka. They commonly suffered and died from polio, yellow fever, hookworm, malaria, measles, mumps, rubella, and smallpox. Has the eradication of these diseases, insofar as they have been eradicated, caused a corresponding loss of something right and good? In other words, would anyone of sound mind wish that we could reintroduce them more generally? What does that say about the world we live in?

What about animals? Arthur Schopenhauer observes, "The pleasure in this world, it has been said, outweighs the pain. . . . If the reader wishes to see shortly whether this statement is true, let him compare the respective feelings of two animals, one of which is engaged in eating the other."[2] The price of all life is death, and it seems that any animal with a nervous system, from the lowest crustacean all the way up the evolutionary ladder, experiences physical pain. Charles Darwin confesses in a letter, "I cannot persuade myself that a beneficent & omnipotent God would have designedly created the *Ichneumonidæ* with the express intention of their feeding within the living bodies of caterpillars, or that a cat should play with mice."[3] The ichneumon wasp lays its eggs inside a living caterpillar. When the eggs hatch, the baby wasps eat their way out. A zoologist observes, "It is better for the genes of Darwin's ichneumon wasp that the caterpillar should be alive, and therefore fresh, when it is eaten, no matter what the cost in suffering."[4] Perhaps the best part of C. S. Lewis's *The Problem of Pain* is the penultimate chapter (right before "Heaven"), entitled "Animal Pain," where he admits that his careful theological explanation of human suffering doesn't really work for our fellow creatures. His ultimate answer to why animals suffer without the ability to make sense of and transcend their suffering? "We don't know."[5]

* * * * * * * * * * *

The etymological root of the word "evil," according to the compilers of the *Oxford English Dictionary*, means primarily "exceeding due measure" or "overstepping proper limits." Because suffering is how we register such overstepping, "evil" has traditionally been used to refer to anything that does harm. To pluck just two examples from the *OED*'s several pages of charming illustrations: Caxton in 1480 complains of "the yelow euyll that is called the Jaundis," and in 1655 Culpepper warns, "In a great Headach it is evil to have the outward parts cold."

As much as we lament jaundice and migraines, especially when our feet are cold, we're a lot less likely nowadays to call them "evil," at least not in earnest. For us, "evil" refers mostly to purposeful infliction of needless suffering. Evil is what Nazi-types do, and the Devil of our mythology is Hitler. An interesting transformation takes place in modernity, which we'll soon discuss, whereby the concept of evil is cordoned off from natural events and circumscribed to the sphere of human action. Jaundice and earthquakes are unfortunate, not evil. Nature just occurs. Shit happens, as we modernists say.

To return us to the more comprehensive idea of evil, one that encompasses human wrongdoing as well as death and misery, I've chosen to use the phrase "pointless suffering." I admit that the phrase is tricky, for this book is largely about how people have found a point in suffering: how artists have found in it the inspiration for our essential works of art, how spiritual seekers have found in it a road to God, how philosophers have found in it atonement with nature and training for our fundamental virtues. But I think the phrase "pointless suffering" works for two reasons.

First, I believe that a certain amount of suffering must appear pointless, at least on first glance. Though we all recognize that some rough spells in life are good things, it's impossible to be a human and not to encounter certain sharp difficulties that just don't seem to fit into any normal scheme of goodness or meaning. Maybe it's our task to see through the appearance of suffering's pointlessness to its ultimate resolution. Or maybe we're to endure its apparent pointlessness with a faith that a rationale exists even though it's hidden from our minds. Then again, maybe the suffering really is pointless in a cosmic sense, and we must figure out some other way of coping—or not. In any case, pointless suffering is where the journey of meaning-making begins.

Second, in the great philosophies of suffering, there's always a paradox, an aching ambivalence, at the heart of our experience of suffering. Yes, suffering is at the core of meaning-making, but some chunk of misery stubbornly opposes even our best efforts at acceptance and understanding. Thus, there's a strong air of mystery to the main concepts that we use to confront evil: God, nature, humanity, art. Just as these concepts and the practices associated with them help us to make sense of and live with suffering, they also contain a lightning-strike of the sublime, something that astonishes our understanding, something that makes them difficult for a contradiction-averse rationality to process. Perhaps certain instances of suffering, after being processed by the active human mind, are better called "undeserved" ("meaningful but undeserved") than "pointless" ("meaningful up to a point and yet still pointless at some level"). But I think it's good to emphasize that our most important cases of suffering, no matter how meaningful, remain in dialogue with pointlessness. For instance, my last chapter shows how the blues is, in part, an attempt to come to terms with slavery and its legacy. The affliction of slavery attains meaning, powerful meaning, in the blues, but it's still *pointless*—not just wrong, but mind-blowingly wrong. When we discover a point in suffering, our hard-fought understanding always contains an element of what we don't understand and can't accept—at least from our human vantage. Pointless suffering is where the journey of meaning-making begins, and it's where it ends as well.

* * * * * * * * * * *

Roughly speaking, there are two important human responses toward suffering, which I'll call the fix-it and the face-it attitudes.

Well, actually there are three, if we don't forget to include the forget-about-it attitude. The forget-about-it attitude may not be philosophically significant, but it's probably the most common. As Blaise Pascal observes in his deadpan manner, "Being unable to cure death, wretchedness and ignorance, men have decided, in order to be happy, not to think about such things."[6] When our friend falls victim to an unexpected stroke, when our community is struck by a terrible crime or natural disaster, when we're diagnosed with some awful malady, it somehow shocks us. Doesn't the fact of our being surprised prove that we live in obliviousness to our surrounding suffering? Mostly we muddle through until our semi-blissful forgetfulness is restored. Sometimes we don't, and our name is added to the list of casualties. In the Hindu epic the *Mahabharata*, the wise hero Yudhisthira must answer a riddle posed by a divine crane, "Of all the world's wonders, what's the most wonderful?" His answer: "That people, though they see others dying all around them, never believe that they're going to die."[7]

In a viral clip from Conan O'Brien's late-night show, our great contemporary Pascalian, the comedian Louis C.K., claims that the main reason we're constantly dinking around on our cell phones is that it's hard to be alone with existence. "Life is tremendously sad, just by being in it," he says. Underneath all our plans and projects is "that Forever Empty . . . that knowledge that it's all for nothing and you're alone."[8] Rather than confront our anxiety at the sadness, we fidget on our tools of infinite distraction. The comedian's observation is perfectly in line with the wisdom of Pascal, who says, "The fact is that the present usually hurts. We thrust it out of sight because it distresses us."[9]

Letting your troubles dissolve in a few drinks, or an exchange of text messages, or whatever your rituals of checking out happen to be, can be as coercive as the need to sleep. To forget about problems that pale in comparison to the really bad deals of the universe, I once watched, rarely getting out of my pajamas, the lion's share of the Little League World Series on television. Far be it from me to disparage the occasional forget-about-it attitude! But ultimately to forget about suffering is to lose our humanity. Louis C.K. goes on to relate an incident, sparked by hearing Bruce Springsteen's "Jungleland" on the radio, when rather than flee his anxiety he stood in its way and let it wash over him. He exclaims, "It was beautiful! Sadness is poetic!

You're lucky to live sad moments! . . . When you let yourself feel sad, your body has antibodies . . . it has happiness that comes rushing in to meet the sadness!" If we never turn off ESPN2 or power down our phones, this one-of-a-kind, tragic, lovely life slips through our fingers. Plants grow and die; animals suffer and ameliorate their pains according to instinct; but we humans must find a way to relate to suffering using our rationality—which brings us back to the fix-it and the face-it attitudes.

When we adopt the fix-it attitude, suffering appears as a grievance to be resolved: we'd be better off if we could minimize, even eliminate, it. Thanks to our fix-it energies, we've used our creative fire to forge all sorts of inventions to better our lives. A large portion of civilization arises out of the fix-it attitude, including a fair amount of science and politics, and nearly all technology.

But there's also the face-it attitude, which characterizes much of religion, art, and the humanities, as well as a certain significant portion of science and politics. This attitude regards nature as something that we must suffer to become who we're meant to be. Confrontations with pain, misery, and death are necessary initiations into a deeper way of being. With our face-it energies, we go through tough times, often not wanting to deal with them at first, and they become a crucial part of our story. Our spiritual antibodies rush in. We tingle with pleasure in contemplating the universe as it is, not as we wish it were. We stand up for liberty, a volatile source of potential suffering, to live together in dignity. At our most inspired, we transform unjust suffering into profound art, culture, and knowledge, and elevate death and injustice into glittering places in visions of beauty, adventure, and salvation.

The fix-it and the face-it attitudes are basic to the human condition. On the one hand, we'll always fight against death, injustice, and misery; on the other hand, we ultimately must accept them as the conditions on which the wonder of existence is given to us. The overarching point I explore in this book is that to be human is to embody a huge paradox: the paradox of having simultaneously to accept and to reject suffering; the paradox of both facing and fixing the same troubles.

Simply to face suffering while renouncing any effort to fix it is heartless: we shirk our wonderful power to better our condition; we become complacent, personally and politically, in the face of injustice. But simply to fix suffering without any effort to face it is shallow: we lose our ability to enrich ourselves through the difficulties, tragedies, and vulnerabilities at the heart of all meaningful things, at the heart of life itself; moreover, we run the risk of unleashing tyranny by refusing to accept freedom in ourselves or uncertainty in the world. What's the balance between fixing and facing suffering? There's no perfect formula. This book is my attempt to examine how our most penetrating thinkers explore and embody the immense paradox at the center of human life.

* * * * * * * * * * *

Part of why I've written this book is that our current age seems to have lost its way with suffering. For several centuries we've been slowly but surely forgetting the mystery itself. In short, our problem is that we've begun to see suffering primarily in fix-it terms. Because the medicines, machines, and political systems that we've traditionally used to combat and correct nature have never been terribly effective, the sheer magnitude of death and suffering has long made the face-it attitude necessary. We've spent so much time having to grin and bear nature, the checks on our fix-it energies have never had to be very strong. Prior to modernity the most serious ways of confronting suffering involved the face-it tools of religion. Our power to modify nature, though it's still limited in what it can accomplish, has suddenly been given a long leash. For the last few centuries our radical technological innovations have changed the terms of our relationship to the world. Long accustomed to taking nature for granted and regarding the sphere of history as the sole space of action, we've now begun to "act into nature," in the words of Hannah Arendt.[10] In Auschwitz and Hiroshima, to take the most dramatic examples, we acted not just as humans but also as gods; in fact, what we did outstripped even the most heinous natural disasters that were once described, in horror and awe, as "acts of God." What's the Lisbon earthquake next to the Holocaust? What's Ebola compared to the atom bomb? We now negotiate the terms of birth and death through biotechnologies, play at omniscience with mass surveillance, design "smart" technologies, and spend our time navigating the virtual worlds that we've created for our amusement. Our power is such that we've begun, however irrationally, to believe that we can—or soon will be able to—dictate the terms of suffering. When we can't fix a problem, our impulse is to ignore it, lock it away, or even destroy those who have it. A surprising number of people in the developed world now go through life not just hoping but seriously believing that they'll be able to acquire and enjoy the uninterrupted goods of a comfortable existence, overcome their diseases and pains, and cruise into a ripe old age. How does their luxurious retirement end? Well, let's not worry about that right now: the Little League World Series is on.

Our increasing commitment to fix-it techniques makes it difficult for many people to accept the face-it basis of institutions like religion, institutions that were once pretty much all we had to confront the onslaught of suffering. Now, when religion is more than an hour-a-week social-club commitment, it's often seen as an impediment to technoscience. According to certain prominent atheists, God is a fairy tale standing in the way of progress. Consider the famous theological conundrum called "the problem of evil," the difficulty of trying to reconcile a belief in an all-good, all-powerful God with the abundance of pointless suffering in creation. Throughout its long history, the problem of evil wasn't so much a problem as it was a fundamental mystery to be wrestled with. Theologians, philosophers, poets, and everyday believers conceived of the world not just as a site of creation but as a site of salvation. They saw in the mysterious personality behind the universe both fix-it and face-it characteristics. But a new way of thinking about suffering was invented in the eighteenth century and has gained steam through the subsequent centuries. Ethics has been increasingly conceived—explicitly by philosophers and often unconsciously by the populace at large—as utilitarianism, which basically holds that suffering is flat-out bad and that the amelioration of pain and death is the basis for all sound moral reasoning. Thus, the problem of evil has been widely used as a clear-cut reason not to believe in God at all, for it seems absurd that a nice, all-powerful biotechnologist would be responsible for a world where children die of cancer. This conception of God as biotechnologist shows just how hard it is for us to imagine the world as anything but a utilitarian construction site.

While I'm grateful for many achievements of modernity's fix-it quest, our society's relationship to suffering can often be unhealthy. We have a tendency to regard grief, old age, bad memories, and even death as foreign invaders of our souls; thus, medicine is inclined to anesthetize all trying conditions, keep us young, and put off our deaths beyond even the point when our lives are meaningful. We have a tendency to envision happiness as the ability to buy stuff and the identities marketers have associated with that stuff; thus, work is conceived as an evil, a treadmill for the sake of consumption, something better done by robots. We have a tendency to believe technology can fix every problem; thus, nature is seen as a mere resource for our enhanced power, or else as a pet we keep locked up in a park. We have a tendency to see politics as simply keeping people safe and making sure the economy is humming; thus, we're increasingly fine with jettisoning democratic practices and striking Hobbesian bargains with our government for security and prosperity. We have a tendency to see education as the mere downloading of future bankable skills and problem-solving knowledge; thus, we're apt to turn away from the face-it disciplines of the arts and humanities insofar they just aren't efficient fixers of problems (in fact, some fear that the harshness of their subjects may trigger traumatic experiences), or else to turn these disciplines, these jewels of human life, into tools for fixing our social problems. Interestingly, the more we see our lives as a ball of grievances to be untangled, the more our entertainment is filled with spectacular dreamlike appearances of death and violence, from zombies to Mortal Kombat. We're forgetting what it means to exist.

It's noteworthy that we often speak of dealing with various troubles in terms of war: the War on Terror, the War on Drugs, the War on Poverty, the War on Crime, the War on Cancer. I can envision a time when we'll mobilize behind the War on Death, a campaign already envisioned at the beginning of modernity by Francis Bacon. It's not enough for us to fight these problems; we talk as if we must conquer them once and for all. In Deuteronomy we read, "The poor shall never cease out of the land."[11] The same can be said about drugs, crime, disease, terror, and death. It's not just that I oppose the hyperbole of talking about our attempt to reduce suffering in terms of war; it's that waging such wars threatens to undermine our humanity and to generate whole new forms of suffering. We must accept immorality, pain, and death as part of the human package, or else we imperil our freedom.

Please don't misunderstand me. Our forgetfulness about the paradox of both accepting and fighting suffering makes calls for the acceptance of cancer, terrorism, and poverty sound like defeatism. I make no plea for complacency. Not to fight against suffering would be as wrongheaded as only fighting against it. Yes, the poor shall never cease out of the land, but we must also remember the next line of Deuteronomy: "Thou shalt open thine hand wide unto thy brother." Acceptance doesn't entail complaisance. While we should respect the backdrop of pointless suffering against which our lives play out, we must work for human goals that are by their nature opposed to pointless suffering. If we're diagnosed with cancer, it makes sense that we submit to chemotherapy. But we should realize that there may come a time when the next level of therapy is no longer worthwhile for the sake of our quality of life. We should also realize, regardless of whether we've been diagnosed with cancer, that suffering is at the core of being alive, that openness to disease isn't simply a glitch, and that we're going to die someday, for such realizations are critical to leading meaningful lives.

My main problem with our superpowered fix-it-ism is that it deprives us of the unique adventure of human existence. It splits us into employers and laborers, marketers and consumers, biotechnicians and patients, entertainers and the entertained, managers and subjects, fixers and the in-need-of-fixing, elites and riffraff, philanthropists and beggars, gods and beasts, when we should be workers, doers, inventors, caregivers, artists, teachers, students, citizens, and human beings—roles that involve an embrace of mutual risk and suffering. We should be people who understand our own vulnerabilities and the vulnerabilities of others, and who can respond creatively to the human condition. To wage war on suffering is to separate us from what makes us human: it inevitably generates abuse and meaninglessness. The War on Terror compels us to curtail our liberties and to torture people, including innocents. The War on Crime compels us not only to incarcerate ungodly numbers of people, including innocents, but to pressure police forces to adopt the equipment and demeanor of occupying armies. The War on Disease has led many to die hooked to bleeping machines rather than holding the hands of friends and family, or to waste away mentally and physically among strangers in old people's homes. These wars also lull the powerful into believing that it's other people who must suffer. We forget that we're of one substance with the waterboarded suspect, the desperate junkie, and the suicidal schizophrenic. Most fundamentally, when we structure our lives exclusively around the fix-it mindset, we spend our days at a remove from what endows them with value: our relationships lack depth, our food lacks savor, our music lacks beauty, our justice lacks mercy, our work seems burdensome, and our leisure activities kill time rather than enliven it. As Michel de Montaigne says of trying to combat the conditions of life itself, "Other wars act outward; this one acts also against itself, eats and destroys itself by its own venom . . . What have we come to? Our medicine carries infection."[12] In short, the attempt to fix all suffering generates its own unique kinds of suffering: the devastation of unintended consequences and, more fundamentally, the deprivation of human value.

The goal of this book is to revive the paradox of accepting and opposing death, misery, and injustice—in short, to recover the mystery of suffering, which is also the mystery of being human. The following chapters are essays on seven different ways of looking at the great paradox of pointless suffering. I begin where we are, or at least where many of us are, by examining the emergence of modernity and the turbulent ways we try to make sense of suffering as we achieve our staggering technological prowess. This first section ends with the idea that we need to rediscover what Hannah Arendt calls "the human condition," even as the traditions that once oriented us within our condition have become imperiled. Thus, in my second section I scour our inheritance to update perennially valuable ways of occupying the human condition in our confrontation with pointless suffering. I see how much meaning still crackles in key terms of confronting the mystery: God, nature, humanity, and art.

* * * * * * * * * * *

After I'd given a reading of my book *The Deepest Human Life* at Prairie Lights Bookstore, Mike Cervantes introduced himself to me and, because I'd mentioned my instruction of ex-cons, asked if I'd be interested in teaching philosophy at the nearby Iowa Medical and Classification Center, a.k.a. Oakdale Prison, where he coordinates educational programs and helps to publish a newspaper. I took him up on the offer and have now been teaching there, off and on, for the past few years. Because the work is pro bono, I've been blessedly free from institutional mandates. I've just gotten to teach philosophy. It's been marvelous!

As a philosopher whose North Star is Socrates, I don't examine ideas as simply historical artifacts or theoretical models, even though history and theory are important. I try to find what's living and dead in great ideas by putting them into conversation with real lives. For all its horribleness, prison has always been a wonderful laboratory for philosophical thought. Immediately I began testing out the guiding figures and ideas of this book among the "guys." (That's what I call the inmates collectively. Though some good-hearted folks object to what they consider the dehumanizing language of "inmate" or "prisoner," I use these terms too, because they're common and clear, unlike politically correct circumlocutions like "persons in prison" or "transitioning citizens." Also, I don't want to soft-serve the fact of the matter. I've been a person in prison; trust me, it's different from being a prisoner.) I figure that prisoners are in a good place to evaluate what Job says about keeping faith in an unforgiving world, or what Epictetus says about maintaining freedom under desperate conditions, or what Nietzsche says about punishment. I hope that my study of philosophy has equipped me to teach the guys something worthwhile for their journeys through this unmerciful, miraculous life of ours. I know for sure that they have something to teach me about how the soul is illuminated or distorted by religion and philosophy. The way I see it, we form an ensemble that enlarges all of us, an invisible republic that includes the ghosts of long-dead philosophers, prophets, and poets—one that includes you too.

My prison teaching, which began with my selfish desire to explore philosophy with interesting folks, soon led to an essential revelation: how we deal with crime is a powerful expression of how we think about suffering. The philosophical problem of suffering is largely about trying to square the seemingly irreconcilable concepts of suffering and justice. What is prison but our practical attempt to reconcile suffering and justice? Punishment is the infinitely mysterious idea of inflicting pain for an idea of the good. The guys are anything but insulated from injustice and misery. Though all of us have inflicted suffering, they're paying a price for doing so. Some of them have inflicted great suffering, including rape and murder. Most of them have also suffered greatly—in their pre-prison lives as well as in prison. As I was working through various philosophers in preparation for this book, I was surprised at how many of them deal with punishment as an integral part of their discussions of the meaning of suffering. I was also surprised at how many of them, from very different perspectives, come out against systematic punishment! The problem of evil is deeply linked to the problem of prison.

Prison is also a clear place where the horrible problems with not thinking seriously about suffering manifest themselves. The War on Crime and the War on Drugs have resulted in 2.2 million of our fellow citizens behind bars—nearly a 1,000 percent increase over the past half century! The United States has under 5 percent of the world's population; we house close to 25 percent of the world's prisoners at the cost of $80 billion a year. What's the success of our extensive "correctional" facilities? A recidivism rate of almost 70 percent. (May these statistics soon prove relics of the bad old days.) In other words, in the name of justice and safety, we're ruining lives, tearing up families, and generating crime! If we want to lead good lives and have a healthy society, we need to take a good long look at what we're doing. We should strive to see injustice as part of us rather than as something that can simply be walled off and reprogrammed. What we do to prisoners is what we do to ourselves. If we want to lead good lives, we must rethink our relationship to suffering. If we want to live in the land of the free, we must rethink the land of prison.

* * * * * * * * * * *

By far the most common response when I tell people I'm writing a book called *Seven Ways of Looking at Pointless Suffering* is something to the effect of "Well, that's grim!" One academic even chastised me, "Philosophy should be about showing people joy and not wallowing in suffering." These responses strike me as symptomatic of our profound forgetfulness of the mystery of suffering. Suffering and joy are not separable. Real joy exacts from us a confrontation with death, misery, and injustice—and not just pleasant death, a little pain, and the occasional moral failing, but the razor-sharp way that all these forms of suffering cut into us. James Baldwin traces what he calls the "double-edged" power of the blues—that most joyous, heartbreaking form of music—to a kind of sensuality, a way of being fully alive in this skin of ours. He says:

> To be sensual, I think, is to respect and rejoice in the force of life,
> of life itself, and to be *present* in all that one does, from the effort of

> loving to the breaking of bread. It will be a great day for America, incidentally, when we begin to eat bread again, instead of the blasphemous and tasteless foam rubber that we have substituted for it. And I am not being frivolous now, either.[13]

I have no desire to be grim. I just don't want to eat tasteless foam rubber.

My hunch is that the endorsement or rejection of philosophical theories is largely determined by temperament. You have a personality such that, when you're inclined to wisdom, you're inclined to the transcendence of Plato, or to the empiricism of Aristotle, or to the peacefulness of Daoism, or to the humaneness of Confucianism, or to the honesty of pessimism, or to the hopefulness of idealism. To study the great expressions of your temperament, to read the best books sympathetic to your ruling pattern, is to become more you. It's one of the most gratifying things about teaching philosophy to see students catch fire and exclaim, "I've always been a Stoic but never known it until now!"

I think that temperament particularly determines how we relate to suffering. Just as a desire for self-control in the face of misery makes Stoicism a necessity for some, an inner drive for righteousness rules it out for others and sways them toward hope in a justice beyond our blood-soaked realities. When I set out to write these chapters, I fully expected to present seven largely incompatible perspectives on suffering.

But as I delved into my various guiding thinkers, hailing from different cultures, working with different temperaments, I found that they alight on the same central paradox of fixing and facing suffering, and differ only in how they manage it. I found myself singing the same song, with admittedly big variations. My last chapter deals head-on with the blues, which, among other things, refers to a repeating chord progression—utterly simple, yet capable of being endlessly freighted with human complexities. I don't want to underplay the differences between Job and Epictetus—or, for that matter, Blind Willie Johnson and Muddy Waters—but I've come to think that there's a deep blues that emerges whenever anyone is serious about coming to terms with being alive and having to die.

Plus, the study of philosophy isn't exhausted by learning only those ideas that ring down the grooves of our peculiar rationality. We become richer selves, more musical souls, when we're able to enlarge our temperaments by challenging our ruling pattern and enhancing those smaller voices also in the ensemble of our selfhood. I'm a philosophical pluralist. To paraphrase William James, I believe that our overall consciousness of truth would suffer if a Platonist were forced, logically or otherwise, to be an Aristotelian, or a Daoist a Confucian, or a Christian a Nietzschean.[14] Each great philosophy articulates a syllable in humanity's never-total message. The more we discover, the more we spell out. Though there are certain fundamental coordinates that should guide us all, I'm primarily interested in expanding our sense of what's possible and enlarging our sympathies. I hope not to solve our moral problems (has a philosopher ever successfully done that?) but to expand our moral imaginations. In my view, the most philosophical philosophers are those who embody humanity so expansively that they stubbornly refuse to be reduced to "a philosophy"—Socrates, Zhuangzi, Montaigne.

Why only seven ways of looking at pointless suffering? In my defense let me point out that the prestigious philosopher Amélie Oksenberg Rorty in *The Many Faces of Evil* comes up with just six! I admit that there are more than six or seven ways of embodying the mystery of suffering. Some of you will be disappointed not to see chapters devoted exclusively to the nuances of Christianity and Buddhism, the first of which takes as its central symbol an image of torture, and the second of which states as its initial truth that life is suffused with suffering. Though there is occasion here to discuss both these traditions (moreover, they guide implicitly much of what I say throughout the book), I figure that the Christian idea of converting pointless suffering into charity and the Buddhist notion of converting it into compassion are relatively well-known, and it's more interesting to wander down related pathways. I'm superstitious enough to think that seven, a lucky number, is plenty of ways to look at what's hardest to look at. Wallace Stevens found thirteen ways of looking at a blackbird. If I found thirteen ways of looking at evil, I worry the last would be that of the Devil himself!

PART ONE

Three Modern Ways of Looking at Pointless Suffering

Busy cutting down human imperfection, they are making headway also on the raw material of good.

FLANNERY O'CONNOR

My former neighbors had a daughter named Ashley who was born with a "broken brain," to use the medical description of one of her sisters. With her extremely severe mental and physical handicaps, the doctors didn't think Ashley would last more than a few days on this earth. When I knew her, Ashley had made it to puberty and was closer to six feet tall than I'll ever be. But she possessed no abilities beyond those of a newborn baby. Bound to a wheelchair, she couldn't talk, walk, crawl, control her hands or legs, or use language whatsoever. She spent her day slumped in her wheelchair, occasionally being fed, frequently screaming.

A baby's cry, however irritating, has the seed of language in it: you know it will someday become articulate. Ashley's cry was a pure siren of misery: it wasn't going anywhere. Though it contained within it the frustrations of birth, growth, and puberty, it wasn't exactly a protest. Her voice gushed out in a flat, constant sound, somewhere between a shriek and a moan: a long vowel of suffering without anger or resentment, like the tuning fork of misery itself. In Sophocles's *Oedipus at Colonus*, the chorus says, "Never to have lived is best, ancient writers say;/ Never to have drawn the breath of life, never to have looked into the eye of day;/ The second best's a gay goodnight and quickly turn away."[1] I generally have a hard time taking those lines as anything but interesting hyperbole. But Ashley made me confront them in all their horror. Would Ashley be better off dead? Was her life genuinely and completely a mistake? Since her life is part of the life we share, is life itself something of a mistake?

One of our most iconic images is *The Scream*, the name given to various paintings and pastels done by Edvard Munch between 1893 and 1910 of a sexless figure crying out on a bridge under an orange sky, with two shadowy figures walking nearby, unfazed by the despair. On certain prints of the image it reads, "*Ich fühlte das grosse Geschrei durch die Natur*" (I felt the great scream through nature). The image is supposed to embody pointless suffering itself, the scream emanating from nature's core, which we try to disregard as we walk across our bridges. Whereas images of suffering from premodern times invoke myths that give meaning to misery (the Crucifixion is an obvious example, with the Resurrection just a few days off), *The Scream* is simply the scream—no story, no past, no future, no redemption, no hope. Frankly, I have mixed emotions about Munch's expressionist masterpiece. I'm not immune to the visual power that makes it one of the rare cultural objects almost everyone knows. But something about the shrieking figure's face and hands strikes me as diluting with exasperation what's meant to be pure despair. It's no surprise that the image lends itself to parodies. In any case, if you want to picture Ashley, imagine the great scream through nature. Munch's iconic figure has nothing on my former neighbor.

* * * * * * * * * * *

In November of 2012 the contemporary philosopher Thomas Nagel argued in the *New York Review of Books* that "whether atheists or theists are right depends on facts about reality that neither of them can prove."[2] A month later, Galen Strawson, another prominent philosopher, wrote in response a brief letter to the editor that shocked me:

> This is not quite right: it depends on what kind of theists we have to do with. We can, for example, know with certainty that the Christian God does not exist as standardly defined: a being who is omniscient, omnipotent, and wholly benevolent. The proof lies in the world, which is full of extraordinary suffering. . . . It may be added that genuine belief in such a God, however rare, is profoundly immoral: it shows contempt for the reality of human suffering, or indeed any intense suffering.[3]

I wasn't surprised to encounter what philosophers call "the problem of evil" used as an argument against God. I'm aware that many intellectuals believe a good God is incompatible with the suffering in the universe. But I was taken aback by Strawson's dismissal of a foundational tradition of Western civilization as "profoundly immoral." I get that it's the job of philosophers to disagree with each other—and everyone else, for that matter. But it flabbergasted me to think that simply name-checking the problem of evil would be sufficient for an otherwise sensitive thinker like Galen Strawson to write off Thomas Aquinas, Dante Alighieri, John Milton, and Dorothy Day as not just mistaken but wicked in their theism. In the midst of his great struggle, Martin Luther King Jr. says,

> My personal trials have also taught me the value of unmerited suffering. As my sufferings mounted I soon realized that there were two ways that I could respond to my situation: either to react with bitterness or seek to transform the suffering into a creative force. . . . If only to save myself from bitterness, I have attempted to see my personal ordeals as an opportunity to transform myself and heal the people involved in the tragic situation which now obtains. I have lived these

last few years with the conviction that unearned suffering is redemp-
tive. There are some who still find the cross a stumbling block, and
others consider it foolishness, but I am more convinced than ever
before that it is the power of God unto social and individual salvation.
So like the Apostle Paul I can now humbly yet proudly say, "I bear in
my body the marks of the Lord Jesus."[4]

Are such convictions "profoundly immoral"?

Charles Taylor begins his marvelous intellectual history *A Secular
Age* by noting that in the 1500s it was virtually impossible not to believe in God, while in the 2000s "many of us find this not only easy,
but even inescapable."[5] After reading Strawson's letter, I was haunted
by a related issue: How is it that through numerous centuries of Western history, despite the fact that unmerited suffering has always been
common, it was considered profoundly immoral to disbelieve in a
good God, whereas now the fact of suffering makes many regard the
belief in a good God as profoundly immoral? What I came to realize is that a certain daring belief has taken root in modernity; in fact,
this belief is almost the essence of the forward-driving momentum of
modernity—namely, *if one can eliminate suffering, one should.* Notice
I say "eliminate," and not just "ease" or "remedy." You see, for most of
our history we've taken suffering as a given, as ineliminable, as something we must work with. Suffering was part of *nature*—nature in the
old sense of a fundamental limit, what we either can't or shouldn't
exceed. We tried to help and heal as much as we could, but we mostly
assumed that disease, pain, and death were ultimately nonnegotiable
rules of the earthly game. There were also "natural" moral laws, fundamental principles about who we were and how we were to use our
freedom. To be in violation of these moral and natural rules was to
put our souls at risk.

This background assumption about the permanence of suffering
was probably built on the simple fact that we didn't have the power to
make any serious changes to nature. Our medicines, though not without effect, were relatively weak. To be healed was to be restored to the

human condition, not to be delivered from pain and death. Famine, plagues, death, and injustice were going to happen, no matter what. Don't get me wrong: there were always fierce protests against suffering, at least since the days of Job; there were also alchemists and explorers who dreamt of fundamentally modifying nature or discovering a fountain of immortal youth. But these protests and wild-eyed projects were relegated to the margins. Primarily our job was to figure out ways of coming to terms with suffering in such a way that we could make it through our difficulties and maybe even find some meaning in them. A common hope was that in a transcendent realm, somewhere beyond this vale of tears, there would be freedom from suffering, at least for the just or the blessed.

In this premodern way of looking at suffering (maybe I should say supermodern way, for it predates modernity and runs through it), the realities of God, nature, humanity, and art all appear as essential mysteries. Christianity—to take the worldview that Strawson finds immoral—is committed to the idea that God, the highest possible object of worship, is good. But Christians simultaneously recognize that God's creation is full of evil. Is nature a testing ground? Did we bring suffering on ourselves through a primal act of sin? Humanity is strangely out of joint with nature. In this world but not of it, the faithful long for a home beyond this earth, the kingdom of God, where suffering will be overcome and perfect justice will hold sway, even as they naturally fear death and cling to their earthly lives. Crafts, medicine, politics, and the fine arts are to embody the fundamental mystery of remedying the troubles of earthly reality while simultaneously affirming the divine justice from which they descend. "The peculiar grace of a Shaker chair," as Thomas Merton says, "is due to the fact that it was made by someone capable of believing that an angel might come and sit on it."[6] On this religious view, we should strive for a human order of health, justice, and beauty but prepare our lives for the heavenly order that at once sustains and punishes us. Humanity needs faith, for reason can take us only so far. For those who still subscribe to some version of this worldview (Ashley's mother is among them),

Ashley appears as a profound enigma to be simultaneously lamented and honored, someone whose soul will be unbroken in paradise.

The central forces of modernity challenge the limits of our acceptance of suffering and press us to eliminate it. God, nature, humanity, and art no longer seem mysterious to those who wholeheartedly embrace the momentum of modernity. In fact, these concepts begin to vanish altogether. With our great technological and scientific advances, we increasingly wield the power of God, so what's the point of religion? The problem of evil redounds on us. The question of why God allows a natural disaster seems outdated in comparison to the question of why humanity is guilty of Auschwitz. The old idea of nature as a fundamental limit is progressively liquidated. Nature is simply what we start with. It's increasingly up to us how much we should keep of it, and how much we should modify. Every day immutable givens fall by the wayside. Even genes seem up for grabs. For some, death itself looks like a disposable nuisance. The concept of humanity is widely believed to be a biological starting point, something to be reconfigured with drugs, surgeries, and social engineering. Our arts—especially our biomedical arts, but also our industry, education, and politics—are ever more directed at solving problems, not grappling with mysteries. The fine arts, traditionally powerful tools for making meaning out of suffering, are seen as "cheesecake," to use the metaphor of Steven Pinker—that is, as pleasant but unnecessary luxuries accidentally concocted from otherwise important problem-solving drives.[7]

On this view, we no longer must take pain or disease as built into the system. Power is meant to correct nature. *If we can eliminate suffering, we should.* Nothing in nature should block us from doing so, except for anything that would cause us more suffering. If we happen to conclude that death and illness can sometimes be good, why not have them on our terms? We shouldn't have to suffer at all. Admittedly, this utopian view rarely appears in its pure form, but it drives our culture for good and ill. The more we embrace this pure principle of eliminating suffering, the more the whole concept of the Christian

God seems like a contradiction in terms. If you insist on clinging to this God, thinkers like Strawson argue, you're clinging to a Biotechnologist in the Sky who actively generates suffering or, at best, stands idly by while it happens, even though He has the means to cure it. To those who subscribe to this worldview, Ashley appears as a horrible mistake. Either we should repair her brain, or, if that proves impossible, there's no reason for her to exist.

* * * * * * * * * * * *

On the morning of All Saints' Day in 1755 an earthquake struck Lisbon, Portugal, a city largely composed of hardworking, prosperous Christians. Thousands of people immediately perished, as fifteen-foot-deep fissures ripped through the town center. Survivors ran to the docks. The ocean bizarrely receded, revealing all the wreckage on the floor of the harbor, and then, to multiply its destruction, returned with a vengeance in the form of a tsunami. The little of Lisbon that wasn't engulfed in water broke out in flames. Earth, air, fire, and water: the four elements teamed up to decimate the population. Historians conservatively estimate that between 30,000 and 60,000 of the city's 200,000 citizens died that day. Lisbon's culture was also laid low. Homes, palaces, libraries, and galleries were left in rubble, to say nothing of its houses of worship.

As Susan Neiman shows in her eye-opening philosophical history *Evil and Modern Thought*, the edifice of thinking about suffering in 1755 was already compromised, and the Lisbon earthquake demolished it as thoroughly as it did the city's churches. The lingering medieval view held that an earthquake was part of the mysterious moral plan of God. In the first half of the eighteenth century Gottfried Leibniz famously argued, in a last efflorescence of the old worldview, that ours was the best of all possible worlds. It was a straightforward deductive conclusion. If God is all-knowing, He must have considered every possible world prior to creation. If God is all-good, He must have wanted to create the best possible world. Since God is all-knowing and all-good, this world must be the best possible world. Insofar as evil exists, it must be necessary for the good to be maximized. By the middle of the century, when the Lisbon earthquake struck, Leibniz's premise that God wasn't an underachieving creator had begun to strain credulity. Our burgeoning new scientific powers emboldened us to think that we could radically improve what God had made. We should no longer accept suffering as a given. Voltaire responded to the Lisbon earthquake first by composing a stinging poem that criticized Leibniz's optimism and then by writing the satire *Candide* in which the splendidly named Dr. Pangloss peers at horrific natural disasters and declares them wonderful.

Leibniz adopts an age-old distinction between natural evil and moral evil (traditionally called *malum poenae* and *malum culpae*). Natural evil refers to the suffering we experience as a matter of course, independent of our choices—for instance, the Lisbon earthquake. Moral evil refers to the abuse of our freedom—for instance, the theft of forbidden fruit. Resting uncritically on an old piece of theology, Leibniz in his *Theodicy* asserts that natural evil is the punishment for moral evil. It might seem trivial—even "profoundly immoral"—to believe that our moral infractions, let alone a distant ancestor's nibble of an outlawed apple, can be justification for the untold death and destruction of nature, from plagues and earthquakes to smallpox and cancer. But, as Neiman says:

> Something trivial is precisely appropriate. What counts in the first instance is not the justice of the connection between what they did and what they suffered, but that there be a connection at all. Why do bad things happen? Because bad things were done. Better to have some causal explanation than to remain in the dark. To connect sin and suffering is to separate the world into moral and natural evils, and to create thereby a framework for understanding human misery.[8]

The belief that natural evil is the consequence of moral evil does a lot of work. It keeps us plugged into the world, upholds the idea of

God as good, gives our suffering meaning, and maintains the idea of a universal moral order.

Alexis de Tocqueville observes, "Evils which are patiently endured when they seem inevitable, become intolerable when once the idea of escape from them is suggested."[9] By the mid-eighteenth century the new sciences and their accompanying technologies had begun to suggest to Europe the idea of escape from evils that had long been patiently endured. Voltaire voices the initial frustration. As Neiman shows in *Evil and Modern Thought*, he's just the beginning of a great tradition that completely rethinks the concept of evil. Leibniz's uncritical connection between moral and natural evil is severed, and a new concept of nature emerges. The old view was that an earthquake is an "act of God," part of a designed plan. The new view, which takes a while to materialize fully, is that nature is a neutral starting point. Things like sunshine and rain and earthquakes just happen. Neither "evil" nor "good," they're the products of cause and effect, of a nonmoral physical order that we can understand through science. Since we don't always like the outcomes of nature, we should, insofar as it's possible, modify our lives or intervene in the causal order to promote better outcomes. We should structure our cities so that the residents are secure from predictable earthquakes. We should seed the clouds when drought comes. We should stamp out disease. We should eliminate crime. This world is, at best, a good start; it's our job to fix it up.

According to this quintessentially modern view, the only place left for evil is human choice. An earthquake is the result of the determinism of plate tectonics, but murder and rape are the results of the free will of humanity. Interestingly, as modernity progresses, even the existence of "moral evil" is challenged. Behaviorists and social engineers hold that human activity, like that of the rest of the natural world, is no more than the product of external forces. Perhaps we too should be diagnosed, arranged, and fixed like any other glitch in nature.

* * * * * * * * * * *

In the *Genealogy of Morals* Friedrich Nietzsche observes, "What really arouses indignation against suffering is not suffering as such but the senselessness of suffering: but neither for the Christian, who has interpreted a whole mysterious machinery of salvation into suffering, nor for the naïve man of more ancient times, who understood all suffering in relation to the spectator of it or the causer of it, was there any such thing as senseless suffering."[10] As the "mysterious machinery" of finding meaning in pain and death becomes decreasingly credible to many in the modern world, philosophers confront suffering on new terms, often inventing their own mysterious newfangled machinery. The three thinkers I examine in this section—John Stuart Mill (1806–73), Friedrich Nietzsche (1844–1900), and Hannah Arendt (1906–75)—are passionate about discovering how to lead a meaningful life in relationship to the misery that's increasingly seen in modernity as pointless. What I particularly admire about them is their refusal to settle for easy answers. They doggedly pursue the messy questions of meaning and value that seem like a waste of time to modernity's technocrats and dogmatists, optimists and pessimists, doe-eyed progressives and sourpuss conservatives.

Modernity's relentless drive to improve the human lot is crystallized in the philosophy of utilitarianism, the central principle of which is that we should ignore outdated ideas of "natural laws" and try to maximize satisfaction and minimize misery for everyone. The philosophers I examine in this section all deal with the difficult legacy of this seemingly straightforward idea. Mill, raised with a strict utilitarian education, never renounces the philosophy of his father, but he seriously complicates utilitarianism with the ideals of freedom and meaning. Nietzsche, by contrast, never misses an opportunity to savage utilitarianism. He insists that life inevitably involves suffering. Not only do we deceive ourselves when we dream of trying to liberate ourselves from pain and misery, we end up tranquilizing our adventurousness and venting our cruelty in sneaky ways. In fact, Nietzsche stands utilitarianism's main idea on its head, arguing that instead of trying to minimize suffering we should embrace suffering, even pointless suffering, including cruelty. Though it would be a bit misleading to say that Arendt is the synthesis of Mill (the thesis) and Nietzsche (the antithesis), the problems recognized and partially generated by the extremes of Mill and Nietzsche do indeed blend together into the great problem of modernity that Arendt spends her philosophical life trying to understand.

Essentially, the problem is that we're tempted to see ourselves as gods rather than as subject to what Arendt calls "the human condition." The utilitarian idea is that we should play the role of a good god and readjust nature to produce our maximum satisfaction. Nietzsche's comparable idea is that we must become the superhuman (*der Übermensch*) by showing that we're spiritually strong enough to be able to embrace whatever happens, even the worst forms of suffering. Both Mill and Nietzsche struggle to find the most life-enhancing forms of their respective philosophies, and I think we learn necessary lessons from each of them about how to think about ourselves in modernity. But the extremes in human nature that they so powerfully articulate—trying to fix the morally chaotic world and trying to embrace the morally chaotic world—threaten to destroy what's meaningful in life. We see the worst of those extremes in the technocrats and terrorists so characteristic of our time. Arendt insists that we must relearn the basic coordinates of being human, even as our technologies and social systems tempt us to into acting like gods or behaving like beasts.

Thank God—or at least thank goodness—for the Enlightenment idea that the human lot can be improved! For all the horrors of modernity, including the earth-threatening perils of technology, few of us would want to trade our lot with a fourteenth-century peasant for whom serfdom and bubonic plague were necessary links in God's great chain of being. But modernity, particularly in its relationship to suffering, poses far-reaching problems. Think of antibiotics as a synecdoche of modernity itself. Antibiotics are a wonderful thing, a life-saving and life-improving triumph of human ingenuity for which we should be deeply grateful. Nevertheless, antibiotics can be overprescribed and overused. We run two big risks: first, rendering the antibiotics useless; second, creating superviruses. Likewise, modernity—of which antibiotics are a part—is a wonderful achievement, an achievement worth embracing and advancing. Yet it can get out of hand. We run two risks: first, meaninglessness; second, inadvertently (or advertently!) unleashing more harm than we set out to remedy.

* * * * * * * * * * * *

Peter Singer, the most prominent contemporary utilitarian, notoriously argues that certain forms of infanticide are morally permissible. In *Practical Ethics* he argues:

> When the death of a disabled infant will lead to the birth of another infant with better prospects of a happy life, the total amount of happiness will be greater if the disabled infant is killed. The loss of happy life for the first infant is outweighed by the gain of a happier life for the second. Therefore, if killing the hemophiliac infant has no adverse effect on others, it would, according to the total view, be right to kill him.[11]

It's interesting that Nietzsche, the opposite of a utilitarian, comes to a similar position. In *The Gay Science*, in a section called "Holy Cruelty," he writes:

> A man who held a newborn child in his hands approached a holy man. "What shall I do with this child?" he asked; "it is wretched, misshapen, and does not have life enough to die." "Kill it!" shouted the holy man with a terrible voice; "and then hold it in your arms for three days and three nights to create a memory for yourself: never again will you beget a child this way when it is not time for you to beget."—When the man had heard this, he walked away, disappointed, and many people reproached the holy man because he had counseled cruelty; for he had counseled the man to kill the child. "But is it not crueler to let it live?" asked the holy man.[12]

Harsh as these quintessentially modern proposals may sound, I confess they're not alien to me when I think of my former neighbor Ashley. It's next to impossible to imagine a utilitarian argument for her existence. I get why someone might think that, since we can't fix her, keeping her scream around is crueler than silencing it forever.

But fundamentally I bristle at the idea of taking her life. As I mentioned, Ashley's mother is religious. She converted to Mormonism shortly after Ashley's birth, in part because of the charity her Mormon neighbors showed her as a new parent in her time of greatest need. I don't think Ashley's mom is under any illusions about the pleasure-pain balance in dealing with her daughter. I also think that incessantly having to care for her disabled child takes hidden psychological tolls on her and her family. Yet she persists in seeing her daughter as sacred, as a soul. What does it mean to see Ashley not simply as a flaw of the universe?

One afternoon I was supposed to help Ashley get off a bus (for a while the special education room at the local public school took her off her parents' hands). I was to take her in the house and wait as her mother got back from an appointment. After wheeling her up the ramp, I found that I couldn't quite finagle the wheelchair into the house. She started to scream. It was cold outside, and she was wearing only an afghan for warmth. Quickly deciding that I needed to carry her over the threshold, I worked my arms under her tall, thrashing frame and hoisted her up into an awkward pietà. I could smell the shit in her diaper. She was moaning so violently that drool frothed at the corners of her mouth. Did she know I was her neighbor? Could she distinguish me from her stepdad, or even her mom? Did she imagine I was kidnapping her? Or was my awkward rescue just one more indistinguishable passage from pain to pain?

Once I got her situated on the couch, she calmed down to her usual steady moan. We looked at each other. At least I looked at her; I wasn't sure if she was processing my face. It occurred to me that she was pretty despite her features' awkward puffiness, which was probably the result of her never having imitated other people's expressions. A few teardrops hovered on her cheeks, and I wiped them away. Her sister's expression "a broken brain" was going through my brain. Ashley wasn't just a problem. She wasn't just a scream. She was also a human being. She was a broken brain, a cracked potential, a shattered human being. She was broken, but she was something of value too—of unfathomable value. Some part of my own broken humanity was being solicited. I thought of a line from Montaigne's essay "Of Cripples," "I have seen no more evident monstrosity and miracle in the world than myself."[13] In that moment, an admittedly fleeting moment, I understood what it means to see Ashley as family, to regard her as one of us, even if she represents the furthest border of our mystery. I understood how fragile my higher identity is—how my thoughts and memories come undone every night in sleep, how they could be totally canceled by a blow to the head or a bite from an infectious mosquito. I'm also constituted by the great scream through nature. I understood why seeing Ashley exclusively as a problem is itself a kind of problem.

ONE

WE SHOULD ELIMINATE

POINTLESS SUFFERING

On John Stuart Mill and the Paradox
of Utilitarianism

It was granted me to derive from that evil my own greatest good.

J. S. MILL

According to William Carlos Williams, "The pure products of America go crazy."[1] Let's modify that observation slightly: "The pure products of modernity go crazy." In the fall of 1826, one such pure product, a twenty-year-old by the name of John Stuart Mill, sank into a suicidal depression.

James Mill, John Stuart's father, was devoted to modernity. Dismissing religion as superstition, he gravitated to the utilitarianism of Jeremy Bentham. James Mill believed that he understood human nature well enough to redesign education from the ground up. Under his rigorous tutelage, his son was proficient in ancient Greek by the age of five; by the age of nine, little John Stuart was reading Latin fluently and making sense of the highest levels of algebra. He celebrated his eleventh year by writing a history of Roman law. When he was fifteen (this would have been when my reading level topped out at X-Men comics, and my great scientific quandary was puzzling out how a bra is unfastened), J. S. Mill had already so mastered classics, philosophy, law, history, economics, science, and mathematics that when he applied to Cambridge University they turned him away because its professors didn't have anything more to teach him. Mill claimed, quite honestly, that he wasn't a particularly gifted child; it was simply that his father had a good system. His education was, in the apt phrase of Isaiah Berlin, "an appalling success."[2]

Mill's education was centered on empowering him to become a great benefactor of humankind, someone capable of realizing Bentham's utilitarianism—of sweeping away premodern beliefs and bringing about the greatest good for the greatest number. Disciplines like philosophy and economics were supremely useful to this end. Religion and poetry, which struck James Mill as accumulations of old-fashioned ignorance and superstition, were not. As in Plato's *Republic*, the poets—those hot-and-bothered types who can't help celebrating love and tragedy—were exiled from Mill's education. (He did read the likes of Homer and Horace for historical context and grammar.) The one art encouraged was music, as it was sufficiently mathematical. In the fall of 1826, when J. S. Mill was twenty years old, he was, by his own admission, an erudite calculating machine whose emotional life was dead on the vine. The buttoned-up young Englishman had a nervous breakdown.

Mill wandered through his life, now devoted mostly to liberal journalism, with a giant emptiness clawing at him. When he turned for comfort to old friends on the library shelves, he found that even his favorite books of history and philosophy were without charm. He soldiered on with efforts for social reform, but his heart wasn't in it. It was as if he really had become a utilitarian machine, only one with a suicidal ghost inside. Even music worried him. Because the combination of notes isn't infinite, and because a tune's charm fades with familiarity, he was tormented by the thought that humanity would eventually grow bored of everything, even music.

From birth Mill had been raised for a single purpose in life: to realize Bentham's—and his father's—dream of reducing the pains and maximizing the pleasures of humanity. With his well-tuned calculative abilities, the twenty-year-old now put his finger right on the problem:

> In this frame of mind it occurred to me to put the question directly to myself, "Suppose that all your objects in life were realized; that all the changes in institutions and opinions which you are looking forward to, could be completely effected at this very instant: would this be a great joy and happiness to you?" And an irrepressible self-consciousness distinctly answered, "No!" At this my heart sank within me: the whole foundation on which my life was constructed fell down. . . . I seemed to have nothing left to live for.[3]

His spiritual and emotional life had been starved, and the goal of his existence no longer seemed worthwhile. But simply realizing that he needed to have feelings and zest didn't give him feelings and zest—any more than realizing you should learn a foreign language allows you to speak the foreign language.

After the dark winter of 1826–27, a near-suicidal Mill chanced on the memoirs of the historian Jean-François Marmontel and read the author's account of losing his father as a boy. Mill started crying, and the fact that he was crying filled him with a paradoxical happiness: "I was no longer hopeless: I was not a stock or a stone."[4] The seeds of an emotional life were stirring. Next he explored the works of the great Romantic poets, particularly William Wordsworth, which further nourished the ecosystem of his inwardness. Life began to have zest again, although it took Mill several years to clamber all the way out of his depression. He realized that if his utilitarian dream of improving the lot of humankind were properly met, certain permanent good things would remain: natural beauty, our sympathy with others, tranquil recollections—the meat of Wordsworth's loveliest work. It's no exaggeration to say that poetry saved Mill's life.

Mill's problem, which is essentially the human problem, was that he was torn between happiness and meaning. We long for some ideal state where suffering is no more, where we would achieve an unalloyed happiness: Mill had been brought up to be able to make progress toward this end. The problem is that the state we wish for is humanly barren. It seems obvious to us moderns that we should simply alleviate suffering. If you have a headache, here's a pill. If you have a fatal disease, let's get you on the operating table. If our political system creates injustice, let's vote it out. That's utilitarianism in a nutshell. But this mindset, for all its wonderful no-nonsense helpfulness, leaves us without poetry—that is, without all the struggles and paradoxes that give life meaning and make it sing. As a pure product of modernity, Mill felt this dilemma like a kidney stone.

Mill's biography illustrates this deep conflict of our nature, and his philosophy is one of the noblest attempts to resolve it. If there has ever been a philosopher who convincingly argues that we should eliminate pointless suffering, it's J. S. Mill. And yet even his humane version of utilitarianism is widely considered to be, in the final analysis, unconvincing, despite the noble ideals that inspire it. Can the refined goals of philosophy be reconciled with the raw humanity of poetry? Is it possible for us to lead meaningful lives and die meaningful deaths without accepting and even embracing a certain ineradicable dimension of pointless suffering?

* * * * * * * * * * *

Throughout most of human history, the so-called problem of evil has been almost exclusively registered as the mystery of evil. The acceptance of suffering has been practically synonymous with faith, which reassures us that this mean old world isn't the end of the story: there's a huge invisible meaning pervading even our most painful or trivial moments if we learn to accept them and grow toward their supernatural promise.

Starting in the eighteenth century, the mystery of evil becomes the problem of evil. The fact of suffering turns into a clear-cut refutation of

God to intellectuals like James Mill. As J. S. Mill says of his father, "He found it impossible to believe that a world so full of evil was the work of an Author combining infinite power with perfect goodness and righteousness." In fact, religion was, in his father's eyes, "the greatest enemy of morality: first, by setting up factitious excellencies,—belief in the creeds, devotional feelings, and ceremonies, not connected with the good of human kind,—and causing these to be accepted as substitutes for genuine virtues: but above all, by radically vitiating the standard of morals."[5] To the James Mills of the world, the idea of worshiping a being that is the ultimate cause of suffering is not only absurd but undercuts the very purpose of morality. It channels energies toward the acceptance of what we should remedy. It makes us worship precisely what we should wish to overthrow.

A big part of the genius of Jeremy Bentham, the Mills' guru, is his ability to follow through on the logic that indicts God. Rather than wait in hope for supernatural justice, we should strive to minimize pain and maximize pleasure in the here and now, the only time we can be sure of having. This is what Bentham calls "the principle of utility" and what Mill often calls "the greatest happiness principle." Bentham isn't officially an atheist; he mostly seems content to talk of God as shorthand for the structuring principles of the universe. When he does analyze the idea of the divine, he comes down as an agnostic who thinks that it's of no real consequence whether we believe in God or not. Yet his philosophy is a powerful kind of atheism, for it's the rejection of the living substance of faith: the fundamental acceptance of suffering as part of the human journey.

Another way of putting the matter is that Bentham's philosophy radically changes our conception of nature. The traditional idea is that nature is a divine set of limits—inalterable physical and moral laws, like gravity, the fact of death, or the Golden Rule—that ultimately punish us when we try to flout them. For Bentham and Mill, nature is simply raw data that we're supposed to modify to humanly acceptable ends. Disease and death, for instance, aren't to be accepted as natural; they're to be combatted and, ideally, remedied. Moreover, there's no "natural law"—that is, no moral code—that governs us; we simply have desires that can be more or less met. On first discovering Bentham as a teenager, the initial excitement for J. S. Mill was precisely his explosion of the old concepts of nature: "phrases like 'law of nature,' 'right reason,' 'the moral sense,' 'natural rectitude,' and the like . . . [amounted to] dogmatism in disguise. . . . Here was the commencement of a new era in thought."[6]

Mill defines nature as "the sum of all phenomena, together with the causes which produce them; including not only all that happens, but all that is capable of happening."[7] Despite his fondness for the Romantics, Mill argues that to revere nature is both irrational and immoral: irrational, because the main point of human reason—think of tools or politics—is to make amends for nature's inability to satisfy us; immoral, because to model our life on what nature does—think of cancer or hurricanes—would be to turn ourselves into moral monsters. As Mill puts it:

> In sober truth, nearly all the things which men are hanged or imprisoned for doing to one another, are nature's every day performances. Killing, the most criminal act recognized by human laws, Nature does once to every being that lives; and in a large proportion of cases, after protracted tortures such as only the greatest monsters whom we read of ever purposely inflicted on their living fellow-creatures.[8]

Mill goes on to compare nature to history's cruelest dictators, only to conclude that the comparison is grossly unfair to the dictators.

"Utilitarianism" is a somewhat misleading term for the moral theory that derives from Bentham. What Bentham means by "utility" is not simply what's useful but what's specifically useful to the attainment of what he claims we all basically want: satisfaction. According to Bentham, pain and pleasure are our "two sovereign masters." The central idea of utilitarianism is that our sovereign masters should lead us not simply to increase our own pleasure and lessen our own pain but to bring about the greatest amount of satisfaction for everyone.

We should aim at what is best. Since pleasure is good, more pleasure is better, and—Bentham reasons—the most pleasure is best. In *Utilitarianism*, J. S. Mill argues, more cogently than Bentham, that the greatest-good principle is the offspring of two impulses in us: the first, our desire for pleasure for ourselves; the second, our inborn moral impulse toward others. Put them together, and you get the idea that we ought to bring about pleasure not just for ourselves but for everyone we influence. If we need a better fancy name for utilitarianism, we could call it "ethical hedonism" or "moral voluptuism"—whatever Greek or Latin term means "maximum-satisfaction-for-everyone-ism."

In short, Bentham wants to put reason in charge of our fate so that life on earth can be improved for as many people as possible. Beginning in the 1790s, his ideas began to catch on—first in revolutionary France and then in reformist England. Some of Bentham's radical proposals slowly but surely came to be taken for granted across the modernizing world: economic freedom checked by a welfare state, equal opportunities for women, the ability to divorce, the separation of church and state, and the decriminalization of homosexuality.

* * * * * * * * * * *

Though J. S. Mill, a dutiful son, never rejects the utilitarianism of his father and his father's mentor, he makes such radical changes to it that it almost deserves a different name. Whether Mill's idiosyncratic version of utilitarianism holds together as a theory is much in doubt; nevertheless, I take Mill's interventions in Bentham's central ideas to be evidence of an impeccable philosophical character: he wrestles with the real paradoxes of being alive, even at the expense of theoretical ugliness.

The first big change is that Mill celebrates political freedom as the best way of bringing about the greatest good for the greatest number. In his masterpiece *On Liberty* (1859) Mill articulates the political principle that becomes second nature to modernity: "The only purpose for which power can be rightfully exercised over any member of a civ-

ilized community, against his will, is to prevent harm to others."⁹ At
first glance, the idea that we can do what we want provided it doesn't
harm others seems like a lovely application of utilitarianism to the
political realm. Oppression, subjugation, and slavery are all obvious
sources of misery, for which a live-and-let-live system of rights seems
like a perfect antidote.

But freedom, especially the kind of pervasive freedom celebrated
by Mill in his masterpiece *On Liberty*, involves a certain nonutilitarian
tolerance of suffering. Take the freedom of speech. On the one hand,
as Mill forcefully argues, this freedom is compatible with the principle of utility insofar as it allows new and potentially helpful ideas to
flourish and bad ideas to be challenged and corrected. On the other
hand, as Mill conveniently ignores, it's easy to find scenarios in which
the suppression of certain kinds of speech could be reasonably justified in the name of the greatest amount of satisfaction. The fear of
terrorism leads some citizens to wish for the suppression of ugly ji-
hadist propaganda, especially the kind of psychological manipulation
terrorists employ on the internet. The fear of regressive political positions leads some students and professors to shut down certain forms
of speech on campus. Could well-tailored laws that limit speech bring
about the greatest happiness and the least misery for the greatest
number? J. S. Mill doesn't recognize even the theoretical possibility
that utilitarianism could be used to suppress the freedom of speech.
"If all mankind minus one, were of one opinion, and only one person
were of the contrary opinion," Mill says in an astounding statement
of principle, "mankind would be no more justified in silencing that
one person, than he, if he had the power, would be justified in silencing mankind."¹⁰ In short, Mill celebrates the value of freedom in ways
that go beyond the greatest happiness for the greatest number; or,
to put the matter differently, his concept of "the greatest good" involves values—like truth or freedom—that aren't reducible to maximal pleasure.

Consider that the Bill of Rights, our country's paean to freedom,
is, roughly speaking, an inversion of the Ten Commandments. God

tells us to worship only the true God; the Constitution tells us that we have a right to worship false gods. God tells us to speak the truth; the Constitution tells us that we have a right to speak falsely. God tells us that we shouldn't kill; the Constitution tells us that we have a right to bear arms. God tells us that we shouldn't commit adultery; the Constitution tells us that we have a right to privacy. God tells us not to bear false witness; the Constitution says that we don't have to incriminate ourselves. In other words, freedom gives us the ability to inflict the kind of evil that almost all moral systems—including Bentham's utilitarianism—try to eliminate. Why, if we want to eliminate suffering, should we celebrate liberty? Why, if we want to fight terrorism and reduce crime and minimize the damage we inflict on each other, should we stick to the Constitution? Wouldn't an enlightened despotism that helps us all to find satisfaction be preferable? Why, if we want to minimize suffering, should we put any trust at all in human freedom?

The main reason to respect rights, for Mill, is that we're not infallible. It's all too easy for us to suppress what seems false and evil only to find out later that it's harmless, or even right and useful. Mill's favorite example of our fallibility is the great Roman emperor Marcus Aurelius, one of the exemplary leaders in world history, a wise sovereign whose Stoic philosophy led him to see all humanity as brothers and sisters; yet "this man, a better Christian in all but the dogmatic sense of the word, than almost any of the ostensibly Christian sovereigns who have since reigned, persecuted Christianity."[11] If a wise ruler like Marcus Aurelius could be so wrong in persecuting a group he thought was a threat to Roman well-being, couldn't any of us lesser legislators be wrong about those whose views we would suppress? Isn't it better for mistake-makers like us to tolerate differences of opinion? Moreover, doesn't the ability to express even assuredly false and wicked beliefs allow us to perceive the truth more vividly and defend it with greater gusto?

Mill's logic here is compelling, but it rubs against the grain of Bentham's faith in human reason. The beauty of Bentham's utilitarianism is its emphasis on how the wisest among us should think through what ails us, come up with solutions, and implement them. According to Mill, liberty isn't just instrumental to decreasing suffering; it's integral to who we are. Isn't such faith in freedom better defended with a concept like dignity or natural rights than with the theory of what maximizes pleasure and minimizes pain? Isn't the principle of utility, at least sometimes, more congenial to paternalism than liberalism?

The second change Mill makes to utilitarianism is that he distinguishes between higher and lower pleasures, a distinction Bentham adamantly rejects. As Bentham famously puts it, "The quantity of pleasure being equal, push-pin is as good as poetry"—or, to rephrase the point, bowling is just as good as Baudelaire, probably better in that bowling is enjoyed by many more people.[12] Though Bentham gives, in my view, an almost comical breakdown of determining the intensity, length, purity, and productivity of certain pleasures, he refuses to accept that the joy of listening to, say, J. S. Bach is necessarily better than the joy of listening to, say, Justin Bieber. If you get a kick out of one or both, wonderful. But it's as wrong for Bach aficionados to disdain Beliebers as for Beliebers to look down their noses at Bach aficionados. If something gives pleasure, it counts as good in Bentham's moral calculus: there's no higher measure than the feeling itself. If the tradition of music schools, instrumentalists, and orchestras necessary for the sustenance of Bach's legacy dies out, it would be no real loss to Bentham, provided that people were still bopping to Bieber.

The prospect of a Bach-less, Bieber-full world strikes lovers of the *Goldberg Variations* like myself as a straightforward *reductio ad absurdum* of Bentham's utilitarianism. In failing to account for a hierarchy of values, Bentham's philosophy likewise seems to misunderstand the nature of what's right or wrong with certain actions. It's easy to imagine a utilitarian celebration of pornography, at least a certain variety of pornography, in that it brings pleasure to many people at the expense of a very few. In fact, let's even imagine a case where a successful pornographic movie is produced without any harm to the actors. Such cases surely do exist, even if they're significantly more infrequent than consumers would like to imagine. Is it really a no-brainer that such instances of pornography are morally good? Is it really a no-brainer that no-harm porn is, in fact, *morally better* than running a marathon or writing a novel, in that running and writing involve an admixture of pain and rarely lead to such widespread pleasure as a moderately successful piece of porn? Aren't there significant values other than pleasure and pain that we should use to judge human endeavors? In fact, don't many of our most valuable activities involve an ineradicable amount of suffering?

Mill tries to rescue utilitarianism from this problem by making a distinction between higher and lower pleasures. Yes, porn is a pleasure to its consumer, Mill would argue, but it's a base pleasure. If it brings widespread pleasure without any harm, it's morally acceptable, but it's still a lesser good than running a marathon, which, though it involves pain for the athlete, brings an intrinsically higher satisfaction than porn. Mill claims that in our application of the greatest-happiness principle we must factor in the quality as well as the quantity of the pleasure brought about by our actions.

Is Mill using something other than units of pleasure and pain on his yardstick of value? He claims that his test for determining quality is completely in line with Bentham's essential idea that pleasure and pain are our sovereign masters. "Of two pleasures," Mill says, "if there be one to which all or almost all who have experience of both give a decided preference, irrespective of any feeling of moral obligation to prefer it, that is the more desirable pleasure."[13] It's clear that sometimes what we take to be higher goods pass Mill's test. But do they always, or even most of the time? In his popular class on political philosophy at Harvard, Michael Sandel shows his students three videos and then asks them to perform and evaluate Mill's test: the first, an over-the-top pro wrestling match; the second, a soliloquy from *Hamlet*; the last, an excerpt from *The Simpsons*. He then asks them which video they find most pleasurable and which they take to be the highest or worthiest. *The Simpsons* always wins the pleasure vote, but Shakespeare always wins the quality vote. Don't the results of this experiment suggest a disproof of Mill's attempt to rescue utilitarianism? Isn't it the case that the higher goods aren't always the most pleasurable? As Sandel puts it, "Mill saves utilitarianism from the charge that it reduces everything to a crude calculus of pleasure and pain, but only by invoking a moral ideal of human dignity and personality independent of utility itself."[14] Mill's only way to rescue utilitarianism from flattening human life is by suspending its fundamental premise. Mill wants to eliminate pointless suffering and enhance meaningful happiness, but he needs a criterion other than the pleasure-is-good/pain-is-bad principle to determine what constitutes pointless suffering and what constitutes a meaningful life.

The Hamlet soliloquy Sandel shows to his students is the monologue of the prince to Rosencrantz and Guildenstern in act 2. It's an interesting choice, for it speaks with uncanny directness to the mental crisis undergone by the young Mill:

> I have of late—but wherefore I know not—lost all my mirth, forgone all custom of exercises; and indeed, it goes so heavily with my disposition that this goodly frame, the earth, seems to me a sterile promontory. This most excellent canopy, the air, look you, this brave o'er hanging firmament, this majestical roof fretted with golden fire—why, it appeareth no other thing to me than a foul and pestilent congregation of vapours. What a piece of work is a man! How noble in reason, how infinite in faculty, in form and moving how express and admirable, in action how like an angel, in apprehension how like a god—the beauty of the world, the paragon of animals! And yet to me what is this quintessence of dust?[15]

I agree with Sandel that it's inadequate to speak of our relationship to a Shakespearean tragedy purely in terms of pleasure. There's certainly much to enjoy about Shakespeare's language, characterizations, and plots, but *Hamlet* does more than simply scratch our itch for entertainment. What's so vital about a play like *Hamlet* is that it does justice to our human complexity: it illuminates and even expands us, it gives us clarifying vistas on our own ups and downs, and it does so by its ability to stir the ineradicable suffering of being human. *The Simpsons* is a great way to pass half an hour, and it's often a brilliant send-up of our culture. But it takes poetry to save the life of someone like Mill who suffers from a fundamental breakdown of values.

We want to be happy, but we also seek out meaning. Often happiness and meaning overlap, but not always. It's not even clear that many of the crucially important things of human life involve a predominance of pleasure over misery. For instance, raising children might prove, on analysis, to involve more headache than fun. But doesn't the very act of trying to measure the value of raising children purely in terms of how much pleasure kids bring seem grossly inadequate? Sometimes the child that brings us the most grief turns out to be the most beloved! And isn't the same thing true of many of our greatest pursuits: sports, literature, work, charity, romance? Yes, they're often sources of satisfaction, but isn't their meaningfulness something that doesn't map perfectly onto the coordinates of pleasure and pain? Mill's deep faith is that what gives us meaning makes us happy, and maybe in some final sense that's true. I sure hope it is. But until that day dawns, we try to balance pleasure and meaning as two sometimes-competing goals.

I have serious doubts that we can find meaning when we calculate our lives in terms of satisfaction. Aristotle shrewdly observes that when we aim at happiness, we're unlikely to achieve it; whereas when we aim at excellence, we have a better chance of being happy. Likewise, when our primary focus is eliminating suffering, don't we often make life worse? Luckily, in his philosophical and political career Mill's focus is less about Bentham's utilitarianism and more about elevating the human character and sustaining the freedom necessary for a variety of interesting and powerful forms of life to duke it out and flourish. Mill's ideal world isn't one of vanishing pain and maximized pleasure; it's a world of freedom, vulnerability, and conflict in which debilitating forms of suffering have been alleviated. His quite reasonable counsel, even if it doesn't add up into a neat theory, is that we should defend freedom and maximize meaning in ways that keep big political instances of suffering to a minimum. What a beautiful idea, no matter how it's justified!

* * * * * * * * * * * *

If we care about Mill's ideals of defending liberty and minimizing gross injustice, we desperately need to reexamine our penal system. I began my own serious reflection on prison with the guys. It was hard at first to get them to talk about the philosophy of punishment. They got derailed. "I don't know what the judge was on when he gave me ten years—seriously, I think he was *actually* on something!" "You're telling me that this child molester is getting half—*half*—the sentence I got!" "Do you know the sentence I would have got in Finland?" "I'm innocent of the charges—well, not totally innocent but innocent enough!"

The first theory of punishment the guys and I finally got around to examining was Immanuel Kant's retributivism. The central idea of retributivism is that the punishment should fit the crime: a serious crime deserves an equally serious punishment, a minor crime an equally minor punishment. This principle restrains our zeal to over-punish. The theory also holds that the punishment should never have an ulterior motive (such as rehabilitation or deterrence); it should be about what the criminal deserves, not what society wishes the criminal would become. This principle extends Kant's idea that we should never simply *use* people: we are obliged to treat others as ends in themselves, including those who have done us grievous wrong. Finally, retributivism states that the government has a strong moral obligation to punish the guilty. In an infamous passage, Kant says that if an island-state was about to be destroyed, and everyone was going to move away, the government should first execute everyone with an outstanding death sentence!

Then we examined the great competing modern theory of punishment, which derives from utilitarianism. According to Jeremy Bentham, the idea of a moral obligation to punish people is one of those concepts of "natural" law that should be eradicated. As he bluntly puts it, "All punishment is mischief: all punishment is evil."[16] Pain is bad; punishment is a pain; thus, punishment—*all* punishment—is bad. That said, the principle of utility is such that certain pains should be inflicted if they bring about a greater happiness. Thus, for Bentham and Mill, the primary goal of our penal system should be to deter future crimes, for crime is a major source of unhappiness in any society. A related goal of our penal system should be the rehabilitation of offenders, for that would allow them to be released nonthreateningly into society. Overall, the big utilitarian idea is that a penal system should be judged solely on its results. Does it increase the happiness and decrease the unhappiness of the maximum number?

The guys roundly rejected the idea that a penal system should be guided by deterrence and rehabilitation. They liked the idea that the penal system should be judged by its results, but they didn't think utilitarian goals panned out. They chuckled at how quickly many of their buddies who'd been thoroughly "deterred" and "rehabilitated" by the system became repeat offenders. Moreover, they shared Kant's irritation with the idea that other people—in this case, wardens, guards, and shrinks—would remake them according to ends that they themselves hadn't chosen.

Jack—one of my favorite students, a robust white-haired inmate who's been in and out of prison—made an astute observation, one that reinvented the analysis of Michel Foucault in *Discipline and Punish* and brilliantly connected it to Kant's central idea. He said:

> The strangest way that I've felt used by the prison system is that I'm forever labeled a criminal. The first time I got out of prison, I realized that everybody looked at me and treated me differently. At first I was mad at them about it. Then I started to realize that I was acting differently myself. In other words, I was treating myself like a criminal! It's that label "criminal" that's the worst punishment. It makes you feel like you're not free even when you're out of prison.

Still, the guys weren't particularly keen on retributivism as an alternative to deterrence and rehabilitation. After deliberation, what some of them came to was essentially a version of J. S. Mill's rights-based version of utilitarianism. When I first started teaching Introduction to Ethics, a student wrote me a brilliant term paper evaluating Kant's and Bentham's moral philosophies. Her thesis was that we should be Kantians on utilitarian grounds: the most efficient way of bringing about the greatest good for the greatest number is to follow Kant's version of the Golden Rule. In our discussion of Mill, some of the inmates came to a similar conclusion. Most of them believed that no system of punishment is ideal. Some were attracted to the idea that society could find a way of restoring the broken communal bonds that cause and are caused by crime—the idea of "restorative justice," which we'll discuss in the chapter on Confucius. But some seemed to think that the best of all possible worlds would be if punishments could be proportioned to the severity of crimes. They all asserted that this was far from the case in our current system, and I don't think anybody who looked at how we've gotten "tough on crime" could disagree with that assessment. Could our current penal system be reasonably defended on any philosophical theory? Not only do we fail to proportion punishments to their crimes, we do a piss-poor job of rehabilitation, and we can be said to deter crime only insofar as we lock up ungodly amounts of people, inflicting a whole lot of suffering for outrageous amounts of money.

At the end of our discussion, I asked the guys a blunt question: "Is prison, as Bentham says, a form of mischief? Is punishment intrinsically evil, even if it leads to something better?" They took the question more seriously than I expected, but they eventually all gave the answer "Yes." I looked to my friend Simon, who has a life-without-parole sentence for the murder of a pimp. Actually, Simon didn't kill or even plan to kill the pimp; he accompanied—"abetted," in legalese—a man who was trying to retrieve a girl from the pimp. His friend and the pimp got into a fight, and the pimp was killed. Iowa is one of the many states that have the un-Kantian felony murder rule that makes anyone involved in a homicide subject to life without parole. The fact that Simon is black probably didn't help his cause. My state, like most of the country, incarcerates black citizens at a disproportionate rate. Cons and ex-cons sometimes refer to Iowa as the International Order of White America. Despite the fact that the judge who was forced to issue the life-without-parole punishment has written letters for Simon's sentence to be commuted, Simon has served nearly thirty years of a life sentence. Soft-spoken but a lively conversationalist, Simon once asked me if I'd trade ideas with him over what's called "o-mail"— email for offenders. I've come to know him by exchanging messages about the weather, philosophy, food, and suffering—the fundamental subjects. When I asked if prison was a form of suffering, he didn't say anything. He didn't need to.

* * * * * * * * * * *

About Jeremy Bentham and James Mill, Isaiah Berlin says, "If someone had offered them a medicine which could scientifically be shown to put those who took it into a state of permanent contentment, their premisses would have bound them to accept this as the panacea for all that they thought evil."[17] A permanent-happiness pill is the most obvious solution to the problem of evil. To their credit, Jeremy Bentham and James Mill never get around to imagining the banality of shiny happy people holding hands because they were too concerned about the million and one evils that would need to be solved before the ditty of paradise could be cued. But in our era, when pharmaceutical companies really do try to convince us that we can buy a bottle of cure-alls, and our politicians promise to fix all our problems, it behooves us to wonder if the greatest good we can imagine is really a life free of suffering, a life of maximum pleasure and minimum pain.

J. S. Mill's philosophy embodies a paradox without really acknowledging it. His deep conviction is that there should be freedom and conflict such that the human character can be enlarged. And he thinks, without much basis, that these freedoms and conflicts inevitably bring about the greatest amount of pleasure with the least amount of pain. In *Utilitarianism* Mill writes, "No one whose opinion deserves a moment's consideration can doubt that most of the great positive evils of the world are in themselves removable, and will, if human affairs continue to improve, be in the end reduced within narrow limits."[18] Is it possible to have real freedom without the risk of evil? Can our lives have the robust kind of meaning that Mill prizes without tragedy and even occasional bouts of depression? Can we ever clearly distinguish productive from unproductive risks, meaningful from meaningless suffering, and successfully fix nature so that our sufferings are always part of a larger happiness? Mill observes, "Every mind sufficiently intelligent and generous to bear a part, however small and inconspicuous, in the endeavor [to remove the sources of human suffering] will draw a noble enjoyment from the contest itself, which he would not for any bribe in the form of selfish indulgence consent to be without."[19] Don't we need the contest itself?

What Mill seems to be driving at is captured less by Bentham's principle of maximizing pleasure and more by the ancient Greek ideal of *eudaimonia*, that notoriously difficult term to translate, which means something like "happiness" or "flourishing." This "happiness" doesn't really refer to pleasure; it's suggestive of a meaningful life, a life that actualizes our powers and is worth being celebrated by its community. Such a life may sometimes involve a predominance of positive feelings and is generally satisfying, but not always. It's often marked by sorrow and strife, and not just accidentally. A flourishing, meaningful life is inevitably involved in projects that involve risk, failure, and struggle. In fact, people who lead meaningful lives often choose struggle over satisfaction. Mill argues that part of the beauty of the freedom of thought is that even when true ideas are ascendant, they still need to be challenged by false ideas lest the truth lose its meaning for us. Shouldn't the exact same logic apply to happiness? Without pain and struggle to test our happiness, it risks becoming meaningless. Only with openness and vulnerability to sufferings that exceed our understanding can there be significance to our lives. Just look at J. S. Mill's autobiography!

Many people, like Simon, suffer needlessly from their inability to participate in the comprehensive goods of being human. All sorts of careers and contributions have been denied to the Simons of the world. It makes sense to use something like Mill's calculus of freedom and happiness to argue for change. It's not simply that Simon's sentence is unfair; he's suffering needlessly. It's next to impossible to tolerate pointless suffering when we know that it's not inevitable. Even though strife and struggle can enhance life's meaning, it's difficult, if not inhumane, to sit idly by when people are hurting in ways that could be alleviated.

My feelings about Simon and his situation resonate with the paradox at the heart of Mill's philosophy. I want to help my friend. I want to relieve the pain of his imprisonment. Though I'm not without hope, I admit my hope is small. I don't see Iowa's legislature overturning the felony murder rule. Even if they do, I don't know if Simon's case would be relitigated. Moreover, Iowa's governors have been incredibly stingy with pardons; basically, you have to do something heroic in prison, like save a guard's life. Simon jokes to me, "Hey, I'd be happy to save a guard's life, but the opportunity doesn't present itself all that often! Plus, isn't it heroic simply not to go crazy after thirty years in prison?"

And yet Simon and I have both learned invaluable lessons from the predicament we want to change. One such lesson I've learned from Simon is about the nature of home. At one point in our correspondence I'd been going on about how I found it interesting that in gospel and blues music "home" generally refers to death—as in "Swing low, sweet chariot, coming for to carry me home." I asked Simon what he thought about home. Could he—or I, or any of us—be at home in this unjust world, even in prison? He wrote back:

> Some prisoners get offended if someone calls prison their home. At times "home" is a place I yearn to get back to. At other moments,

when I'm accepting life on life's terms, "home" is the here and the now. For me to have any semblance of peace I must accept "home" as the here and now! I guess, to me, "home" is a state of mind *and* a place I desperately yearn to get to. Any place. Clearly, knowing that at any moment in the night a prison guard can holler at me, "Let me see some skin," and I must come from underneath my warm blanket to reveal an arm or leg, doesn't make prison particularly homey! And yet I can feel at home on earth—out in the sunshine, under the clouds, with friends, writing to you.

I've reflected a lot on that letter. There's an awful, beautiful paradox in what Simon says. We're at home on this earth, and we're not at home on this earth. We desperately wish to get away from the unjust circumstances that are inevitable to our condition, and yet, as Robert Frost says, "Earth's the right place for love."

* * * * * * * * * * *

Speaking of love, I've failed to mention the most important part of John Stuart Mill's biography, more important than even his mental breakdown and subsequent discovery of Romantic poetry. In 1830, when Mill was almost out of his depression, he met and fell in love with Harriet Taylor, who was already married with children. Scandalizing their fellow Victorians, they spent most of the next two decades joined at the hip: Taylor even established a separate residence from her husband so she could have uninterrupted time with Mill. In 1851, two respectable years after her husband died of cancer, Harriet Taylor became Harriet Taylor Mill. I've been following the custom of referring to works like *On Liberty* as exclusively Mill's, but Mill himself claims that they're the result of his intellectual collaboration with his friend, lover, and eventual wife: "All my published writings were as much her work as mine; her share in them constantly increasing as years advanced."[20]

The history of literature blazes with songs and stories of passionate love, but rarely does it crackle and glow more warmly, more companionably, more admiringly than in Mill's tribute to Taylor.

> Alike in the highest regions of speculation and in the smaller practical concerns of daily life, her mind was the same perfect instrument, piercing to the very heart and marrow of the matter; always seizing the essential idea or principle. The same exactness and rapidity of operation, pervading as it did her sensitive as well as her mental faculties, would, with her gifts of feeling and imagination, have fitted her to be a consummate artist, as her fiery and tender soul and her vigorous eloquence would certainly have made her a great orator, and her profound knowledge of human nature and discernment and sagacity in practical life, would, in the times when such a *carrière* was open to women, have made her eminent among the rulers of mankind. Her intellectual gifts did but minister to a moral character at once the noblest and the best balanced which I have ever met with in life. Her unselfishness was not that of a taught system of duties, but of a heart which thoroughly identified itself with the feelings of others, and often went to excess in consideration for them by imaginatively investing their feelings with the intensity of its own. The passion of justice might have been thought to be her strongest feeling, but for her boundless generosity, and a lovingness ever ready to pour itself forth upon any or all human beings who were capable of giving the smallest feeling in return.[21]

My rough-and-ready theory of true love is that it involves the reconciliation of two seemingly impossible tasks: our beloved must give us everything good that our parents gave us, and our beloved must give us everything good that our parents failed to give us. True love makes us feel simultaneously at home and on an adventure. We all have intimations of it. I think of first reaching out to hold the hand or kiss the lips of someone I'm falling in love with: it's a terrifying risk, charged with wild desires, but it's also permeated by my deep-rooted longings for tenderness and acceptance. Is it possible to put the complicated jigsaw puzzle of true love together in a lasting way? Well, Taylor seems to have puzzled out Mill! Harriet shared the philanthropic aspirations and intellectual vigor that John Stuart so loved in his father, *and* she embodied the poetry and compassion that he never got from his upbringing: "What was abstract and purely scientific was mine; the properly human element came from her."[22] It's not a stretch to say that Mill and Taylor's love is the embodiment of their philosophy, a noble blend of Jeremy Bentham's utilitarianism and William Wordsworth's poetry.

TWO

WE SHOULD EMBRACE
POINTLESS SUFFERING

On Friedrich Nietzsche and the
Challenge of the Eternal Return

I love you, enigmatic life . . .
Throw both your arms around me.
If you have no more happiness to give,
Well then, give me your suffering.

LOU SALOMÉ

As a precocious thirteen-year-old who'd lost his father to a mysterious brain malady, Friedrich Nietzsche wrote an essay, his first philosophical effort, on the problem of evil. "As for the 'solution' of the problem I posed at that time," Nietzsche teasingly reflected years later in the *Genealogy of Morals*, "well, I gave the honor to God, as was only fair, and made him the *father* of evil."[1] His last deed before sinking irretrievably into the catatonic depths of his own brain malady was, when he saw a horse being beaten in a Turin piazza, to embrace the creature and weep. In the three intervening decades he never stopped trying to trace evil to its origin and throw his arms around suffering.

Bertrand Russell says that Nietzsche's whole philosophy is contained in a few lines of *King Lear*: "I will do such things—/ What they are yet I know not, but they shall be/ The terrors of the earth."[2] Russell is thinking of passages in Nietzsche like "Who will attain anything great if he does not find in himself the strength and the will to *inflict* great suffering? Being able to suffer is the least thing . . . but not to perish of internal distress and uncertainty when one inflicts great suffering and hears the cry of this suffering—that is great, that belongs to greatness."[3] Or, "'Evil has always had great effects in its favor. And nature is evil. Let us therefore be natural.' That is the secret reasoning of those who have mastered the most spectacular effects, and they have all too often been considered great human beings."[4] Mill says that the worst human actions pale in comparison to natural disasters. Nietzsche says that the most magnificent human actions aspire to the same power as horrific natural events! He calls on us to confront suffering on terms that stand the problem of evil on its head. Insofar as modernity elevates us to the position of God or, to use Nietzsche's term, the superhuman (*der Übermensch*), we must be willing to embrace suffering enthusiastically—even to the point of becoming the new fathers of it. We should stop running from pointless suffering. We should turn around and embrace it! We should dance with pointless suffering!

* * * * * * * * * * * *

Friedrich Nietzsche was born in 1844 to an overbearing mother and a kindly Lutheran pastor in Röcken, a small town near Leipzig. His relatively happy childhood was scarred by the sickness and death of his dad in 1849. Except for a few rowdy lapses, Nietzsche was a good student who, in hopes of becoming a pastor himself, headed off to the University of Bonn. There he realized that God had recently been murdered, even if the murderers—mild-mannered historians and scientists—didn't yet realize the extent of their crime. To his mother's chagrin, he switched to the study of philology at the University of Leipzig, where he distinguished himself as the most promising classicist of his generation. After a brief tour in the Prussian military, he became a professor at the University of Basel at the tender age of twenty-four. Falling under the sway of the philosophy of Arthur Schopenhauer and the friendship of Richard Wagner, Nietzsche soon abandoned the stolid academic life and became an itinerant philosopher who at the end of his sanity could declare with only slight exaggeration, "I am no man, I am dynamite."[5]

What compelled Nietzsche to give up on his Christianity was a combination of science and the new historical research into religion. Belief suddenly seemed silly.

> A god who begets children on a mortal woman; a sage who calls upon us no longer to work, no longer to sit in judgment, but to heed the signs of the imminent end of the world; a justice which accepts an innocent man as a substitute sacrifice; someone who bids his disciples drink his blood; prayers for miraculous interventions; sins perpetrated against a god atoned for by a god; fear of a Beyond to which death is the gateway; the figure of the Cross as a symbol in an age which no longer knows the meaning and the shame of the Cross— how gruesomely all this is wafted to us, as if out of the grave of a primeval past! Can one believe that things of this sort are still believed in?[6]

Nietzsche never disproves God, because he doesn't believe that we come to beliefs through proof and disproof. They rise and fall according to our complex psychologies, in which reason is mostly a figurehead. Nietzsche believed that he was experiencing in his own complex psychology the early stages of a crisis of faith that would rip apart civilization, the institutions of which were all entwined, explicitly or implicitly, with religion. As he puts it with characteristic flair, "Have you not heard of that madman who lit a lantern in the bright morning hours, ran to the marketplace, and cried incessantly: 'I seek God! I seek God!... Whither is God?... I will tell you. We have killed him—

you and I. All of us are his murderers. But how did we do this? How could we drink up the sea? Who gave us the sponge to wipe away the entire horizon?'"[7]

According to Nietzsche, all living beings are driven by "the will to power," the desire to grow, to assert, to overcome—not merely to find pleasure and avoid pain, as utilitarianism would have it. Even evolutionary theorists, whose science Nietzsche generally appreciates, fail to understand that survival and reproduction are simply side effects of our power increasing. The struggle for existence isn't the whole show; it's just the occasional fracas in a wild world devoted to growth, expansion, and superiority.

The problem is that our will to power has now broken the reins of religious belief that for centuries had guided it in a credible direction. For two millennia Christianity channeled the will to power into a great civilization and endowed our suffering with a cosmic meaning. We now risk hurtling into a meaningless world, what Nietzsche calls "nihilism." One of the reasons that many believers in God appreciate Nietzsche is that he sees clearly just how integrated religion is into culture. At least he appreciates the significance of religion, they figure, even as they consider his conclusions a horrifying *reductio ad absurdum* of atheism. Whereas many atheists abandon belief in God like it was giving up belief in the tooth fairy and then live as unconscious parasites on the slowly dying carcass of the culture born of that God, Nietzsche understands that our liberal democratic institutions and habits are nourished by sacred background beliefs. The concept of "justice," for instance, relies on the idea that there's an order of right and wrong transcending politics: our democracies are *under God*. The concept of "rights" relies on the idea that this transcendental order can be found in each of us: we possess unalienable rights *endowed by our Creator*. Even our concept of "truth" often presumes that there's an unchanging natural system that can be grasped by a mind that hovers outside the system. Nietzsche is too alert to the complex architecture of thinking to believe that we can simply get rid of the myths, images, and practices that undergird our culture and still expect it to maintain itself.

What really gets under Nietzsche's skin is the human type that predominates without a higher set of values—a "god"—to give meaning to the will to power. Nietzsche calls this human type "the last man" (*der letzte Mensch*, which is actually "the last human," but I'll stick to the term "the last man" because it's acquired authority in English). Essentially, the last man is a wimpy utilitarian: "'We have invented happiness,' say the last men, and they blink."[8] Because the last men lack any kind of invigorating beliefs, they aspire to nothing more than creature comforts. They work for no higher reason than to meet their basic needs or to fend off boredom. They come home from their jobs and immediately seek out tranquilizing entertainment. Pain and hardship—prerequisites for any kind of serious accomplishment—are dismissed as evil and daunting, to be avoided if possible. The last men prefer comfort over aspiration, normalness over greatness, immediate gratification over long-term struggle, insurance over risk. They shun history because they have nothing to learn from it, or they mock it because they want to bring it down to their level. They worship the idea of "progress," which means trying to make life easier and longer. Their lives are so disconnected that they exercise their will to power, in complete safety, in the form of violent spectacle and entertainment. Because they have little fight in them and are driven by gratification, they're easily herded and manipulated by charismatic leaders who promise them security and prosperity.

Christianity, when it was genuinely believed in, gave everyday people—the "herd," to use Nietzsche's disdainful term—beliefs, symbols, and rituals that made them part of something greater than scratching their itches. The last men keep Christianity's sense that suffering and death aren't the true destiny of humanity, but they jettison the beliefs and disciplines that produce greatness. They represent the triumph of the herd. By believing in paradise without seriously believing in God, the last men try to remake life into something lifeless. Nietzsche encourages us not to tranquilize ourselves but to embrace life to the fullest, which means to embrace the suffering that's inseparable from life: "You want, if possible—and there is no more insane 'if possible'—*to abolish suffering*. And we? It really seems that we would rather have it higher and worse than ever. . . . The discipline of suffering, of *great* suffering—do you not know that only *this* discipline has created all enhancements of man so far?"[9] Nietzsche's big objection to the last men is their mediocrity: "The time is coming when man will no longer give birth to a star."[10]

* * * * * * * * * * *

As a budding philosopher coping with the death of his father, the teenage Nietzsche wrestled with the theological problem of evil. Grappling with the death of God, the grown-up Nietzsche upends the problem: "Under what conditions did man devise these value judgments good and evil? *and what value do they themselves possess?*"[11] The traditional problem of evil involves the search for the moral rationale for suffering: How can we have faith in God when there's so much evil in the world? Nietzsche seeks instead suffering's rationale for morality: How does evil compel us to put our faith in goodness?

In the *Genealogy of Morals*, his most systematic work of philosophy, Nietzsche argues—drawing on his philological training at Leipzig—that we initially see the world in terms of the value judgments "good" and "bad." "Good" refers to whatever enhances us (health, power, beauty, victory), "bad" whatever diminishes us (sickness, weakness, deformity, loss). "Good" is the successful expression of the will to power, "bad" the frustration of our fundamental drives. In this way of thinking about values, suffering isn't bad—particularly when we get to inflict it! Suffering and death are built into a healthy life: no pain, no gain. The warriors and the wise claw their way up in society—and enjoy doing so. The strong throw themselves into hardships because they recognize that the enhancement of their powers is possible only through the thrill of struggle and battle. They actively seek out challenging friends and welcome equally strong enemies, for they have the power to repay good with good, bad with bad.

It's the weak who come to see suffering as bad, because suffering for them involves humiliation and domination, the thwarting of their

WE SHOULD EMBRACE POINTLESS SUFFERING | 61

will to power. A big part of their suffering is that they're looked down on by the strong and come to see themselves as low, common, plebeian. Their concerns shrink to mere utility, the maximizing of their pleasures and the minimizing of their pains through obedience and deference. Though they put on a nice face to placate their masters, they seethe with what Nietzsche calls *ressentiment*—the French word for a special kind of resentment where we blame others for our suffering to protect our self-image. To borrow a parable from the *Genealogy of Morals*, it's understandable that lambs don't like being attacked by their predators, but it's *ressentiment* when lambs start claiming that being a predator is evil.

Then something happens that Nietzsche regards with equal parts horror and respect: *ressentiment* becomes creative. Certain priestly members of the slave class—first in ancient Judaism and then with Christianity in the Roman Empire—engage in a wholesale reinterpretation of morality. What the master class considers "good" suddenly becomes "evil," and what the master class considers "bad" suddenly becomes "good." Natural outpourings of power and dominance are viewed as wicked, whereas meekness and humility are recognized as signs of blessedness. Glory goes no longer to the victors but to those who turn the other cheek. The downcast and downtrodden are valued just as much as, if not more than, the nobles of society. Everyone is equal, and the poor are paradoxically great. Rooted in *ressentiment*, "the slave revolt in morality" involves an "imaginary revenge," in which the slave's thwarted will to power is given a new value system to express itself. Under the new dispensation, the meek are promised inheritance of the earth. What begins as bitterness at the master's success turns into revenge on worldly success itself. The same good-evil psychology that sings the praises of universal brotherhood comes to imagine an ultimate state of justice where the good—the weak—rise to dominion in paradise, and the evil—the strong—are cast into hell. In other words, what presents itself as meekness and love is, in fact, a gigantic triumph of vengeance and dominance, for the slave revolt in morality doesn't just defeat someone or something; it defeats the very concept of worldly defeat. It gloats in an imaginary heaven over those who once gloated on earth.

But the slaves pay a big price for their newfound morality. Because they recognize domination as evil but still burn with the will to power, they're forced to see existence as intrinsically sinful. The will turns against itself, punishing itself for simply existing. The price is what Nietzsche calls the "bad conscience": "Hostility, cruelty, joy in persecuting, in attacking, in change, in destruction—all this turned against the possessors of such instincts: *that* is the origin of the 'bad conscience.'"[12] When we can't beat up others, we beat up ourselves. The beauty of Judaism and Christianity is that they give us symbols, myths, and rituals that allow us to channel our bad conscience into powerful modes of life. The downside is that these modes of life are self-punishing; their highest expressions involve ascetic practices of fasting, self-flagellation, abstinence, constant repentance, constant guilt—all for an interpretation of life meant to make life better! Nietzsche observes, "Although the shrewdest judges of the witches and even the witches themselves were convinced of the guilt of witchery, this guilt nevertheless did not exist. This applies to all guilt."[13] Along similar lines, he says, "The Christian resolve to find the world ugly and bad has made the world ugly and bad."[14]

* * * * * * * * * * *

Nietzsche's call to reject the legacy of morality and to embrace cruelty can sound . . . well, cruel. The problem is exacerbated by the fact that Nazism, arguably the cruelest political movement in a century with many strong contenders for the title, embraced aspects of Nietzsche's philosophy. When I introduced the *Genealogy of Morals* to my prison class, a new student raised his heavily tattooed arm and asked, "Is Nietzsche a Nazi?" Usually when students ask that question, I assume they're looking to get out of reading a philosopher on the loophole of his being a moral monster. Certain of this guy's tattoos made me wonder if saying yes wouldn't be a way of selling him on the thinker!

It's thrilling to read Nietzsche's description of his books as dynamite. It's disturbing to find oneself in the position of handing weapons to Leopold and Loeb.

Like most teachers, I have a knack for putting off tough questions. I replied to my inked-up student, "Before we tackle Nietzsche and Nazism, let's be clear that Nietzsche isn't saying, 'Rather than be kind, be cruel,' at least not exactly. His view is that all human action is motivated by the will to power. What he calls 'cruelty' is the inevitable power play in whatever we do. The choice isn't between cruelty and kindness, it's between a self-aware, self-directed 'cruelty' and a sham 'cruelty,' one that exerts power in ways that are secretive, self-destructive, guilty, and often crueler than the openly cruel."

As I was fending off the Nazi question, I suddenly realized that Nietzsche's best example of how moralism can be crueler than open "cruelty" was all around us: the penal system itself. According to Nietzsche, our moral ideas, when closely examined, all channel the will to power. Even Kant's high-minded categorical imperative, that we should always treat others as ends in themselves and never merely as means to an end, is used to justify—even demand—that we inflict serious punishment on others. As Nietzsche puts it, "The categorical imperative smells of cruelty."[15] We could say the same thing about Bentham, who argues that all punishment is mischief and then goes on to envision an elaborate prison where inmates are constantly monitored. The guys and I talked about how the idea of a penal system can be traced back to Christian morality and the bad conscience. Lawbreakers didn't spend much time in prison prior to Christianity's introduction of the ideal of penance: they were mostly exiled, beaten, or executed. The radical new idea of Christianity was that prison could be a place of cure, a cell of solitude in which to become penitent—a *penitentiary*. Then, in the late eighteenth and early nineteenth centuries, as Michel Foucault demonstrates in *Discipline and Punish*, this idea of the penitentiary blended with utilitarianism to become a strange moralized extension of industrialism: masses of prisoners were "corrected" and surveilled in a maximally efficient reformatory.

In other words, prison became a unique way of inflicting physical and psychological harm on others *for their own good.* It's prolonged cruelty in the name of efficient kindness!

According to Nietzsche, punishment is fundamentally an act of dominance, a drama of asserting power over those who've offended us. Under master morality, punishment is usually short and sharp, if it's even necessary. It's either "You've offended me, so now I'm going to hurt you" or "You've offended me, but since you're beneath my concern, get out of my sight." The offender is promptly killed, humiliated, or ignored. Under slave morality, punishment becomes much more elaborate. It's turned into a prolonged drama, rationalized with any number of meanings, and applied universally. It becomes a covert celebration of power behind the curtain of morality. Nietzsche says, "Without cruelty there is no festival: thus the longest and most ancient part of human history teaches—and in punishment there is so much that is *festive!*"[16] I tend to think of the decapitations and hangings that were once boisterous public spectacles, or all the delicious depictions of hell throughout Christian history. But the guys pointed out more contemporary examples of the festiveness of punishment: the court and prison dramas that provide us with so much entertainment, the long-standing political theater of getting tough on crime, the smug satisfaction taken by those who haven't been convicted in physically and psychologically separating themselves from the "bad guys," our jokes about prison rape.

Nietzsche's point is that we find the true justification of our penal system in our social assertions of dominance rather than in any positive effects on the incarcerated. In this light, we discussed the following passage from the *Genealogy*:

> It is precisely among criminals and convicts that the sting of conscience is extremely rare; prisoners and penitentiaries are not the kind of hotbed in which this species of gnawing worm is likely to flourish. . . . Generally speaking, punishment makes men hard and cold; it concentrates; it sharpens the feeling of alienation; it

strengthens the power of resistance. If it happens that punishment destroys the vital energy and brings about a miserable prostration and self-abasement, such a result is certainly even less pleasant than the usual effects of punishment—characterized by dry and gloomy seriousness.[17]

I asked, "Does prison actually make you hard and cold?" That was too easy a question for them. Their only question was how you face the constant thwarting of your will and hardening of your heart. Even the adamant Christians and Muslims admitted to the psychological reality that Nietzsche describes. One prison convert said, "We see everything he's talking about on a regular basis: the hardened, the alienated, the resisters, the gloomy. I do have stings of conscience, but not because of here. This place feels like one big machine meant to break you down." He reflected a moment, as if taking some private pleasure, and continued, "It seems funny that people ever think that prison is supposed to cure you. The challenge for us, in spite of prison, is to figure out how to hold on to some of what he's calling our 'vital energy' and use it to do something good."

Nietzsche enjoys teasing us by using charged words like "cruelty" to make us rethink our values to the core, but whenever he gets specific with his encouragement to inflict suffering, his proposals sound graceful rather than indecent. The fact is that a crude injury done to others makes them more difficult to manage.[18] Those who've been through our penal system have a nearly 70 percent recidivism rate after three years—not a great record for the ideals of penance and rehabilitation! According to Nietzsche, we shouldn't be afraid of doing things that make others hurt for the sake of enhancing life; nor should we shy from being hurt. But there's little to be gained by bullying or punishing others; moreover, it's usually the inwardly weak who feel the need to bully and punish. The virtues recommended by Nietzsche have little to do with cruelty as we normally conceive it. In *Daybreak* he envisions the strong soul to be honest ("towards ourselves and whoever else is a friend to us"), brave ("towards the enemy"), magnanimous ("towards the defeated"), and polite ("always").[19] Nietzsche's prophetic alter ego Zarathustra says, "That man be delivered from revenge, that is for me the bridge to the highest hope, and a rainbow after long storms."[20]

When the guys read Nietzsche's proposal "Let us do away with the concept *sin*—and let us quickly send after it the concept *punishment!*" they had a good chuckle.[21] Omar—who'd been first introduced to Nietzsche in a California prison, where older inmates passed down *Thus Spoke Zarathustra* as wisdom literature to the newbies—spoke up about how we need to eliminate even more than sin and punishment. He was interested in the idea of life as a kind of art project, a continual process of reimagining and remaking ourselves. He spoke eloquently of how Nietzsche inspired him in making art and living life to be unafraid of delving into the darkness and thus emerging with a new, enriched self. Along these lines, Omar argued that we need to get rid of the idea of the offender altogether. Nietzsche is indeed fond of the idea of killing off the subject behind our actions. As God dies, so does the soul. We say that "lightning strikes," as if there were something called lightning that decides to strike, whereas the striking and the lightning are one and the same. The electricity just happens.[22] Likewise, expressions of power just happen. We don't always have to like these expressions of power, and it's natural sometimes to resist them, fight them, perhaps even punish them. But Nietzsche thinks it's an illusion of grammar to believe there's some underlying actor who, say, ten years after the fact, is still guilty. I think of people like Omar or my friend Simon. Whatever they were guilty of in their twenties, aren't they radically different now in their late fifties? Are the lightning bolts that struck three decades ago still pertinent to this season's weather? To think that prison reforms the underlying soul of the criminal is, according to Nietzsche, metaphysically absurd. There's no guilty party underneath the crime. We're always being reformed wherever we find ourselves.

* * * * * * * * * * *

"Oh, what months I have had, and what a summer!" Nietzsche wrote to his friend Franz Overbeck in 1861, in a letter composed in Latin so Overbeck's wife couldn't read it.[23] On the one hand, that summer Nietzsche had been having violent stomach cramps, unrelenting bouts of nausea, and debilitating migraines. "Pain is vanquishing my life and will," he explained. "I have experienced as much torment to my body as I have seen changes in the sky. Every cloud conceals some form of lightning that can hit me with surprising force and altogether destroy my hapless self. I have already summoned death as a doctor and hoped yesterday would be my final day—but I hoped in vain." On the other hand, that summer Nietzsche experienced the central inspiration of his life in the mountains of Sils Maria, Switzerland: "a revelation—in the sense that suddenly, with indescribable certainty and subtlety, something becomes *visible*, audible, something that shakes one to the last depths and throws one down.... One hears, one does not seek; one accepts, one does not ask who gives; like lightning, a thought flashes up, with necessity, without hesitation regarding its form—I never had any choice."[24]

Like his teacher Schopenhauer, Nietzsche understands that pain, misery, and death aren't just occasional bugs in the system; they're central features of existence. What are we supposed to make of that? The last men shrug their shoulders, hide away in the comfiest corner they can find, and try their damnedest not to think about human fate—numbing themselves with work, entertainment, alcohol, and other anodynes. The religious refuse to accept that this vale of tears is our destination. They believe that this world must be a testing ground for a supernatural afterlife where suffering and death shall no longer rule the roost. Many modernists, like utilitarians or Marxists, also regard this world as a vale of tears; however, they don't believe in an otherworldly solution to our misery. They want to bring about heaven on earth, or at least a world of ever-diminishing suffering, through the vigorous interventions of political systems, science, or technology. Is there another way of relating to the fact that life is suffering? Is there a more life-enhancing way of relating to those awful migraines?

The rapture atop the Alps in the summer of 1861 was Nietzsche's discovery of the eternal return. The idea is first introduced to the public in *The Gay Science*, in a chapter called "The Greatest Weight."

> What, if some day or night a demon were to steal after you into your loneliest loneliness and say to you: "This life as you now live it and have lived it, you will have to live once more and innumerable times more; and there will be nothing new in it, but every pain and every joy and every thought and sigh and everything unutterably small or great in your life will have to return to you, all in the same succession and sequence—even this spider and this moonlight between the trees . . ." Would you not throw yourself down and gnash your teeth and curse the demon who spoke thus? Or have you once experienced a tremendous moment when you would have answered him: "You are a god and never have I heard anything more divine."[25]

In his notebooks Nietzsche toys with the idea that the eternal return is an actual scientific fact. Basically, we're the product of combinations of matter and energy, which began in the misty depths with Event A, which then led to Event B, and so on, all the way to you now reading this book. Nietzsche reasons that since there's a finite set of combinations of matter and energy and an infinite amount of time, eventually the universe will chance again on Event A, which will then lead to Event B, and so on, all the way to you now reading this book, which will eventually lead back to Event A, which will then lead to Event B, and so on, all the way to you now reading this book, which will eventually . . . you get the picture. But are the combinations really finite? And how can we know that time won't come to an end before we ever bump into Event A again? Nietzsche never publishes his "scientific" doodlings with the eternal return. It probably makes the most sense to understand the eternal return as the spiritual challenge that's presented to us in *The Gay Science*.

Are you willing to say yes to this life? Are you willing to do it all over again—every stretch of waiting at the bus station, every crummy relationship, every hangover, every migraine? It's a tough challenge to get the mind around. Start by considering a random snippet of life, something "unutterably small," neither earth-shatteringly awful nor world-changingly wonderful—an uneventful week of seventh grade, for instance. For me that involved getting up painfully early to catch a ride with my dad, forcing myself to down breakfast (I've never been a morning person), dull class after dull class, mediocre to disgusting school lunches (but for Thursday's glorious chili with a warm cinnamon roll on the side), aching glimpses of Maggie's beauty in her Guess jeans, being menaced in the bathroom by high-schoolers or otherwise peeing in fear of that menace, inane joking with my pals by the column radiator, the alarming awkwardness of random erections, laboring like a machine over easy math problems in study hall, the ridicule of peers, the pressures of passing notes, the aroma of the new X-Men comic in the mail, Mom's mashed potatoes and pork gravy, utterly forgettable sitcoms and game shows, mixed success in taping my favorite songs off the radio, insomnia. Do I really want to do that over again? Gottfried Leibniz, the philosopher who infamously calls ours the best of all possible worlds, observes that most of us would be willing to live life over, provided we didn't have to live *the same life* over.[26] Maybe. But despite the magnificence of things like Maggie's smooth curves and Mom's fluffy mashed potatoes, I'm not sure that I want to live any version of seventh grade again.

We're right back at the basic problem of evil. We rebel against the world as it is. We don't like the fact of seventh grade, let alone the fact of migraines or rape. But Nietzsche's radical idea with the eternal return, the "greatest weight," is that we must reconcile ourselves to this very world. There's no "better" world awaiting us. When we stop imagining a world other than the one in which our existence is possible, we open ourselves up to a rapturous joy, which Nietzsche links to the Greek god Dionysus, the god of wine and ecstasy. According to myth, Dionysus lives, dies, and is reborn, again and again, in a great celebration of existence. Like the grape, he must grow and be crushed, year after year, for the world to be intoxicated. Jesus is also conceived as a dying God, and his blood is also drunk as wine. But Christ's resurrection signifies a rebirth into a different life. Dionysus is continuously reborn into this life. The tragic festivals associated with him are celebrations of the pain and glory of this world.

For Nietzsche, we're now entering a new stage of human existence, one where we abandon the old ways of coping with suffering: the primitive idea of thinking of evil's origin as a god we can barter with, the Christian idea that the misery of this life is somehow deserved, and the utilitarian idea that we should eliminate suffering through technology and politics. We must now embrace suffering without justification. The eternal return is a kind of anti-theological "theodicy," one where we take all our star-birthing powers and use them to energize ourselves with the dynamism of being alive. By accepting the challenge of the eternal return, we rise out of our mere humanity into the space once populated with gods: we become the superhuman, *der Übermensch*.

But what about poor Nietzsche and his migraines, which were so next-to-impossible to embrace that they made him long for death? A clue to understanding Nietzsche's attempt to affirm his migraines can be found in *The Gay Science*, where he makes the fascinating claim that modernity's central problem with suffering is that we've grown unaccustomed to suffering. Pain and misery were once taken as givens, so we found strong ways of dealing with them, even of benefiting from them. But because we're now able to immunize or dull ourselves to agony, we're extremely touchy when tragedy does strike, even when it doesn't touch us directly. The mere thought of pain turns us into pessimists about life. The harsh facts of the universe suddenly seem like an obvious disproof of a good God. "There is a recipe," Nietzsche writes, "against pessimistic philosophers and the excessive sensitivity that seems to me the real 'misery of the present age'—but this recipe may sound too cruel and might itself be counted among the signs that lead people to judge that 'existence is something evil.' Well, the recipe against this 'misery' is: *misery*."[27] Nietzsche comes to see his miserable migraines as a defense mechanism against the soul-destruction of modernity.

Surely Nietzsche has his own bouts with pain and suicide in mind when he muses, "The most spiritual human beings, assuming they are the most courageous, also experience by far the most painful tragedies: but it is precisely for this reason that they honor life, because it brings against them its most formidable weapons."[28] If we're going to affirm any of life, we must affirm all of it, including the pains and troubles that shape and reshape us, for "if our soul has trembled with happiness and sounded like a harp string just once, all eternity was needed to produce this one event."[29] Ultimately, Nietzsche's migraines give him insight into what life really involves: inherent antagonism. They purge joy of phoniness. "The perfect brightness and cheerfulness, even exuberance of the spirit," he says at the outset of his philosophical autobiography, "is compatible in my case not only with the most profound physiological weakness, but even with an excess of pain. In the midst of the torments that go with an uninterrupted three-day migraine, accompanied by laborious vomiting of phlegm, I possessed a dialectician's clarity par excellence."[30] Nietzsche's most famous line is "What does not kill me makes me stronger."[31] Who knows, without his migraines Nietzsche might have become one of the herd, a wimpy utilitarian, a last man!

It's certainly not that pointless suffering leads to more overall good than bad. The idea is that Nietzsche wants us to embrace the whole of our lives, lives with plenty of senseless pain in them. Alexander Nehamas's *Nietzsche: Life as Literature*, one of the best secondary sources on the philosopher, is premised on the idea that Nietzsche asks us to stand in relation to our lives as artists do to their art. Nehamas's analogy is particularly helpful with the eternal return. Think of the tense and tragic moments in a great work of art: as hard as they are to bear, we don't want them to be otherwise, because they enhance the overall effect. Or, for that matter, think of how artists can find grist for their mill in random and horrible events—a turn of phrase, a natural disaster, a bug meandering across a sunbeam, heartbreak. Nietzsche encourages us to live our lives artistically, making use of what seems pointless or silly or tragic to forge something meaningful, satisfying, whole. We're "to live dangerously."[32] Our biographies might turn out to be tragedies rather than comedies, involving a triumph of pain over pleasure. But can't tragedies be profound? Isn't there something inspiring about Omar's vision of prison as the great antagonism where he forges the artwork of his life?

Throughout his life, Nietzsche experienced in art, especially ancient tragedy and modern opera, an overwhelming feeling of joy and possibility. In *The Birth of Tragedy*, his first book, he identifies the beauty of Greek tragedy as the ability to celebrate life's wondrousness even though our actions ultimately have no effect on the essential repetitions of nature, even though we all suffer and die according to random twists of fate. In the modern world, music is our great art, capable of infusing spiritual grandeur into frustration and sadness. "Without music life would be a mistake," Nietzsche bluntly states.[33] With the eternal return, he imagines what it would mean to make music of life, to fuse Dionysian rapture with what otherwise appears the mistake of existence, and thus to experience "the happiness of a god full of power and love, full of tears and laughter, a happiness that, like the sun in the evening, continually bestows its inexhaustible riches, pouring them into the sea, feeling richest, as the sun does, only when even the poorest fisherman is still rowing with golden oars!"[34]

* * * * * * * * * * * *

Friedrich Nietzsche died in 1900. The Nationalsozialistische Deutsche Arbeiterpartei—the Nazi Party, for short—wasn't founded until 1919 and didn't rise to power until 1933. Plainly, Nietzsche wasn't a Nazi. Admittedly, his sister, Elisabeth Förster-Nietzsche, did become a Nazi and pushed highly edited versions of her brother's work on the fascists. Both Hitler and Mussolini read Nietzsche with enthusiasm, especially those parts of his work that praise domination and disparage liberalism, Judaism, and pacifism. There's a particularly unsettling picture of Hitler with his trim mustache gazing longingly at a bust of Nietzsche with his supermanly mustache. In Nietzsche's defense, he found the prospect of having to deal over and over with his stupid, future-Nazi sister the chief impediment to being able personally to accept the eternal return.

Because he disdained anti-Semitism, ridiculed mob mentality, and savaged nationalism and its facile rationalizations, Nietzsche would have been anything but a supporter of National Socialism. The real question, in my view, isn't if Nietzsche is a proto-Nazi. He clearly isn't. The question is if Nietzsche's philosophy offers us the resources we need to criticize the worst of what Nazism stood for and accomplished. That the gas chambers were defended with anti-Semitism is stupid, but can the philosopher of the will to power and the eternal return express our moral horror at the gas chambers themselves? Again and again Nietzsche savages the idea of equality and praises acts of rising up and overpowering. Isn't part of the horror of Nazism precisely its agreement with Nietzsche on this score?

The contemporary Italian philosopher Giorgio Agamben reformulates the eternal return ever so slightly: "One day or night, a demon glides beside a survivor [of Auschwitz] and asks: 'Do you want every instant, every single detail of the camp to repeat itself for eternity?'" Agamben answers, "This simple reformulation of the experiment suffices to refute it beyond all doubt, excluding the possibility of its even being proposed."[35] It's not a matter of whether we're spiritually strong enough to accept Auschwitz. It's not just that we can't will the Holocaust to happen again, let alone to be on repeat. The very idea of imagining Nietzsche's test in light of such evil is wrongheaded. It's not our role to will the entire universe. Perhaps our task really is to recognize and act on certain moral truths—for instance, "Don't slaughter innocents." Isn't the proper goal of the human will after the Holocaust "never again," not "always again"?

It's next to impossible for us to endorse the world. We can't get over our revulsion at events like Auschwitz or Hiroshima. Should we even try to? Our great No cries out for something beyond this world, something beyond power and conflicting wills, something suggestive of old-fashioned good and evil, if not holiness. Maybe there's a source of good and evil deeper than *ressentiment* that bubbles up out of human nature, or nature itself, or the divine, just as thinkers have been saying for ages. It seems right, as Nietzsche says, that there's no going back to superseded beliefs, but maybe it's necessary to return to the deep realities that inspired those old beliefs to begin with. It's admittedly hard to recognize a moral dimension to human life amid all the swirling power dynamics that Nietzsche so brilliantly exposes. His psychological diagnosis of humanity seems about 99 percent right. But that 1 percent he misses might be the most significant thing about us.

Another way of getting at Nietzsche's blind spot to morality is to consider his assault on pity, which he always describes as the source of his "greatest dangers."[36] He says in *The Anti-Christ*, "Pity stands in antithesis to the tonic emotions which enhance the energy of the feeling of life: it has a depressive effect. One loses force when one pities. The loss of force which life has already sustained through suffering is increased and multiplied even further by pity. Suffering itself becomes contagious through pity."[37] As with his attack on morality, there's so much right about this analysis. Pity is often a covert power trip that pointlessly multiplies misery. Nobody with any self-respect likes to be pitied, so it's understandable that Nietzsche asks us to stop regarding pity in positive terms. Yet isn't there a moral response to other people's pains and sorrows, not far from pity, something like compassion, something I like to call "blues-understanding," where we enter the common suffering of being alive and meet not as masters and slaves but as equals? Isn't pity, as dangerous as it can be, the initial stirrings of this blues-understanding? Doesn't pity register, at least sometimes, our basic sense that that we're connected to others, and that their suffering can be bad? And can't "slave moralities" like Christianity and Buddhism occasionally lead to acts of charity or compassion that aren't completely reducible to the will to power?

It's hard for me to read Nietzsche's attacks on pity—his "great temptation," which he feared would lead to his undoing—and not think, with pity, of his undoing by pity in Turin on January 3, 1889.[38] As he was walking down the Via Carlo Alberto, he saw a frustrated cabdriver whipping an unbudging horse. Something in Nietzsche snapped. He ran up, threw his arms around the horse's neck, and began sobbing. His landlord eventually took him home. After two days of motionless silence, he sputtered his last words, "Mother, I'm an idiot." For a decade his family took care of the demented philosopher until he finally died of pneumonia. Amazingly enough, there's video footage, a little over a minute, of Friedrich Nietzsche from 1899, in the depths of his catatonia. A shot of his hand moving almost imperceptibly. Shots of him in uncomfortable slouches, looking at nothing at all. Shots of him in bed with his head propped up on a pillow, zoned out like someone watching late-night TV. A final shot of him with brightened eyes, somewhere between bemused and idiotic. Watching the haunting footage over and over, a kind of mini eternal return, I wonder whether the visionary is still there behind the blank stare, or whether what slave moralists call his "soul" has been annihilated. Could the philosopher who lived and thought so thrillingly, whose courage allowed him to embrace life despite constant bouts of suicidal agony, have willed eternally his final decade of catatonia? Can I will his mental illness to happen again? Can I will it even once for myself? There's a popular bit of graffiti that goes "'God is dead' —Nietzsche. 'Nietzsche is dead' —God." When I watch that footage of his final days, I think something nearly identical: "'Suffering is overcome' —Nietzsche. 'Nietzsche is overcome' —Suffering."

I also think about another philosopher, my hero William James. In a notorious passage from *The Varieties of Religious Experience*, in the chapter called "The Sick Soul," he relates an "acute neurasthenic attack with phobia" that threw him into depression a decade before Nietzsche broke down in Turin.

> There arose in my mind the image of an epileptic patient whom I had seen in the asylum, a black-haired youth with greenish skin, entirely idiotic, who used to sit all day on one of the benches, or rather shelves against the wall, with his knees drawn up against his chin, and the coarse gray undershirt, which was his only garment, drawn over

them inclosing his entire figure. He sat there like a sort of sculptured Egyptian cat or Peruvian mummy, moving nothing but his black eyes and looking absolutely non-human. This image and my fear entered into a species of combination with each other. *That shape am I*, I felt, potentially.[39]

James goes on to say, "I remember wondering how other people could live, how I myself had ever lived, so unconscious of that pit of insecurity beneath the surface of life." What's so invigorating about Nietzsche in his lucid years is his resolve to dance with pointless suffering. What's so tragic about Nietzsche in his decade of dementia is his utter collapse into pointless suffering. When I obsess over that footage of him, I keep hearing James's words, "That shape am I."

THREE

WE MUST TAKE RESPONSIBILITY FOR POINTLESS SUFFERING

On Hannah Arendt and the Banality of Evil

Science has made us gods even before we are worthy of being men.

JEAN ROSTAND

We're only a pomegranate seed away from wielding the power of God, according to our oldest myths. The most well-known of them is the story of how primordial man and woman are punished for a nibble of fruit that makes them "like God, knowing good and evil." But there are many other old tales, like that of Pandora or Gilgamesh, that relate our inborn curiosity to the necessity of suffering and death. The greatest trauma of humankind, it seems, was the emergence of humankind. A puny animal, suddenly able to reflect on the world and itself, recognized the fact of its mortality and longed for something transcending its condition. Out of the birth pains of our species comes the entire grammar of our existence: language, art, technology, religion, philosophy—all the ways we try to imagine or reshape the world into visions beyond what is naturally given.

The German American philosopher and political theorist Hannah Arendt (1906–75) begins most of her works by pointing out that humankind has just been through a trauma comparable to our emergence as rational animals. The Holocaust, the atom bomb, totalitarianism, and space travel are Arendt's most dramatic examples of this new trauma, though she believes that the crisis is bigger than even these epochal events. This recent trauma is a fulfillment of our oldest trauma. When J. Robert Oppenheimer first exploded the atom bomb, the only words he found up to the task were from an ancient Hindu epic about the beginning of the Age of Chaos, "Now I am become Death, the destroyer of worlds." It's like we've weaseled our way back into the Garden and stolen another bite of forbidden fruit, this time off the Tree of Life.

Arendt herself uses a "myth," a distinctively modern one, to depict our disorienting situation. She begins her book *Between Past and Future* with a short parable by Franz Kafka.

> He has two antagonists: the first presses him from behind, from the origin. The second blocks the road ahead. He gives battle to both. To be sure, the first supports him in his fight with the second, for he wants to push him forward, and in the same way the second supports him in his fight with the first, since he drives him back. But it is only theoretically so. For it is not only the two antagonists who are there, but he himself as well, and who really knows his intentions? His dream, though, is that some time in an unguarded moment—and this would require a night darker than any night has ever been yet—he will jump out of the fighting line and be promoted, on account of his experience in fighting, to the position of umpire over his antagonists in their fight with each other.[1]

In Arendt's analysis, Kafka's parable portrays us in our current predicament, cut off from a living tradition, yet caught between the conflicting forces of the past and the future. The past is not our burden or our blessing: it's the set of inherited ideals and problems that forces us awkwardly into the future. Likewise, the future is not what we're progressing into; rather, it's the fear of the future that throws us back onto our historical identities.

But the essential point in Kafka's parable for what I'm calling our current trauma is that we fantasize about rising above our condition—jumping out of the battle and being promoted to "the position of umpire." To rise above our condition would be to become like God, and playing God is bound up with our current trauma. As Arendt puts it, we've begun "to act into nature."[2] The Holocaust and the dropping of the bomb, in fact, surpass the most awful of what we once thought of as God's actions into nature. By the middle of the twentieth century thoughtful people could no longer say what John Stuart Mill said in the late nineteenth century, "Anarchy and the Reign of Terror are overmatched in injustice, ruin, and death, by a hurricane and a pestilence."[3] What's the Lisbon earthquake in comparison with Auschwitz? What's a flu epidemic next to Hiroshima? The very names Auschwitz and Hiroshima stand for a whole new kind of suffering, a terrible vast self-inflicted suffering: the liquidation of humanity by humans.

It's not just in these extremes that we unleash titanic forces on our own species. We have the power to extend life, manipulate birth, and alter the planet's atmosphere. We study ourselves as guinea pigs, often in hopes of redesigning our behavior. We photograph our home planet while standing on its satellite. We design "smart" technologies that replace our own jobs or reduce us to the status of servants. All these radical changes, even when they make some of our lives easier, fill us with what Arendt calls a "peculiar kind of loneliness"—the loneliness of the assembly-line worker, the loneliness of the astronaut, the loneliness of the inmate, the loneliness of the guinea pig, and the loneliness that eats at so many otherwise comfy lives shuttling among bureaucratized work, highly mediated social life, and tranquilizing downtime—the loneliness of the young utilitarian J. S. Mill, the loneliness of Nietzsche's last man, as well as the loneliness of his superhuman.[4] It's a special kind of suffering, the condition of feeling abandoned by our humanity, a loneliness that can even be experienced—indeed, is commonly experienced—among great masses of people.

Our official ways of thinking split us into gods and the raw biological life on which the gods work their magic: biotechnicians and patients, marketers and consumers, managers and employees, scientists and their data, droppers of bombs and blips on the screen. In her first major work, written in the immediate wake of World War II, Arendt observes, "It is as though mankind had divided itself between those who believe in human omnipotence . . . and those for whom powerlessness has become the major experience of their lives."[5] When we are so divided between technological god and biological beast, we lose the distinctive space of being human, the shared space where we discover and reveal who we really are through our words and deeds.

But we're neither gods nor beasts, neither utilitarian supercomputers nor Nietzschean superhumans. The people who executed the Final Solution were—people. Those who detonated the atom bomb went to the bathroom shortly thereafter. Though Arendt doesn't offer a comprehensive solution to our problem, she gives us the reminder of what it means to be human, something our current trauma causes us to repress. In large part, her philosophical work is the demonstration that our language is still up to the task of orienting us as human beings. To show us how to think and move in Kafka's disorienting gap between past and future, she recalls the distinct meaning of words, words like "labor" and "work," "behavior" and "action," "violence" and "power," "private" and "public." In the midst of our great trauma Arendt asks herself, "What remains?" Her answer is "The language remains."[6] Her philosophical task is to compile a dictionary of being human.

* * * * * * * * * * *

Born into a secular family of German Jews, Hannah Arendt grew up in Könisberg, the hometown of Immanuel Kant. From an early age she suffered from our basic need to understand: "I can either study philosophy, or I can drown myself."[7] Trying not to drown in Heidelberg, she came under the influence of Martin Heidegger, one of the most original philosophers of the twentieth century in the midst of his fundamental breakthroughs. They fell tumultuously in love, and she became his mistress and muse. They broke up several times, the last in 1929. Later that year she married her first husband.

In 1933 Martin Heidegger made an enthusiastic foray into the Nazi Party, and Hannah Arendt fled Germany for France, where she worked on behalf of Jewish refugees, divorced her first husband, and married Heinrich Blücher, a poet, military historian, philosopher, and fellow émigré. Arrested by the Vichy regime for being a "foreign Jew," she was sent to an internment camp, though she was eventually allowed to leave the country. In 1941 Arendt moved to the United States, along with her husband and mother, and lived and worked as an American for the rest of her life.

In 1943 Hannah Arendt began to read reports about Auschwitz. She didn't believe them. They made no human sense. She and her military-historian husband knew that the Nazis were the lowest of the low, and one couldn't put anything past them. But what possible sense—militarily or politically—could there be in building factories in the midst of war to exterminate a race of people? As the year wore on, she realized in the face of undeniable evidence that the unthinkable had indeed happened: "It was really as if an abyss had opened. Because we had the idea that amends could somehow be made for everything else, as amends can be made for just about everything at some point in politics. But not for this. *This ought not to have happened.*"[8]

We sometimes use the word "dehumanizing" to describe an affliction that pushes humanity to our limits—slavery, rape, war. Evil as such things are, they still have contortions of our humanity in them. The slave's humanity is denied and yet somehow also accepted. The rape victim is both object and subject. The enemy is a monster and also a soldier. For these classic forms of evil, reparations of a kind can be made—not to make things even (an impossible task), but to return some semblance of justice. By contrast, according to Arendt, the victims of the Holocaust were treated in a purely dehumanizing fashion. Their deaths were not simply the twisted result of rage, lust, or the conventions of power. They died at the end of an assembly line. No amends could be made. The Holocaust wasn't just undeserved suffering: it was pointless suffering. As Hannah Arendt put it in a 1946 reflection on the "death factories":

> They died together, the young and the old, the weak and the strong, the sick and the healthy; not as men and women, children and adults, boys and girls, not as good and bad, beautiful and ugly—but brought down to the lowest common denominator of organic life itself, plunged into the darkest and deepest abyss of primal equality, like cattle, like matter, like things that had neither body nor soul, nor even a physiognomy upon which death could stamp its seal.[9]

Obviously the victims of the Nazis were dehumanized. But so were the Nazis themselves. Though slavery and rape—and, to a degree, war—deform the character of not just the victim but the victimizer, they're justified in the name of the victimizer's humanity. For instance, slavery's official purpose as a social institution was to free up others to have a genteel existence. But Nazism, as well as Soviet totalitarianism, attempted to liquidate the concept of humanity altogether—for everyone. It wasn't simply that a bunch of thugs got power and did some really bad things; a new space opened in which masses of people could be mobilized toward dehumanized and dehumanizing ends. As much as Nietzsche would have cringed in horror, the Nazis were supposed to become superhuman. Not only do we have the problem of why God makes a world where certain things absolutely should not happen, but we now must ask why *we* make a world where certain things absolutely should not happen. The problem of evil is reborn.

In *Origins of Totalitarianism*, her first book after World War II, Arendt doesn't make the mistake that she made when she first read of the Holocaust. To understand Nazism is precisely *not* to be shocked by the gas chambers. The elimination of the human being and the control of the human animal were the heart and soul of its ideology. Terror is at the core of totalitarianism. Just as we have traditionally lived in holy terror of God striking us down at any moment, the subjects of a totalitarian system are supposed to live in a similar holy terror of the regime.

At first Arendt names this institutionalized terrorism "radical evil": "a system in which all men have become equally superfluous."[10] With her customary carefulness with words, she eventually abandons the expression "radical evil." As extreme as the problem is, she comes to believe that evil possesses no real depth and hence can never be "radical." Only good can be radical.[11] But she doesn't abandon the idea that an evil order in which humanity has become superfluous has emerged. She famously renames this new order "the banality of evil."

* * * * * * * * * * *

That we sometimes use the words "behavior" and "action" synonymously is a sign of how our current trauma has disoriented us. "Behavior" properly refers to what's done according to an outside rule. It's predictable, like the behavior of bacteria in a petri dish or the behavior of your knee when tapped by a rubber mallet. When we tell a bunch of rowdy kindergartners to get in line and "behave," we mean that they should all be following our orders. "Action," by contrast, refers to the disclosure of who we are through what we do and say. It's what reveals us as individuals. If behavior is about following an outside rule, action involves freedom—that is, authorship of ourselves. Thus, action is judged as good or bad, praiseworthy or blameworthy. If our kindergartners refuse to behave, they're "acting up," and we're likely to scold them. Soldiers on the battlefield turn and run: we judge their action as cowardly or prudent. Others stay and fight: they're brave or foolhardy. Meanwhile citizens back home declare their support or opposition to the war: they're just or unjust, wise or unwise. What we do and say acts out who we distinctively are. In a big way, it is who we are.

Arendt says that action is ultimately rooted in "natality," a word she coins to mean the fact of being born *as a human being*, the flip side of mortality. If you've ever held a newborn in your hands, you've had the visceral experience of natality. Beyond all your cooing at the cuteness, you're overwhelmed by the dizzying, wondrous question of who this kid is going to grow up to be: a business mogul, a scoundrel, the president of the United States, all of the above? "Action" refers to what boys and girls grow up to do and say. It's what lets us know who they are; it's what surprises us. Our natality is the ultimate source of all our faith and hope, as when the Gospels sum up the gladdest tidings, "Unto you a child is born."[12]

The other peculiar word Arendt uses in connection with action is "plurality." What she means is that we live among people who share the human condition with us but who are individually unique. We're not just a mass of rough copies of the same nature, as is a swarm of bees. We're too surprising. We pop out people as radically distinct as Mozart and Hitler, you and me. Our deepest sameness as humans comes from our differences. We're plural. The very condition of action is plurality, because action is all about revealing who we are, and we need someone to distinguish ourselves from and reveal ourselves to.

One upshot of plurality is that action requires a public sphere where we can reveal ourselves through our words and deeds to others. Think literally of public spaces, like the town square or the mall (those places the ancient Romans synthesized into the Forum) where we arise from our common slumpiness, dress ourselves up, and strut our stuff. But think also of the opinion page, the battlefield, a conference, a protest, those periods of work where we interact with the public—a "forum" where we have a chance to make a distinct impression through what we do or say, where we're not just organisms sliding by but humans disclosing ourselves for good or ill.

A big part of our current trauma is that spheres of action are being reduced to zones of behavior. We increasingly talk of the acting up of schoolchildren as "problematic behaviors" and try to design systems to guarantee smooth-functioning subjects of education, which itself is commonly "delivered" with standardized methods and curricula and "assessed" by standardized tests. Workers often must recite scripts in their interactions with the public. High-powered social scientists use "big data" to craft laws, predict elections, trade stocks, and arrange compatible lovers. Acts of war are translated into drone strikes after the available data have been analyzed with algorithms. We turn our modern efforts to modify nature on ourselves.

When something inevitably goes awry in our systems (and, given the unpredictability embedded in our natality and the weakness of our rational designs, it always does), we demand accountability. The standard retort is "Hey, I just work here." Unsatisfying as it is, the retort is basically right, for these systems operate by liquidating responsibility. Even when a system does achieve its end successfully, we still lose the value of action, the ability to show who we are, the ability to be judged as individuals. "The trouble with modern theories of behaviorism," Arendt witheringly observes, "is not that they are wrong but that they could become true."[13] Or, to update the point a bit, the trouble with modern theories about how computers are intelligent is not that they are wrong but that they're becoming true: our souls and the institutions that sustain us are increasingly becoming computer-like. We're ceding our natality to number-crunching programs. These programs are sold as more "intelligent" than we are, and maybe at their best they are better at minimizing suffering and maximizing certain positive outcomes. Even so, they undermine the meaningfulness that makes our institutions worthwhile in the first place. Moreover, they rarely work as billed; and when they fail, we've subtly destroyed the basis for the accountability we inevitably demand.

Arendt's controversial *Eichmann in Jerusalem* makes the argument that Adolf Eichmann, the Nazi lieutenant colonel who managed the mass deportation of Jews to ghettos and extermination camps, exemplified how behaviorism is becoming true. In the one pan of Lady Justice's balance was the purposeless murder of millions of innocents; in her other pan was a traveling salesman for the Vacuum Oil Company. In his defense Eichmann essentially argued, "Hey, I just worked there." A law-abiding citizen of Germany, he was doing his duty as a member of the military. It just so happened that this humdrum carrying-out of his duty led to the mass murder of innocents. This is, in Arendt's words, "the fearsome, word-and-thought-defying banality of evil."[14]

Since the publication of *Eichmann in Jerusalem*, it's been a minor industry to prove that Eichmann wasn't a nice-guy functionary but a true believer in Nazism. Recently it's been discovered that in Argentina, where he fled after the war, he was at the center of a coven of Nazis who entertained dreams of a new Führer's triumphant return. For those like the intellectual historian Richard Wolin, this discovery disproves Arendt's analysis: "Arendt had her own intellectual agenda, and perhaps out of her misplaced loyalty to her former mentor and lover, Martin Heidegger, insisted on applying the Freiburg philosopher's concept of 'thoughtlessness' (*Gedankenlosigkeit*) to Eichmann. In doing so, she drastically underestimated the fanatical conviction that infused his actions."[15]

A common defense of Arendt's book against such criticism is that her general analysis is correct; it's just that she applies it to the wrong man. There's truth in this defense. Regardless of the facts about Eichmann, it's a profound insight that nasty regimes are partially powered by many otherwise unobjectionable family men and women who aren't existentially committed to a murderous ideology but whose "behavior" puts blood on their hands. An Auschwitz commandant illustrates the point: "We were all so trained to obey orders without even thinking that the thought of disobeying an order would never have occurred to anybody."[16]

But I'm not completely convinced that Arendt is guilty of fingering the wrong guy. Her central criticism of Eichmann, as Wolin says, is that he couldn't "think." She doesn't mean that he didn't have thoughts rattling around in his head. Thoughts were definitely rattling, many of which gave off a distinctively Nazi tone. But the beauty of the Nazi ideology for people like Eichmann is that it relieves them from having to think for themselves. It excuses them of the inner dialogue necessary for morality. And it does so in part by eliminating a public sphere in which they are to be judged for their actions. At one point in his trial, Eichmann brings up in his defense Kant's categorical imperative, the idea that we should always act on a principle we could will all people to act on—the very essence of the inward dialogue of morality. But how does Eichmann interpret it? He thinks that it means a Nazi should always follow the Führer! Following the Golden Rule means always doing what you're told by those in power! Here we see the grotesqueness of thoughtlessness masquerading as thought.

Eichmann's inner life, in Arendt's analysis, was a tissue of clichés. Grabbing at a contradictory mixture of stock phrases and thin rationalizations, he was unwilling to stand by whatever principles he fancied were his. He was mediocre. He was thrilled by the power Nazism lent him and thus happy to go along with it. His craven defense in the courtroom and his passionate waiting for the return of a new Führer in Argentina perhaps prove rather than challenge Arendt's thesis that totalitarian ideologies thrive on the inability of their members to think. If Arendt had used the expression "normality of evil" rather than her judgment-laden "banality of evil," would there be fewer objections? Perhaps we're so losing a sense of what it means to think and act that we can no longer recognize banality. Perhaps being normal is becoming way too normal!

It's funny that intellectuals often have trouble getting what Arendt means by "thinking," whereas when I teach her ideas to community college students, many of whom have laborious jobs, they have no problem at all in understanding the idea and appeal of thoughtlessness. Those who work in stores that instruct them about when to smile and how to greet customers, those who put in time at the factory next door to the college, those who in junior high and high school were bumped from one behavioral modification program to another—they understand the appeal of "shutting off your brain," to use an expression that inevitably crops up in our discussions. They also understand the phenomenon of the "company man" who becomes a thoughtless true-believing repeater of institutional clichés.

Obviously, the comparison between a Nazi war criminal and a grocery-store functionary goes only so far. My point is that the appeal of not thinking and the systems that encourage thoughtlessness are neither hard to understand nor simply artifacts of a distant generation of Nazis. When we rise through the ranks of such systems, it's incredibly difficult not to become banal. The consequences of our obedience aren't always evil, but we can become hollowed-out as humans. Moreover, when we get into the habit of the I-just-work-here mindset, we're tilling the ground for totalitarianism to take root in our minds.

The problem with rendering a judgment on the banality of evil is that our moral and legal systems are wisely built on the idea that people aren't truly guilty if they didn't intend to do the crime. So, should Eichmann—or anyone who's just doing his or her job even though it leads to something terrible—not have been held accountable for what he did? (A similar question has been asked about all those traders and bankers whose self-serving, albeit legal, actions contributed to the financial collapse of 2008.) Critics of Arendt often argue that Eichmann really did do a few horribly abusive things to Jews: evil actions that warranted the death penalty. While it's true that Arendt doesn't have all the lowdown on the guy, it's also the case that it wasn't simply acts of good old-fashioned evil that Eichmann was being accused of. He was being tried not just for a few acts of brutality but for the Holocaust.

Regardless of his intentions, Arendt thinks that Eichmann *should* be held responsible for the Holocaust—and, by extension, that we must all take some responsibility for the pointless suffering that our participation in dehumanizing systems enables. The crime of the Holocaust demands that those who committed it are held responsible, even if a Nazi did just work there. Eichmann's crime is that he didn't think and act when he should have, that he was apolitical in the midst of politics. His crime was that he didn't intend anything in opposition to the Holocaust. He might have been a behaving cog in the Nazi machine, but the machine itself was acting, and the machine was human, the result of thousands of people's acquiescence. Here's how Arendt imagines the proper verdict:

> Politics is not like the nursery; in politics obedience and support are the same. And just as you supported and carried out a policy of not wanting to share the earth with the Jewish people and the people of a number of other nations—as though you and your superiors had any right to determine who should and who should not inhabit the world—we find that no one, that is, no member of the human race, can be expected to want to share the earth with you. This is the reason, and the only reason, you must hang.[17]

* * * * * * * * * * *

The banalization of human life doesn't stop at politics. It creeps into the workplace, another sphere where our identities are forged. Just as our trauma sometimes makes us elide the difference between action and behavior, so too it inclines us to blur the difference between labor and work.

"Labor" properly refers to the unskilled, repetitive tasks that we must do to get by. The main, almost the sole, motivation for laboring is necessity. The most basic form of labor is—labor. Women must "go into labor" to deliver a child. No woman, let alone man, ever says, "I'm really interested in going into labor; I just don't want to have a kid." The reason that trillions of women throughout history have willingly and unwillingly gone into labor is simple: babies. Labor is repetitive because the ends of labor are fed right back into the process of life itself. The point of labor is to consume the labor. Why do you wash the dishes? So that you can make them dirty again. Why do you pick the crops? So that you can put food on the table so that you can eat so that you can pick more crops. Why do you have babies? So that they can grow up to have babies of their own.

It's hard, even a little silly, to take pride in labor itself. Labor itself is largely meaningless. Don't misunderstand me: it's critical that labor gets done, and it's natural and good to take pride in providing for yourself and your family, let alone in enduring what it takes to have a kid. But it's a bit much to call in your friends and family after you've done the dishes and say, "Let's all just admire my labor." As someone who's been accused of being a bad dishwasher, I don't want to overplay this point, but basically a washed dish is a washed dish. The difference between your labor and mine is slight; at a certain level of easily attained competence it's nearly nonexistent. We can take pride in having provided the necessities, but we don't find our distinct selves in labor (in fact, monks engage in labor precisely to liberate themselves from the self). Because we find so little personal meaning in labor itself, we generally try to get out of it. The upper classes have made slaves do it. Men have made women do it. The rich pay servants to do it. Parents force kids to do it. Technologically advanced societies invent machines to do it. Labor doesn't reveal our natality.

Work, by contrast, is meaningful and does reveal our surprising humanity. "Work" properly refers to a skilled activity that contributes something lasting to the world. Craftspeople and artists work. They build and make things that are not, like the products of labor, fed right back into the system but that stick around and make us feel like we're at home on this planet—things like houses, hats, shoes, coats, paintings, songs, aqueducts, and temples. "Work" also refers, in a secondary sense, to what people in the trades do, those who repair what has been made so that it can last longer. Your work has something of you in it. You do rightly call your friends and family after you've built a house or woven a hat or fixed a combustion engine and say, "Admire my work." Like action, work discloses who you are as an individual, only it does so in a concrete way. We work not simply because we have to but because we can delight in it. Just think of all the hobbyist makers and fixers who willingly give their weekends over to tinkering with completely unnecessary projects.

Not only does our work tell us something individual about us, it tells us something about our way of life, our culture—what Arendt calls "the world." If you want to learn about another culture, say, ancient Egypt, you can find out a lot by looking at their pots and their papyri, their tombs and their temples. In fact, a big part of why work is so personally meaningful is precisely that we're contributing something important to the world.

Just as action is being reduced to behavior, work is being degraded into labor. From John Locke and Adam Smith to Frederick Taylor and Henry Ford, humanity has been discovering the astonishing amount of power in labor itself. By butchering work into little laborious tasks—the "division of labor," arranged and overseen by what Taylor called "scientific management"—we're able to unleash a tremendous amount of productive power. We create untold numbers of jobs (which are, however, increasingly done by robots), innovate like never before, and generate hitherto-unimaginable amounts of wealth. But we pay a huge price for these gains. The Marxist criticisms of capitalist labor are well-known: the failure to pay laborers for the essential value they add to their products, the long hours, the shipment of jobs to the cheapest labor source, the subsequent uprooting and destruction of communities. Arendt's point is even more far-reaching. Whether in capitalist or communist economies, the unleashing of labor power has seriously diminished our opportunities to find meaning in our work. Turning work into labor has eliminated a crucial place of self-discovery and meaning-making.

The most obvious example of this degradation is the assembly line. When Ford first got his factory up and running, it was hard for him to find anyone willing to work in it. Building a car from scratch, or even just fixing cars, was once a job of some distinction. Who'd want to trade such real work for the monotony of an assembly line's menial tasks? Who'd want to be Charlie Chaplin at the beginning of *Modern Times* with the job of twisting widgets over and over? (It's never clear in the movie what his factory is making, because, from the perspective of the laborer caught in the banality of the system, what difference does it make?) The Little Tramp becomes so overtaken by his machinelike task that his whole body is sucked into the inner workings of the assembly line in an eerie moment of atonement of man and machine. *Modern Times* is a brilliant revelation of our insidious new problem of evil: we reduce ourselves to machines in the name of progress.

But it's not just assembly lines. Buzzwords of the business model— "objectives," "research-based," "assessment," "quantifiable," "efficiency"—have now insinuated themselves into "white-collar" jobs, as they once did into "blue-collar" jobs—even, I regret to say, into education. One of the central points of Matthew Crawford's *Shop Class as Soulcraft* is that office jobs have been subjected to the same kind of "scientific management" that once reduced the jobs of craft-workers to factory labor. Crawford describes a job he got at Information Access Company where he naïvely assumed that he'd be doing the serious intellectual work of closely reading and carefully summarizing scholarly articles. He soon found out that he wasn't actually to read the articles, just to apply a method of scanning them. At first he was expected to do fifteen articles a day. Soon he had to do twenty-eight scholarly articles a day! Crawford uses the values-laden language of Arendt to describe the effect of turning intellectual work into labor: "The job required both dumbing down and a bit of moral reeducation."[18] He had to learn how to be irresponsible, to be thoughtless.

Why would we ever subject ourselves to such labor? What possibly could motivate us to give up contributing something meaningful to our community for doing replaceable labor in the service of lame goals? Remember the point of labor: we labor so that we can consume the products of labor. In other words, we do our jobs so that we can make money and buy stuff. Many laborers in the world (for instance, the Bangladeshi children who made in a sweatshop some item of clothing currently worn by you or me) do their jobs simply so that they can feed themselves. The "white-collar" laborers who make more than enough to take care of themselves and their families use their paycheck to engage in what we aptly call consumerism, which usually amounts to trying to buy back the identities that have been stolen from us.

Crawford's apt phrase for our predicament is "the Easy Bake Oven of consumerism."[19] He's referring to Betty Crocker, the company that in the 1950s realized consumers want not just to buy a product but to acquire an identity. We want to eat our cake and have our identity as bakers too. The solution? Sell cake mixes to which we must add eggs. Presto! The cake is now "homemade." Such easy-bake identities are at the heart of most marketing campaigns. Only rinky-dink local ads bother to describe the product being hawked. The big-time ads associate their products with an identity we long to acquire: rugged individualist, cool sex object, can-do fixer, artist, leader, outfoxer of circumstances, even ironist of consumerism. "Just add our product to your life," the marketers say, "and—presto!—a real identity will be yours."

The problem is that without work in Arendt's sense, most people have no way of forging a real identity out of our natality, so we try desperately to get one in some other way. Not only do we try to buy our identities with the right blue jeans, motorcycle, or political candidate, we're forced to interpret an identity out of what we do. This is nowhere so apparent as in the pointless activities invented by middle management—"team-building exercises" and whatnot—that serve to justify their jobs. It's not sufficient for administrators simply to do crossword puzzles while others do the labor central to the company's mission; they have to be "leaders" and "facilitators," basically made-up terms to describe identities that have been obscured in the bureaucracy.

By depriving us of the sphere in which real identities can be formed, the labor-consumption cycle turns us into slaves—in some cases, pampered slaves, but slaves nevertheless. Beyond that, this cycle eats away at the world itself. We begin to acquire an appetite to consume everything and anything—clothes, houses, politics, news, even the earth itself. "Consumption," Arendt says, "is no longer restricted to the necessities of life. . . . [It] harbors the grave danger that eventually no object of the world will be safe from consumption and annihilation through consumption."[20] The ideals of work—durability, stability, meaning—are sacrificed in favor of a world designed for obsolescence. In the name of efficiency, jobs, and money, we hollow out our lives and trash the planet. This is a very peculiar, very sad thing for us to be doing to ourselves.

* * * * * * * * * * *

With the degradation of action and work, and the desiccation of the public spheres where we can forge fully human identities, we run the risk of undermining the conditions of social and political order. The more a bureaucracy—the rule of Nobody—holds sway, the greater our anxiety grows about keeping things together. What generally arises in such circumstances is some form of terrorism, an increasingly powerful force in our current age. To understand the terror quintessential to our times, Arendt believes, we must distinguish between power and violence.

A single person might have strength, but "power" refers to the ability to act together. A government has power. Without power, in fact, there's no community at all. Basically, power comes from shared beliefs and practices. Think about the orderliness of any society. Most of us stop on red, refrain from robbing our neighbors, register for selective service, pay our taxes, and pull over when the sirens flash. Why? We might give any number of prudential reasons (like "Otherwise I could go to prison"), but the fact of the matter is that we mostly follow our laws because we're in the habit of doing so, because we believe in them, consciously or unconsciously. We stop on red even when nobody's around. The laws have power.

Violence relies on fear rather than shared belief. Mao Zedong famously said, "Power grows out of the barrel of a gun." Arendt regards this as dangerous nonsense. There's a huge difference between political power and political violence. What grows out of the barrel of a gun is terror. It's certainly true that terror can often move people to do what terrorists command, but as soon as their instruments of terror are neutralized, their "power" vanishes. Real power is an end in itself, for it grounds our ability to live together. Violence, in sharp contrast, is instrumental—both in the sense that it can coerce people to do things and that it relies on instruments like guns and bombs.

Power and violence are not only very different, they're opposites, Arendt believes: "Where the one rules absolutely, the other is absent."[21] If power is total, what need is there for violence? If violence is ubiquitous, no institution or person has any power at all. Of course, it's never the case that either rules absolutely. Governments always need their military and police forces, just as tyrants and terrorist regimes require a certain amount of shared belief from informers and comrades.

Violence has always had a dangerous, though sometimes proper, place in human life. At its worst, it's a system of plunder that allows a regime of power to be maintained. At its best, it has a clear-cut strategic end: to defend ourselves, to protect others, to redress an injustice, to revolt. But our sense of the place of violence has become scrambled. We're inclined, like Mao, to overlook the importance of belief and to glorify violence as the essence of political power.

The event that most scrambled our sense of violence was the detonation of the atom bomb. Nuclear weapons make violence seem like everything and nothing. To have them is to be taken seriously as a world power. But they fill us with the fear of not just our own death but our race's death—in fact, our whole world's death. This is a new version of apocalyptic fear: the fear that not God but humanity will destroy the earth. It renders courage moot. In his poem "Aubade" Philip Larkin says, "Being brave/ Lets no one off the grave./ Death is no different whined at than withstood."[22] That's patently false. It makes a huge ethical difference whether you're killed while groveling or you're killed while resisting. But Larkin's defeatist lines are perfectly true about facing a nuclear weapon. Before such massive violent force there's no longer any such thing as courage or cowardice. We all die equally as raw biological life-forms.

In response to this godlike technological violence, many lose their taste for violence altogether and become attracted to nonviolence. Sit-ins and peaceful protests are ingeniously substituted for riots and attacks. Nonviolent protests nevertheless function a lot like violence in that they can be an effective strategy for accomplishing a clear-cut end. In the case of the civil rights movement Arendt admires how nonviolent protests successfully led to the elimination of discriminatory laws. But she also points out that such protests "proved utter failures and became counterproductive when they encountered the social conditions in the large urban centers—the stark needs of the black ghettos on one side, the overriding interests of white lower-income groups in respect to housing and education on the other."[23] Just like violence, nonviolence is limited in what it can accomplish when it comes to the realm of power. The only way to change a power structure is to change people's hearts and minds.

Another response to our godlike technological violence is that a select few become attracted to terrorism. Violence begins to look like an end in itself, a way of forging a strong identity. This is a deep mistake, as deep as mistaking the labor-consumption cycle for a sphere of identity formation. It's made not just by ISIS and mass shooters but by intellectuals like Jean-Paul Sartre and Franz Fanon. Bureaucratic state power is so diffuse, so often blindly unjust, and so consolidated by overwhelming instruments of violence that terrorist acts against it have a certain dash. Arendt defines bureaucracy as "the form of government in which everybody is deprived of political freedom, of the power to act; for the rule by Nobody is not no-rule, and where all are equally powerless we have a tyranny without a tyrant."[24] The person who clearly expresses freedom in a total bureaucracy is a criminal, a terrorist, or a tyrant. Suicide attacks are a particularly powerful way of acting—of exiting what's regarded as a corrupt all-encompassing system.

Totalitarian regimes integrate terror into their bureaucracy. Part of their very concept of political order is to reestablish a lost authority, an almost godlike authority, by means of random, mass terror. As our own history has shamefully demonstrated, liberal democracy is also not above using its massive instruments of violence to create "shock and awe" where we fantasize about consolidating or establishing our power. The predictable backlash is what we recognize as terrorism.

"The practice of violence, like all action, changes the world," Arendt warns us, "but the most probable change is to a more violent world."[25]

Beyond the random interruptions of violence and terrorism, we frequently experience a pervasive sense of disconnect with our humanity. We get more and more "freedom" to gratify and distract ourselves, while the actual power of the world is wielded by vast systems, their knowing engineers, and the occasional tyrant who unleashes their horrible power. Speaking of the bureaucratized world of modern life, in which there's an ever-widening gap between the impersonal power structure and the lives that we lead, Milan Kundera says, "What can a citizen, with all his rights, change about his immediate environment, about the parking lot being built below his house, about the howling loudspeaker set up across from his windows? His freedom is limitless, and powerless."[26]

* * * * * * * * * * * *

We've always made social and political conditions that make us suffer, from slavery to serfdom, from timocracy to tyranny. Arendt's point is that we now inflict on ourselves the kind of suffering that's usually made us ask "Why me?" to the gods. Totalitarianism is the most extreme type of this self-inflicted suffering, but it's apparent in consumerism, "scientific management," terrorism, and the various forms of destroying the public sphere that characterize contemporary society. We're depriving ourselves of our own humanity, usually in the name of a utopia. We're depriving ourselves of not just this or that human good but the very sources of good and evil. We're all becoming prisoners of a kind, prisoners of our own power.

What are we supposed to do with our new kind of self-inflicted suffering? What's the solution to the peculiar kind of loneliness that comes with being half-technological-god and half-evolutionary-beast? Arendt doesn't have a political program or an ethical solution. Instead of giving us new rules for what some call the Anthropocene, she reminds us that we're still human. Our humanity depends on thinking for ourselves, finding and preserving public forums, acting in those

forums, finding real work, forging rather than consuming our identities, taking responsibility. In our deprivation we've been given the
opportunity to see what we most need. In our suffering we've been
given the chance to renew the world. It's a lesson Arendt first learned
when she fell in love.

Arendt wrote numerous poems about her tumultuous relationship with her teacher Martin Heidegger, a man who was married with
children and seventeen years her senior. Part of their relationship's
intensity came from the magical bond between a brilliant teacher in
the midst of his essential breakthroughs and a brilliant student able to
peer over the wall and see the same mysteries. They were two people
sharing the secret of truth itself. Yes, she was his muse, but he was
her muse too. Their relationship was doomed, not just because he
was married but because there was something incompatible between
them—productively incompatible, but incompatible nevertheless.
To put a fine point on it: Heidegger was an anti-Semite attracted to
aspects of Nazism and repulsed by Roman and American political
philosophy, and Arendt was a Jew attracted to Roman and American
political philosophy and repulsed to her core by everything the Nazis
stood for.

Arendt drew her initial, fundamental insight about suffering from
their tumultuous relationship. In a prose poem from when she was
twenty-five and head-over-heels, she wrote: "To suffer and to know,
to know every minute and every second with full awareness and cyni-
cism, that one has to be thankful even for the worst of pains, indeed
that it is precisely such suffering which is the point of everything and
its reward."[27] She was realizing the old Homeric wisdom that we suffer
so we can sing.

It's only a bit of a stretch to say that Arendt's youthful lesson about
suffering and love can be applied to how we should relate to the terrorism that humanity inflicts on itself. In love we inflict a divine suffering on each other, and in the modern world we also inflict a divine
suffering on each other. In both cases, we reach down into the depths
of who we are. In both cases, we emerge either broken or alive. As

John Berger says of our contemporary condition, "Liberty is slowly being found not outside but in the depths of the prison."[28] To confront the suffering of erotic love the youthful Arendt turned to the language of poetry. To confront the suffering of the modern world the mature Arendt turned to language itself. Her magnum opus, *The Human Condition*, she originally planned to title *Amor Mundi*, which means "the love of the world."

Though we shouldn't underestimate the forces that threaten to deprive us of our humanity, we also shouldn't forget all our powerful counterweights to the degradation of thought, action, and work. When Arendt arrived in the United States, having fled first from Nazi Germany and then from occupied France, she wrote her teacher Karl Jaspers about the many downsides to America: the social oppression (especially of black citizens), the willful ignorance of death, the deep-rooted anti-intellectualism. But she was pleasantly surprised by, and deeply grateful to, her new country: "There really is such a thing as freedom here and a strong feeling among many people that one cannot live without freedom. The republic is not a vapid illusion."[29]

She reminds us that no matter how bad things get, the entire human condition, with all its peculiar natality, nestles inside every new child born unto us. The capacity for the regeneration of human value, in surprising new forms, lies in you and me. In *Men in Dark Times* Arendt celebrates certain figures—Rosa Luxemburg, Karl Jaspers, Isak Dinesen, Randall Jarrell, among others—who endured and confronted the monstrosities of the twentieth century but were not made monstrous by them. It's not that such figures have the single correct philosophy or religion that salvages their humanity, even though various philosophies and religions can certainly help. It's that the human condition is always open, always rekindling itself.

> Even in the darkest of times we have the right to expect some illumination, and . . . such illumination may well come less from theories and concepts than from the uncertain, flickering, and often weak light that some men and women, in their lives and their works, will

kindle under almost all circumstances and shed over the time span that was given them on earth.[30]

Arendt doesn't give us much guidance about what to do within the human condition. But she's superb about lighting the way to where the human condition can be found.

Not long ago I went to a talk by an ex-con who had benefited from my alma mater's liberal-arts-in-prison program. After describing his study of neurobiology and philosophy, he mused, "For the first time in my life I felt like a real citizen." I was struck by the comment, but also puzzled. What does the study of neurobiology, fascinating as it is, have to do with making you into a citizen? After one of my sessions at Oakdale Prison, I casually asked the guys if they understood what the ex-con meant. My lifer friend Simon raised his hand and volunteered:

> I know exactly what he was getting at. All my life I've felt like it's me against the world, like I've had to fight for everything I get. But in this class it's different. I feel like what I say matters. Even when people disagree with me, it's not a life-threatening thing. What's in my brain has some dignity, and I feel like what I'm learning is giving it more dignity. I feel like a real citizen in here, just like what the ex-con felt like in his classes. Who knows what could happen?

The prisoners around our makeshift seminar table nodded in agreement. One added, "Yeah, I like this citizenship thing." Despite our justifications and rationalizations for prison, it's often largely a place to break down people's humanity as a form of vengeance. But it's astonishing how humanity can persist even there. It makes you love the world. As Zbigniew Herbert says, "And even if the City falls and one of us survives/ he will carry the City inside him on the roads of exile/ he will be the City."[31]

INTERLUDE ON THE
PROBLEM OF EVIL

Some people tell me
God takes care of old folks and fools,
But since I've been born,
He must've changed the rules.

FUNNY PAPA SMITH

What philosophers call "the problem of evil" is now usually presented as a court case against a defendant whose guilt would mean his nonexistence. Why would God—reputedly an all-good, all-powerful being—allow all the misery of the world? Why does creation veer so far from our moral expectations? Why does evil often triumph over good? Given the fact of, say, a child's debilitating cancer, the case against a good divinity seems clear-cut. If God is all-powerful, then He would have the power to cure the child's cancer, or, perhaps more to the point, create a world where children never suffer from cancer. If God is all-good, then He clearly would want to bring about the world where the child doesn't suffer and die. Because humanity has been all-too-commonly subject to such heartbreaking circumstances, it's unreasonable to believe in an all-good, all-powerful God. It seems even immoral if the logic of your beliefs forces you to conclude, "Therefore, you deserve it, little one."

The (in my view) weak version of the atheist's case against God, sometimes known as "the strict logical disproof," is that a perfectly good God is logically incompatible with even a drop of bad. A totally white piece of paper means that there are no black splotches on it. An all-white creator would create nothing but an all-white creation. Likewise, the creation of a perfect God absolutely entails that there would be nothing opposed to perfection in it. Generally speaking, the imperfections come in three varieties: death, misery, and wrongdoing. If life is good, why shouldn't it be endless? If pain and misery are bad, why should they ever arise? If sin is evil, why shouldn't our most agonizing ethical dilemma be what flavor to select at the gelateria? The fact that there are evil splotches on creation absolutely disproves the existence of a perfect God.

But "the strict logical disproof" has serious problems. Nearly all of us accept as important *some* death, suffering, and abuses of freedom. If we never died, either there would be terrible overpopulation or the possibility of new life would be eliminated. Plus, a life can be meaningful only if it unfolds out of a finite past into a finite future.[1] If pain and negative emotions weren't built into us, we'd have no alert systems for our bodies and minds. It's a disorder when people have a congenital insensitivity to pain. They bite off the tips of their tongues. Their infections fester. Broken bones go unnoticed. Negative emotions—sadness, worry, fear—serve a similar function of helping us to figure out what's valuable and attuning us to the world. And if we didn't have the ability to make some bad choices, we wouldn't be able to build character. Parents, coaches, and teachers—if they possess the slightest bit of wisdom—know that we can't encase young people in pain-free, risk-free, choice-free environments without stunting any number of goods that arise from the confrontation with risky choices, pain, and even death. John Keats, in a lovely letter to his brother and sister-in-law, speaks of our difficult existence as an arena of "soul-making." Isn't he at least partially right?

But the atheist can make a much stronger case than "the strict logical disproof." The problem, on this view, is not death but early death, not pain but excessive pain, not mistakes but gross abuses of freedom.

Suffering may well be compatible with an all-good, all-powerful God, but the overwhelming amount of suffering renders such a divinity extremely unlikely. I remember a *Saturday Night Live* skit in which a Ferris wheel's highest setting was "So Fast That People Fly Off." In a way, that little joke sums up what's sometimes called the "evidential" case against God. Why on the wheel of biological existence can death be dialed up not just for eighty-year-olds but for eight-year-olds? Why do the settings for human suffering include schizophrenia and migraines? Why can the Ferris wheel of human freedom be cranked up all the way to child rape and genocide? Sure, we understand that a good God is compatible with *some* pain and death, just as being a good coach is compatible with putting athletes through some pretty tough exercises. No pain, no gain. But if we look at this bloody world to draw conclusions about its creator, wouldn't it be reasonable to think that it was designed not by a coach trying to make us all into the best spiritual athletes possible but rather by a drunk, abusive coach only sometimes trying to improve us, who often takes a baseball bat to our shins for the hell of it? Or maybe we should conclude, like Hume's Philo in the *Dialogues concerning Natural Religion*, "This world . . . was only the first rude essay of some infant deity, who afterwards abandoned it, ashamed of his lame performance: it is the work only of some dependent, inferior deity; and is the object of derision to his superiors: it is the production of old age and dotage in some superannuated deity."[2]

Religious folk, in the presence of misery, sometimes say that it's all part of God's plan. I have great respect for the inkling that there's meaning to be found in suffering. But if they're saying that every pang and shriek of suffering is merited, they're profoundly mistaken. All holy texts, including the Bible itself, rule it out: "God maketh his sun to rise on the evil and on the good, and sendeth rain on the just and on the unjust."[3] There's a profound bit of light verse by a nineteenth-century English judge that goes:

The rain it raineth on the just
And also on the unjust fella;

> But chiefly on the just, because
> The unjust hath the just's umbrella.

Crime often pays. Bad things happen to good people. Well, maybe "good" is a stretch to describe the likes of us. But what happens to people is very often worse than we deserve. To look at the world in even a cursory manner and think that the level and location of suffering are right where they ought to be is worse than absurd: it's wicked. If the belief in God implies such callous unreasonableness, then we should probably all be atheists.

Yet the logic of the evidential case against God, let alone the strict logical disproof, betrays our failure to understand how the mystery of pointless suffering is fundamental to our humanity. What we think of as distinctively human—technology, art, religion, politics, philosophy—depends on a gap between how the world is and how we think it should be. If there were no gap, we'd never have developed tools: What improvement could they offer? We'd never have painted images on a cave wall or anywhere else, for our imagination would have no impetus: Why should anything be different? We'd have no politics: How could things be organized better than they naturally are? No religion or philosophy either: everything would already make sense. In fact, the very concept of moral goodness would disappear, for virtue would be indistinguishable from selfishness. It would be a world of boring biographies in which the big dramas were those times when we selected pistachio over orange-blossom ice cream, or—worse!—didn't get to have dessert after supper. A world without human thought, without human freedom, without humanity itself. It's not simply that technology, politics, and philosophy deal with pointless suffering; it's that they wouldn't exist without it. To battle pointless suffering is a fundamental task of ours—and that means there must be pointless suffering! I'm not saying that the evidential version of the problem of evil is wrong. It's quite right in its way: the world *is* incompatible with our visions of goodness. We can certainly imagine a better world than this one; in fact, it's our job to do so and then to try to bring about that better world. But what we can't do is to imagine a *meaningful* world where some remainder of suffering doesn't seem excessive. What Kant says in the opening to his masterwork is right on the money: "Human reason has this peculiar fate that in one species of its knowledge it is burdened by questions which, as prescribed by the very nature of reason itself, it is not able to ignore, but which, as transcending all its powers, it is also not able to answer."[4] To think that the world should be without some pointless suffering is a suicide wish. No evil, no us. The problem of evil disproves God only by refuting humanity!

* * * * * * * * * * *

To drive home my idea that pointless suffering is built into our humanity, let me show how the "problem" of evil dogs us regardless of whether God is in the picture. Our society, driven as it is by a vague utilitarianism, is drifting toward a situation where we're beset by our own unique problem of evil, what could be called the "anthropological problem of evil." As Arendt shows us, we're beginning to cry out "Why me?" to ourselves. Our radically increased scientific knowledge and technological powers have put us in an increasingly awkward position. With our superpowered fix-it-ism, we have become like the gods and are now occasionally confronted by the fundamental question of the Creator: what's the best among all the conceivable worlds that we should try to bring about? If we start with the premise that all excessive suffering should be fixed, we soon find ourselves in insoluble muddles.

It's common in contemporary discussions of the theological problem of evil to encounter questions like "Why does God ever allow mass murderers like Adolf Hitler or Adam Lanza to be conceived?" Soon we may be asking, "Why do *we* ever allow someone like Adolf Hitler or Adam Lanza to be conceived?" In fact, scientists have been analyzing Adam Lanza's DNA to see if there are any glaring abnormalities. Let's say that they isolate a genetic sequence for certain traits associated with extreme violence. (I happen to believe that this research is based on a faulty view of the role of genes, but I'll use "genes" as shorthand for the possibility of discovering the root causes of violence.) What should be done? Should we allow the genes to stand and risk evil? If so, wouldn't someone who suffered from any negative consequences of our decision cry out to us, "Why didn't you stop this?" If instead we destroy the risky genes or kill the fetuses that carry them, even setting aside serious moral qualms about abortion and eugenics, where do we draw the line with genetic sequences that pose similar risks? Would we allow genes for violence but not mass violence? Sexual harassment genes but not rape genes? Couldn't people on the suffering side of our line, provided they hold to the principle of maximizing pleasure and minimizing pain, still cry out in protest?

Curing children of cancer and other life-taking diseases is clearly part of the best of all humanly imaginable worlds. But is there an age where we should accept lethal diseases, even if we have the power to eliminate them? The problem is that diseases like cancer are structurally necessary for the maintenance of various goods associated with death, pain, and freedom: population control, the opportunity for new generations to rise and flourish, the heroism of struggling with suffering, the meaningfulness generated by the ever-present possibility of death. Yet any given instance of that structural necessity is hard to bear when you have the power to eliminate it. If we imagine an "enlightened" use of our technologies such that we allow only so much disease for the good to be preserved and even predominate, wouldn't someone that we allowed to suffer "fairly" from the disease cry out, as once to God, "Why me?"

But what happens if we don't put limits on the use of our biotechnological powers? Until recently it was unthinkable that we'd have the problem of overcuring diseases, of living too long. But in a striking personal essay called "A Life Worth Ending," Michael Wolff recounts the story of his mother as a case of just this phenomenon. At eighty-four she required major heart surgery to live. Though she was already showing minor signs of dementia and was hesitant to go through with such a major procedure, the doctors successfully operated on her, initially to the great relief of the author. Now that his mother was in good physical health, her dementia progressed quickly and horribly. Wolff writes, "Circumstances have conspired to rob the human person—a mass of humanity—of all hope and dignity and comfort. When my mother's diaper is changed she makes noises of harrowing despair—for a time, before she lost all language, you could if you concentrated make out what she was saying, repeated over and over and over again: 'It's a violation. It's a violation. It's a violation.'" He ends his essay, "I do not know how death panels ever got such a bad name. Perhaps they should have been called deliverance panels. What I would not do for a fair-minded body to whom I might plead for my mother's end."[5]

Hospitals and nursing homes have no shortage of those whom Wolff calls "the old old." Should these suffering people, these modern-day Tithonuses, have been allowed to die of their cancers and heart diseases prior to when their lives became violations of their humanity? Let's imagine a deliverance panel that tells families like Wolff's that certain life-saving surgeries aren't authorized for patients who fail to meet certain conditions. While such decisions, at least in theory, might be wise and just, it's inevitable that they'd lead to a situation where a contemporary Job would cry out to the panel of fellow human beings: "How can you have so much power and claim to be good when you allow my parent to die, my child to suffer?"

One way of trying to wiggle out of this difficulty would be to say, "If only these sufferers could think as clearly and wisely as our deliverance panel, or the doctors, or philosophers, or me! The best instances of utilitarian legislation don't really suffer from the problem of evil. At most they suffer from an *apparent* problem of evil." This defense is no different in kind from the common theodicy that says what appears to be evil is actually a part of God's plan. The big difference, however, is that the theist can lean on God's infinite wisdom and goodness, whereas our deliverance panel wobbles on the dubious assumption that certain confident philosophers, politicians, scientists, doctors, or citizens are in possession of the ability to conceive and successfully draw the ideal limit to suffering.

Another way of trying to wiggle out of our problem of evil would be to say that people shouldn't be forced against their will to sacrifice for the greater good; it should simply be a legal option for each of us to choose whatever is compatible with a reasonable conception of the greatest good. Michael Wolff seems attracted to this position with euthanasia: "Meanwhile, since, like my mother, I can't count on someone putting a pillow over my head, I'll be trying to work out the timing and details of a do-it-yourself exit strategy. As should we all."

But this libertarian-utilitarianism, even if it has plausibility as a political fix, doesn't really get us out of the philosophical problem. What do we do if people don't avail themselves of the good-maximizing option? Either we're allowing evil when it could be prevented, or we must tackle the problem of freedom itself. Why on utilitarian grounds should we tolerate free choices, particularly when free choices so often lead to evils? If freedom is simply one positive utilitarian good among others, why should its protection trump the elimination of pointless suffering? Maybe we should get rid of freedom altogether and have philosopher-monarchs force people to do what's best for them.

Better yet, why not develop techniques—drug treatments, hypnosis, psychological nudges, social systems—that give people the feeling of freedom but subconsciously direct them to do only what's good? The extremes of totalitarianism furnish us with degrading and wicked examples of the desire to refashion free humans into flawless behavior systems. Nanny-statism is a well-meaning version of the same ambition. In the 1950s Robert G. Heath, a psychiatrist at Tulane University, used electrodes in the brain to modify the behavior of patients prone to violence. He also surreptitiously used his experiment to try to prod them in other "good" directions—for instance, to "cure" gays. Anthony Burgess's idea in *A Clockwork Orange* of "Ludovico's Technique," which manipulates human desire so that we avoid committing certain injustices, is the famous literary expression of Heath's dream. The novel's protagonist, the violent hooligan Alex, with his eyes propped wide by specula, is forced to watch brutal movies under the influence of a nausea-inducing drug. Thus, like a Pavlovian dog, he's brainwashed into experiencing debilitating repulsion whenever he thinks of committing a crime. Though he's indeed rendered docile by the treatment, the downside is that the score to the violent movies is Beethoven's Ninth Symphony. Not only is Alex cured of crime, he's unable to listen to the "Ode to Joy" without wanting to puke.

If we could perfect "Ludovico's Technique," even if we could somehow manage not to do stupid things like trying to cure gays, we'd ultimately undermine the values of heroism, dignity, courage, hope, love. The concept of biography would lose all its interest, if not all its meaning. As Anthony Burgess teaches us, there'd be no more Ludwig Beethoven, no more odes to joy! Kant points out that if doing the right thing always paid off, it would eliminate the moral worth of doing the right thing: "Suppose we could attain to scientific knowledge of God's existence . . . all our morality would break down. In his every action, man would represent God to himself as rewarder or avenger. The image would force itself on his soul, and his hope for reward and fear of punishment would take the place of moral motives."[6] Without the space to make bad choices and a world marked by a gap between our morality and how things go, the difference between acting selfishly and acting morally would vanish. We need a morally incoherent world to have morality at all! We need a backdrop of pointlessness for life to have a point!

We just can't escape "the problem of evil" without eliminating our humanity. A genuinely human existence requires a structure of death, suffering, and freedom. We must label as "evil" some instances of death, suffering, and freedom. To have a line between necessary and unacceptable suffering is essential for human existence. Any version of that line, whether drawn by God or a panel of philosophers, will and must appear unfair at some level, at bare minimum to someone on the suffering side of it, unless we check our rebellious brains at the door. Our situation is such that we're conceptually torn between justice and suffering. If God isn't available to rip us in two, we'll do the job ourselves.

The problem of pointless suffering doesn't refute God, nor does it refute us. It constitutes God. It constitutes us. The question is not about "solving" a problem but about living examined lives in relationship to what Gabriel Marcel calls a mystery, "a problem which encroaches upon its own data, invading them, as it were, and thereby transcending itself as a simple problem."[7] To speak practically, I don't want to see "deliverance panels," but I would like us to have advisory groups made up of doctors, nurses, psychologists, and philosophical or spiritual advisers, who converse with patients and their families about their most serious medical decisions in ethical terms. The point would not be to solve the problem of evil by drawing ideal lines of pain and death; the point would be to face the mystery of suffering together—to confront the value-laden matters of life and death and to seek out as a community the never-perfect balance between accepting suffering and utilizing our limited technological powers to fight it. The point would be to help patients make decisions for themselves—by their very nature, *agonizing* decisions—in examined transcendence of the technical problems of pathology, medical treatments, maximized life, and minimized pain.

I was recently at a funeral for my dear friend Mike's brother Steve Judge, who suddenly and unexpectedly dropped dead at the age of fifty-four. Steve's life was a case study in suffering. As a young man, he had everything going for him: smarts, good looks, athleticism, kindness, dutifulness. While a star at the Air Force Academy, he was bitten by a mosquito and came down with encephalitis. He spent weeks in a catatonic state. After he emerged from it, he was diagnosed with chronic and severe schizophrenia. For the next thirty years, until his heart finally broke, he was haunted by delusions, anxiety, and paranoia. The universe, like a naughty child, had taunted Steve and his family with towering promise only to knock it down like so many carefully constructed blocks. Yet Steve and his family found a new, quiet, unglamorous heroism in facing the challenges of mental illness with what fortitude, kindness, and even gratitude they could muster. Thanks to his mother's advocacy, Steve was put on an antipsychotic that eased his delusions and allowed glimpses of his former self. At the funeral, Steve's sister, Kate, shared a few brief incandescent re-membrances, some from the age of gold, some from the age of chaos. She concluded, "It took me a long time to realize that the question is not 'Why did this happen?' but 'How are we to respond?'" Yes, that is the central question.

PART TWO

Four Perennial Ways of Looking at Pointless Suffering

It is a precious and rare gift
like a noose of diamonds.

ANNA SWIR

In 1506 Pope Julius II was told about some interesting statues dug up in a vineyard near Santa Maria Maggiore. He sent two of his acquaintances with an enthusiasm for the ancient world, the architect Giuliano da Sangallo and the artist Michelangelo Buonarroti. When they climbed down into the pit where the statues had been unearthed, Giuliano gasped, "It's the *Laocoön*! The one that Pliny mentions!" Michelangelo had already begun to draw it.

The *Laocoön*, which has been on display in the Statues Courtyard in the Vatican Museums basically ever since its discovery in the Renaissance, is one of humanity's unforgettable images of suffering. Laocoön is the priest who, when the Greeks attempt the ruse of the Trojan Horse, tells his comrades, "Don't trust the horse, whatever it is: I fear the Greeks, even when they're bearing gifts," and then hurls his spear at the hollowed-out wood. But it's preordained that the Greeks are to defeat the Trojans, and the gods don't want a prophetic priest to mess up the plan. So Minerva sends two giant sea serpents to kill not just the skeptical Laocoön but also his two sons.

Giuliano and Michelangelo were so thrilled because Pliny hails the *Laocoön* as "a work superior to any painting or bronze."[1] It did not—and does not—disappoint. The marble statue, a linguini of limbs and snakes, is so intense it seems like it would wriggle if you touched it. One of Laocoön's sons, bitten by the serpents, has almost given up the ghost. The other son, still trying desperately to fight the beasts, looks to his father with a mixture of disappointment and petulance. In the middle, Laocoön passes into the private world of agony as his splayed body grapples with the monsters.

Part of what's attractive about the sculpture is Laocoön's physique. It's the perfection of those muscles that surely inspired Michelangelo: his feel for the beauty of the male body was intense. According to Pliny, there were three sculptors: Agesander, Polydorus, and Athenodorus. For all I know they chose maximum agony as a subject for no other reason than that it gave them an opportunity to show what it looks like when every muscle flexes simultaneously. After all, suffering is one of the many chisels of beauty.

The image is also compelling because it crystallizes a fundamental, perhaps *the* fundamental, aspect of the human situation. The story it tells is about how suffering presents itself as pointless. Here's a man whose agony and death are *because* of his being virtuous! And it's not just Laocoön who's punished; even his children must suffer and die! How do the subjects relate to this bitter fact of the universe? One child, who embodies human reason's initial attitude, rebels. The other child, who represents the eventual defeat of human reason, is deprived of the luxury of rebellion: a look of "Why me?" shades into a limp acceptance of inevitable death. Laocoön represents the synthesis of the postures on his left and right. On the one hand, his powerful body exerts itself to the utmost to fight off the serpents. On the other, his face is free of all petulant rejection of his fate. He's simply suffering, simply crying out. His agony returns him to an animal innocence.

In this sense, the sculpture translates the lines from Virgil's *Aeneid* (or perhaps Virgil's lines translate the sculpture—the exact date of the *Laocoön* is unclear):

> While simultaneously his hands tore at the knots,
> His fillets blotted by saliva and dark venom,
> He simultaneously pierced heaven with a horrid scream,
> Like the bellowing of a wounded bull fleeing the altar,
> Trying to shake off its neck the ill-aimed axe.[2]

The repetition of "simultaneously" (*simul* in Latin) is crucial, underlining the complex situation of being human. We must use our rationality to combat our condition in which we seem to have been hit by an ill-aimed axe; we must also—paradoxically, simultaneously—live out our condition as ignorant creatures in an order that sustains and destroys us. Before the drama with the serpents, Laocoön sacrifices a bull to the gods. Now he's the sacrifice.

Virgil's paradox is sharper yet. Had Laocoön been successful in warning the Trojans about the Greek ruse, the Greeks would never have conquered Troy. Had the Greeks never conquered Troy, Aeneas would never have fled the city. Had Aeneas never fled the city, he'd never have gone to Latium. Had he never gone to Latium, Rome would never have been founded. Thus, had the innocent Laocoön not suffered, there would be no Rome. No tragedy, no civilization. No pointless suffering, no humanity. Does this somehow eliminate the pointlessness of the suffering? Well, yes and no. The *Laocoön* joins the Crucifixion as one of the fundamental images where the suffering of innocence is so intense, so excessive, that it spills over into maximal meaningfulness.

* * * * * * * * * * * *

A few years ago I had the pleasure of attending Betty Cooper's hundredth birthday party. I knew that her ancestors had come to Virginia on the same ship as the family of Thomas Jefferson. As we shook hands, I thought about her having shaken hands with one of her elders as a child. I reckoned I was only two or at most three handshakes away from Thomas Jefferson!

If we continue my fantasia, using the Bible's seventy-year lifespan as a rough guide, we're only six handshakes away from William Shakespeare, eight or nine from Joan of Arc, not even thirty from Jesus. In other words, if on a football field we lined up a string of contiguous lives between us and Jesus, and we were at the end zone, he'd be somewhere around the twenty-yard line. We'd barely have to raise our voices to have a conversation. Socrates is thirty-five handshakes away. Add ten more handshakes, and we arrive at Laocoön and the other players of the Trojan War. I could probably throw Achilles an accurate pass. Cam Newton could get one to a painter of the Lascaux cave. It amuses me to imagine some distant future when our ancestors think of the period from, say, 1,000 BC to AD 3,000 as one fairly homogenous lump of time (the Symbolic Age?), the way we tend to blur together the many millennia of the Neolithic Age.

It's true that the thinkers I examine are subject to a unique history and could be approached in an antiquarian light, but my point with the handshakes is that we're not so distant from any moment in recorded history. What your grandpa or great-grandma or fifty-times-great-grandparent has to say about life might not be so out of touch. The Job authors and Confucius—chapters 4 and 6—are standing somewhere between Socrates and Homer; and Epictetus—chapter 5—is on our side of Jesus. Sidney Bechet, the subject of my last chapter, is but one handshake away. I don't intend to downplay the importance of history. If anything, I'd like to see more fine-grained work on how the zigzags of history influence and are influenced by the philosophy and culture of suffering. Nevertheless, I believe certain ideas and images aren't exhausted by their immediate contexts. Much has changed since the days of Laocoön, but the fact that we suffer and die despite our virtues hasn't changed a whole lot over the years.

Confucius says, "Reviewing the old as a means of realizing the new—such a person can be considered a teacher."[3] It's an essential part of being human to revive what's valuable in our inheritance—to "break bread with the dead," in the words of W. H. Auden.[4] In communing with the dead, our contemporary minds learn something old and thereby make something new. The goal is renaissance. One of the teachings of Zbigniew Herbert, the great Polish poet and essayist, who happens to be one of my heroes, is that with the right kind of mental work we can belong to the same epoch as Leonardo, that we can still have living encounters with Socrates, that the first human who ever applied red ochre to a cave wall can be our contemporary. As he emerges from the cave paintings of southwest France, Herbert feels on his palm "the warm touch of the Lascaux painter" and declares, "I am a citizen of the earth, an inheritor not only of the Greeks and Romans but of almost the whole of infinity."[5] In his essay "Pact," he describes an archaeological discovery of a damaged human skeleton from the middle Stone Age, the right arm of which rests on the skeleton of a five-month-old puppy. The tender gesture moves Herbert to say, "Stone Age man spoke to us in a whisper full of love. He affirmed the pact made twelve thousand years ago, a covenant more lasting than all the treacherous treaties of tyrants fallen into the dust of oblivion and scorn."[6]

There's no going back to old ways of life, thank God. If the project of modernity poses some big problems for us, it's only because it's solved a thousand others. But those big problems remain, and the finest spirits of the modern age have always insisted on trying to correct for our overcorrections to nature. The past is indispensable when it comes to seeing our limitations and reorienting our sense of what's most valuable. We aren't so separate from our twelve-thousand-year-old brother petting his puppy. Let's ignore the treacheries of tyrants, large and small, and continue to affirm his pact.

* * * * * * * * * * * *

This section examines four perennial ways of looking at suffering. There are also at least four perennial ways of *not* looking at suffering.

In *On Death and Dying* Elisabeth Kübler-Ross famously identifies stages of how we react to a terminal illness. The first four are denial, anger, bargaining, and depression. Life itself is a variety of terminal illness. We often carry on in varying stages of oblivion, indignation, or melancholy; and our technological way of life is built on the attempt to bargain suffering away. Denial, anger, bargaining, and depression are four ways of refusing or failing to find meaning in suffering. They're all understandable. I've researched each of them carefully in my personal life!

The last of Kübler-Ross's stages, the most honest and liberating stage, is acceptance. If the first section of this book was devoted to exploring the destiny of the idea that pointless suffering is to be eliminated, this part of the book is devoted to exploring the extent to which pointless suffering can and should be productively accepted. It's probably no coincidence that three of these perennial ways of looking at pointless suffering are premodern, and the fourth is rooted in the pervasive political oppression of black Americans. These ways of dealing with pain, injustice, and death are under no illusion that paradise is just a few pills or laws away. Yet they all involve more than simply shrugging one's shoulders and giving up in the face of suffering. The point is to recognize our unique vulnerability such that we're atoned with each other and the universe. These ways of looking at suffering all empower us to use our faculties to the fullest and live as truthfully, justly, beautifully, and joyfully as we can.

There's a grim meme that involves asking people if, given the possibility of time travel, they'd zoom back and kill the infant Adolf Hitler. In my view, it's a bad sign for human nature that the question is always posed in terms of murdering a baby rather than, say, going back to the night of Adolf's conception and sounding a fire alarm before Alois could get in Klara's *Höschen*. Counterfactuals are a little silly, but one way of getting at the central paradox embodied by the thinkers in this section, the paradox of accepting and combatting suffering, is to consider if, given the history-altering time machine, you'd rescue Laocoön and Jesus, knowing that by doing so you'd also negate

Roman civilization, Christianity, and all their offshoots. Would you spread word in Troy of Odysseus's ruse before the gods have a chance to silence Laocoön? Would you rile up the crowd so it yells "Jesus!" instead of "Barabbas!" when Pontius Pilate offers it the choice of commuting a sentence? On the one hand, there's something unimaginably horrible about allowing the excruciating fates of Laocoön and Jesus if you have the power to help. On the other hand, there's something horribly unimaginable about poofing Western civilization out of existence. Even if you want to indict Rome and Christianity as having brought about more pain than happiness in their often-brutal reigns, there's a pricelessness that they've brought to human life—if need be, think of highlights like Cicero, Shakespeare, Bach, or your aunt—that exceeds, as by a whole other dimension of value, the admittedly terrible suffering Western civilization has exacted. Would you save Laocoön and Jesus? What should we do about the pointless suffering at the foundation of humanity?

This section is an attempt to sketch the *Laocoön*—not the physical image, but the spiritual paradox embedded within it.

FOUR

POINTLESS SUFFERING

REVEALS GOD

On the Book of Job and the Significance of Freedom

It is true that the unknown is the largest need of the intellect,
though for it, no one thinks to thank God.

EMILY DICKINSON

I'm going to inflict yet one more injustice on Job. In just a moment, I'm going to commit what the literary critic Cleanth Brooks calls "the heresy of paraphrase" on the chapter of the Bible that deals unflinchingly with the question of pointless suffering. Unlike God, I'm willing to give a rationale for my violence.

One of the poetic books of the Hebrew Bible's Ketuvim, the Book of Job is itself the result of an injustice. According to historians, the version that everyone knows is a mishmash, compiled between the seventh and the fourth centuries BC, of two or more very different texts by very different authors: a simple folk tale about a patient Job who keeps his faith through tough times *and* a complicated philosophical discussion in verse featuring an angry Job who challenges God. This textual injustice, it seems to me, turns out to be justice in disguise, for the mishmash is truer to the complexity of our reality than either version would be on its own—though I myself prefer the long, boring middle part to the charming folk tale that sandwiches it.

The first thing I taught at Oakdale Prison, at the suggestion of Mike Cervantes, was the moral philosophy of Immanuel Kant. That led to an interesting session on the concept of evil. And that led to the problem of evil and the Book of Job. Since parts of the text are rough going, rather than give the usual canned lecture as a prelude to our discussion at the prison, I figured it would be efficient and interesting to do a readers-theater performance as distilled into more-or-less contemporary voices. So, for the good of the criminals, I committed a crime against the Bible by paraphrasing the Book of Job. Heresy is sometimes the first step of holiness.

The Book of Job: An Unjust Paraphrase
Dramatis Personae

GOD or YHWH, the creator of everything, reputed to be both all-good and all-powerful. *The part was played by yours truly, not out of some power trip, at least not primarily, but because I wanted to ensure that His sublimely sarcastic tone at the end came through loud and clear.*

THE DEVIL'S ADVOCATE (in Hebrew, *hassatan*, "the satan"), God's most trusted adviser, whose role is to be skeptical and probing. *Numerous inmates volunteered for the part!*

JOB, the man who has it all: health, wealth, a great family, and a moral character that makes him deserving of his good life. His exact religion is unknown, though he's not Jewish (or, obviously, Christian or Muslim). *Job was played by a young man who'd been given a life sentence at the age of nineteen for having sexually abused a girl for eight years (in other words, a girl he began to molest when he was eleven).*

JOB'S WIFE, a no-nonsense lady. *I had misgivings about assigning a lady's part to one of the inmates in the all-male prison, so I had my sister Amanda—who volunteers teaching Spanish in the prison—come along to play the female role.*

ELIPHAZ, BILDAD, and ZOPHAR, Job's friends. *Three prisoners—a Christian, a self-proclaimed Gnostic, and an atheist.*

ELIHU, a young know-it-all. *He was played by Simon, my friend who's served almost thirty years of a life sentence for being involved in the murder of a pimp.*

The narration was read by Mike Cervantes, the coordinator of the educational programs.

> NARRATOR: In a quiet spot in the Middle East lives a man named Job—a good husband, father, businessman, neighbor, and servant of God. Above him, in heaven, God and the Devil's Advocate are chatting.
>
> GOD: . . . I know, I know: humans have been a surprisingly bad invention. But I take consolation in Job. Just look at him! I wish all people were so genuinely good.
>
> THE DEVIL'S ADVOCATE: Is he *genuinely* good? I don't deny that he hasn't done wrong. But it's easy for Job to do right, given the life he leads. Surely you've read Immanuel Kant, who argues that in order to have true moral worth a human must do what's right because it's right, not simply because it leads to good outcomes. The only way to test Job's goodness would be to see what he'd do if deprived of his cushy life. Myself, I don't think he'd remain committed to goodness.
>
> GOD: Want to bet?
>
> THE DEVIL'S ADVOCATE: You read my mind.
>
> GOD: Then let's let him have it.

NARRATOR: The following months are a horrible ordeal for Job. An imperial army from the West attacks his quiet homeland, launching drone strikes in the name of peace and justice that destroy all Job's property and kill every last one of his employees. Though the imperial army quickly loses its will to fight and leaves, Job's ten children are traumatized. He encourages them to go to a party to forget their troubles. A tornado strikes the house of the party, leaving all ten of Job's children dead in the rubble.

JOB'S WIFE (*in grief and anger*): So this is what our upright life has gotten us? If we want to save a shred of dignity, there's only one thing to do at this point: curse God. He may hold all the cards, but we don't have to kiss His ass.

JOB: No, I will not curse God. I didn't ask "Why me?" when things were going well for us, and I'm not going to complain now that things are terrible. God gives, God takes. That's His right.

NARRATOR: They return to grieving.

GOD: See! Job is still good!

THE DEVIL'S ADVOCATE: He does still have his health . . .

GOD (*without much hesitation*): Fine, let's give him a disease.

NARRATOR: Job is struck with the excruciating Hyperimmuno-globulin E syndrome. To remember the atrocious symptoms, medical students learn the acronym FATED (coarse or leonine Facies, cold staph Abscesses, retained primary Teeth, increased igE, and Dermatologic problems). Job's friends—Eliphaz, Bildad, and Zophar—come to Job. They see how much he's suffering, physically and mentally, and they sit quietly by his side for a week. Finally, Job speaks.

JOB: Life is evil. I wish I'd never been born.

ELIPHAZ: You're overreacting. Don't give up! Think of the advice you used to give people when they were going through hard times: the good will win out. Plus, you're no angel. God sees everything, even your hidden motivations. It should be no surprise that you must be punished for your sins.

JOB: Some friend you are! So God has been watching me and tallying up my smallest infractions and now in punishment has destroyed my property, murdered my children, and thrown in a dose of excruciating skin disease for good measure?! That's really comforting. Thanks.

BILDAD: You're being self-centered, Job. This isn't God's fault. Wars are what imperial powers do. Partying is what kids do. Bad things happen as a result. Are you really so spotless in your behavior? Do you really deserve no bumps on the road of life? God has a plan for it all. Our ancestors have always believed in a fair God. Surely you don't think that you're wiser than they were!

JOB: Look, I'm not trying to put God on trial. I'm simply asking, "Why doesn't humanity get a trial?" I'm in excruciating pain. My children are all dead. My property is destroyed. Where's even a scrap of evidence that people like me deserve their fate? It's like God has let evil rule the world.

ZOPHAR: I'm with Bildad and Eliphaz. God is good and powerful. You happen to be suffering. We're going to doubt you before we ever doubt God.

JOB: That's because you all have your heads up your asses. Do you think that God is going to like it that you're trying to flatter him with lies? (*To God*) If it was worth watching my family and me so closely that you've tallied up every little thing we've ever done wrong, isn't it worth a few minutes of Your time to give me an answer? What have I done? Why do You hide from me? When I die, I'm going to be gone forever. Is it really my fate to live, suffer, and perish without any understanding?

ELIPHAZ: Who are you to challenge God?!

BILDAD: Think about someone other than yourself for one minute, Job. How do most of us get through the day? We believe that things are going to work out. Are you seriously trying to destroy the one thing that gives us hope?

JOB: First God tortures me, now my friends torture me. I just
can't give up thinking that I deserve an answer!

ZOPHAR: Don't go over to the dark side, Job! The wicked never
prosper. They're always dogged by a bad conscience.

JOB: Are you kidding? The wicked prosper all the time. Right
about now I wish I were one of those happy wicked people.

ELIPHAZ: Job, we've tried to be nice here. But let's face it. You're
evil. You've lived in wealth while poor people around the
world were suffering. You call that being good? And now in
all your selfishness you demand that God come down from
His task of ruling the whole universe and give you a detailed
list of the thousand and one ways you've ignored the needy
or hurt others. If anything, you should be glad that God isn't
making you suffer more!

JOB: I'm sick and tired of this! I want God, though I have no
idea where to find Him. If God were to put me to the test, I
know He'd find that I haven't done anything to deserve
my fate.

NARRATOR: Job and his friends all start talking at once, vehemently restating their positions. Finally, Job's voice rises
above theirs.

JOB: I don't care what anyone says! As long as I'm alive, I'm going
to speak the truth. We've figured out every last place to drill
for oil, but we still haven't figured out where a drop of wisdom is found. All we can do is speak the truth as best we can
in hopes that we someday find it. . . . If only I could go back to
the good old days! I'm a decent person. May my wife screw
someone else if I'm lying!

NARRATOR: A young man has been listening in on the conversation. He finally speaks up.

ELIHU: People always say that you should listen to your elders.
Well, I've listened to you, and it turns out that I have the answers that you "wise" men have been groping for. First, you
complain that God doesn't speak to you. Have you ever had a

dream? That's God speaking to you. Second, God is perfect. He has no need of our goodness, and He isn't at all bothered by our badness. All He cares about is doling out justice. So you definitely deserve what you're getting, Job. Third, even if you are suffering too much, it's good for you! Suffering makes you into a better person. Fourth, have you ever seen a thunderstorm? That's God at work. You never know what He's going to do! So, basically that should answer all your questions.

NARRATOR: God has been listening in on the conversation and suddenly appears in the form of the tornado that killed Job's children. All hide their faces in terror except for Job, who looks straight into the whirlwind.

GOD: Am I hearing you right, Job? Did you say that you want to have a trial? Fine by me. Man up and answer my questions. First, have you ever designed the set of interlocking ecosystems necessary to make a living planet like the one you're on now? Please, tell me in detail how you would go about doing so—you know, the kind of planet where when you finish it all the angels burst out in applause? Wait, maybe we should start with an easier question. Have you ever simply built an ocean? Tell me about your idea of the perfect balance of condensation, water levels, photosynthesis, amoebas, sharks, salinity, and so on. Or, let's go even easier yet, how would you make sunlight produce the colors of dawn on the earth's atmosphere? Also, you know how the universe eventually comes to an end . . . what's on the other side? And you know how your life comes to an end . . . what happens then? Feel free to start answering at any point. Or maybe you'd first like to talk about even easier topics, like the generation of snowflakes, the destruction of the world, the relationship of the winds, the value of hail, the necessity of desert flowers, the formation of dewdrops, the history of the Ice Age, the language of lightning, the interlocking evolution of lions and antelopes, the aesthetics of ostriches, or the ophthalmology of falcons. Since you know just how the world should work, I really want to hear from you. . . . Speak up, I can't hear you. . . . Cat got your tongue?

JOB: I'm sorry. I've said too much already.

GOD: I thought that you had a problem with my judgment? Go on, dress up like God, sit on the throne a while, administer the whole world as you see fit. Be my guest. Punish everyone you deem evil. Reward everyone you deem good. Destroy the gap between how humans think the world should be and how it is. Admittedly, you don't know the first thing about how to run a universe . . . but I'm sure that your judgment would be infallible, and everything would work out perfectly. . . . Look, let me let you in on a couple of my inventions. First, consider something that you don't even have a name for. Let's call it Behemoth. It's the life-force. Sexual desire. The wildness that makes life. If you want to picture it, think of a giant crocodile. Why don't you put this huge, ravenous, man-eating beast on a leash and go on a little stroll? Second, consider what we'll call Leviathan. Think of an enormous whale. The vast unknown. Infinity. The chaos out of which life emerges and against which all life struggles. Do you want to put Leviathan in a fishbowl? Do you want to cut up Leviathan into pieces of sushi? If you even got a glimpse of him, you'd drop dead. He sneezes lightning. He looks down on everyone but Me. Behemoth and Leviathan: though their wildness is critical to the meaning of your existence and the existence of all life, go ahead and tame them. Let's see what happens.

JOB: I've tried to stuff the unnameable into the puny categories of humanity. I've doubted the only universe in which my life is possible. Up to now I'd only heard about God. Now I see God. Now I truly know I'm human, and I'll shut up.

GOD: Eliphaz, Bildad, and Zophar, get over here. (I'm not even going to bother with you, Elihu!) If you think I was mad at Job, you were wrong. I'm mad at all of you. Job asked honest questions, and you gave him phony answers. As is his usual custom, Job acted like an honest human being. As is the usual custom of religious types, you acted like phonies. You need to repent. And if I choose to forgive you, it's going to be because of people like Job.

NARRATOR: Job is healed, his property is restored, and his business becomes even more successful than before. He and his wife have ten more children, who turn out to be smarter and better-looking than their previous children. Living to see his grandchildren and great-grandchildren, Job dies peacefully at a ripe old age.

THE END

My paraphrase is certainly an injustice, a deep one. I've strip-mined the world's most majestic poetry. The Book of Job's linguistic nobility, even in its finest translations, isn't just an ornament to the message: it is the message. God's speech is beyond paraphrase. Not only is His poetry about the vastness and intricacy of creation unparalleled, it's all the grander for being delivered with heavy irony.

> Hath the rain a father? or who hath begotten the drops of dew?
> Out of whose womb came the ice? and the hoary frost of heaven,
>   who hath gendered it?
> The waters are hid as with a stone, and the face of the deep is frozen.
> Canst thou bind the sweet influences of Pleiades, or loose the bands
>   of Orion?[1]

Only God has the authority to speak sarcastically about the Milky Way! But it's not just God's poetry that's crucial to the poem. Job's speeches are heart-wrenching in their honesty.

> For there is hope of a tree, if it be cut down, that it will sprout again,
>   and that the tender branch thereof will not cease.

> Though the root thereof wax old in the earth, and the stock thereof
> die in the ground;
> Yet through the scent of water it will bud, and bring forth boughs
> like a plant.
> But man dieth, and wasteth away: yea, man giveth up the ghost, and
> where is he?[2]

My paraphrase is also sinful because there are many passages that suggest multiple—seemingly endless—interpretations. As the Rabbi Harold Kushner notes, "In the English translation of Job that I use, virtually every page has a footnote that reads 'meaning of Hebrew uncertain.'"[3] In short, I've translated an odd-numbered Beethoven symphony into a jaunty work for a jug band.

One thing I hope my paraphrase does suggest is a point that's crystal clear in the text. When God appears at the end, He emphasizes several times that Job's friends have not spoken rightly about Him, and that Job has spoken rightly. It's striking, because Job's friends do all they can to defend God, and Job insists on the injustice of his suffering. Job doesn't curse God, but he flings, like so many grenades, devastating questions at the coherence of God's creation. In his moaning and musing Job says all sorts of harsh things, some of which contradict each other. Nevertheless, God says that Job in his insistence on the pointlessness of suffering has spoken rightly.

In other words, the Book of Job is a profound defense of philosophy and the other liberal arts. Speaking rightly doesn't mean saying what you think God or society wants to hear. It means trying to find a language that's true to reality in all its boredom, horror, and glory. It means cutting through the crap and trying to see things as they are. It's the kind of speaking where honest questioning is better than easy answering, where contradictions in the name of trying to get things right are preferable to harmonies that paper things over. In other words, it's the practice of philosophy, science, literature, and the rest of the liberal arts—not simply as a bunch of ideas to be memorized and mastered, not simply as handy tools for getting jobs and manipulating nature, and definitely not as a bunch of fancy theories that explain everything, but as adventures of understanding. The Book of Job demonstrates a kind of spooky freedom in God. But it also shows us the freedom of philosophy, which is wrung from the unjust suffering and grandeur of the universe. Such was the freedom of the prisoners in our discussion of the Book of Job following our performance.

* * * * * * * * * * *

The atheists found plenty of ammunition in the Book of Job, as did the believers. Interestingly, though I didn't ask them to maintain their masks, the inmates mostly defended the position of the character they played. For instance, the guy who played Job kept insisting that God never really explains Himself: there's no possible rationale for a large sum of the world's injustice, the young inmate argued. Because under the surface of abstract discussions often lurk very real aches and anxieties, I wondered about the extent to which my far-from-innocent Job was coming to terms with the fact that he'd inflicted so much pointless suffering. I also wondered about the extent to which he himself felt like a victim of divine injustice. Here, after all, was someone who began molesting a girl when he was eleven years old. If he's truly guilty of his crimes, then something was horribly wrong with his life, something not altogether or even primarily of his own doing. I wondered if there isn't an infinitely gentle, infinitely suffering thing at the heart of us all, even the most hardened or sociopathic criminals, let alone this bright-eyed, broken, guilty, young Job. I was starting to feel that hurt at the core of a tragedy by Sophocles or a blues by Sidney Bechet, the hurt that Job so wrenchingly expresses. I was just beginning to frame my reflections in more generalized terms when our conversation was interrupted: one of the more talkative inmates had to say his final goodbyes before being shipped to another prison. After hugs and handshakes, his parting benediction was "I pray with all my heart that every one of you finds what you're searching for, whatever path you're on."

Prior to our performance of the Book of Job, I taught the prisoners the classic problem of evil, the problem of how to reconcile an all-good, all-powerful God with the existence of pointless suffering. The way that the most committed believers reacted to the problem pre-figured almost exactly the reactions of Job's "pious" friends. "Why," I asked, "are some children born with debilitating diseases that lead shortly to their deaths?" One replied, "Maybe the child was going to grow up to do something horrible, and now God has spared us." Someone else said, "The child is being punished for the past sins of humanity." Yet someone else suggested, "Maybe because of the child's cancer, we'll find a cure that will save millions of other people." None of these responses explained why *this* little Job had to suffer. "Would anyone," I asked, "be willing to offer these explanations to the faces of suffering children and their parents at the local hospital?"

On the authority of the Bible itself we can see that such "pious" responses to suffering are false—perhaps not dishonest, but not in good faith. Those who offer them aren't trying to find an explanation as much as they're trying to protect their identity as believers. They're rationalizing, as surely as Job's false comforters. It's less that they ac-tually believe God to be good than that they fear what would happen if they didn't say He was good. (To be fair, atheists who bring up the problem of evil are also generally rationalizers looking for a neat trick to poof away the Big Daddy they learned about as kids.)

In *The Interpretation of Dreams*, Freud discusses how the mind often uses self-contradictory logic in service of wish-fulfillment. He could easily be talking about the speeches of Job's comforters.

> The whole plea . . . recalls vividly the defence offered by a man who was accused by his neighbour of having returned a kettle in a dam-aged condition. In the first place, he said, he had returned the kettle undamaged; in the second place, it already had holes in it when he borrowed it; and in the third place, he had never borrowed it at all.[4]

I see Elihu's speech, in particular, as revealing the kettle logic of our standard religious defenses of God: "First, God has explained pointless suffering already. Second, there's no pointless suffering to explain. Third, your pointless suffering makes you into a better person. Fourth, shut up, God might be listening and inflict some pointless suffering on you!"

One of the splendid things about reading the Bible (as opposed to our usual strategy of acting like we've read it to praise it as the word of God or to dismiss it as a bunch of superstitious nonsense) is discovering how hard the Holy Book is on religious people. Mostly when people are doing things in the name of religion in the Hebrew or the Christian Bible, they're acting stupidly or even maliciously. I teasingly reassured the prisoners, "I myself believe that the Bible is somewhat off on this point. Though religion is often vacuous and vicious, I think that it has its good points too, and we shouldn't dismiss religion solely on God's word."

God doesn't explain the universe. As G. K. Chesterton says, "Instead of proving to Job that it is an explicable world, He insists that it is a much stranger world than Job ever thought it was."[5] Instead of giving Job an answer, God takes Job's puzzlement and squares it—and then cubes it. It's not only suffering that can't be fathomed: the universe itself can't be domesticated to human understanding. Even after our furthest-reaching scientific advances, even after our most profound philosophies, even after our most sublime art, even after our grandest religions, even after our Einsteins and our Bibles, there's always an incorrigible strangeness and plurality in the cosmos that far outstrips them, a bottomless reserve capable of inspiring more science, philosophy, art, and religion. We're children of Behemoth and Leviathan. The Book of Job completely supports the basic logic of the atheist's version of the problem of evil, only it then flips the atheist's logic on its head. *Of course, the world isn't morally coherent. We need a fundamentally chaotic world, albeit one that forever insists on being worshiped and explained.* (After our discussion, one of the inmates took me aside and showed me his copy of the Bible. He'd pasted postcards and magazine cutouts that depict the grandeur of nature next to passages in God's speech to Job about the dazzling, puzzling glory of creation.)

Chesterton also says, "In the drama of scepticism God Himself takes up the role of sceptic. . . . He does, for instance, what Socrates did."[6] Yes! Socrates is the master of leading those who think they know to recognize their ignorance. This newfound ignorance, when fully embraced, is meant to be the highest kind of wisdom attainable to human beings. As Socrates says, "I am certainly wiser than this man; it is only too likely that neither of us has any knowledge to boast of; but he thinks that he knows something which he does not know, whereas I am quite conscious of my ignorance. At any rate it seems that I am wiser than he is to this small extent, that I do not think that I know what I do not know."[7] All of philosophy for Socrates, as for all philosophers worth their salt, takes place against the backdrop of our ignorance.

* * * * * * * * * * *

Robert Frost commits his own injustice against Job in *A Masque of Reason*, his 1943 comedy that purports to be the lost concluding chapter of the Book of Job. In Frost's version, Job, like my inmate Job, remains frustrated at God's refusal to answer the question of why He hurt him so. Job even despairs, "The chances are when there's so much pretense/ Of metaphysical profundity/ The obscurity's a fraud to cover nothing." (This is not just Frost's judgment on God; it's also his judgment on T. S. Eliot.) Eventually, God gives His comically, horrifyingly banal answer: "I was just showing off to the Devil, Job,/ As is set forth in chapters One and Two."[8]

But it's in one of Job's earlier exchanges with God in *A Masque of Reason* that we find the more profound answer to why we suffer pointlessly. God thanks Job for establishing that "There's no connection man can reason out/ Between his just deserts and what he gets." Our suffering is less important for us than for God!

> My thanks are to you for releasing me
> From moral bondage to the human race.

The only free will there at first was man's,
Who could do good or evil as he chose.
I had no choice but I must follow him
With forfeits and rewards he understood—
Unless I liked to suffer loss of worship.
I had to prosper good and punish evil.
You changed all that. You set me free to reign.
You are the Emancipator of your God.[9]

Do you feel the strangeness of Frost's insight? In Proverbs we read, "No ill befalls the righteous, but the wicked are filled with trouble."[10] If it were actually true that no ill befell the righteous and the wicked were always punished, then God would be a slave to our morality. His vast universe would have to bow to little old us, at least insofar as we achieved moral goodness. God would be, in this case, singularly ungodlike.

The fact that when we suffer pointlessly we liberate God—or at least demonstrate God's freedom and sublimity, His *godliness*—isn't much comfort, admittedly. But it does put us into a new relationship with ourselves. Just as God is liberated by Job's suffering, Job is liberated by his suffering at the hands of God. I mentioned Kant in my version of the Devil's Advocate's quizzing of God in part because the inmates and I had discussed Kant's moral philosophy, but mainly because the Book of Job is a very Kantian book (Kant himself has an admiring essay on it). The great philosopher argues that an action appears as free only when it's done for reasons other than its benefit to us. If my every gift of charity also happens to bring me lavish praise and a big tax deduction, how can I ever know if I'm truly charitable? If Job's morality corresponds perfectly with what brings him happiness, isn't his morality invisible? Plus, our moral worth appears only in a world that doesn't fit our morality, a world where we suffer in ways that overmaster what we deserve. Job's questioning of God in the intense middle chapters is the work of self-knowledge. It's Job's way of painfully breaking through our fantasies to know himself as a genuine moral agent. It's a breakthrough that many of my students, particularly those who had converted in prison, knew well.

Because the fact of pointless suffering makes YHWH free as God, and Job and the rest of us free as human beings, God and humanity can now have a meaningful relationship. If God's task were simply to reward us for moral action, He'd be our slave, a genie in the bottle of our morality. If our task were simply to get rewards for good behavior, then we'd be no more than dogs on the leash of a kindly universe—or, more likely, dogs in the pound for bad behavior. But because we're both free, our goodness means something, and the universe means something. Pointless suffering puts us in touch with ourselves as unique moral creatures and puts us in touch with the kind of universe that makes the gift of our existence possible. Pointless suffering brings us to God.

* * * * * * * * * * *

I worry that theological language, once so charged with meaning, now strikes many ears as out of touch, if not downright nonsensical. "God is dead," in Nietzsche's infamous phrase. As the inmates and I discussed the idea that "pointless suffering brings us to God," I could see that to some of the eyebrow-raised atheists it sounded like I was saying, "Pointless suffering helps us to see leprechauns riverdancing on the lawn." That's too bad, because the point transcends our beliefs about scientific descriptions of entities in the universe. Theological language is actually about something, even if it's very difficult, if not impossible, to explain what that something is. Throughout our history people have used religious speech as the most fine-tuned way of talking about the infinite meaning in the world: they haven't just been whistling "Dixie."

My way of trying to broaden the point beyond the believer-atheist divide was to retell one of the best known stories from the Moth, a nonprofit group dedicated to storytelling. The comedian Anthony Griffith relates the bitterly ironic fate of coping with the agonizing death of his two-year-old daughter while simultaneously performing comedy to pay her medical bills. At just the moment when he hits rock bottom, as Griffith tells it with fiery passion:

> A voice in me comes up, like Denzel from *Training Day*, "Man up, Nigger! You think you're the only one losing kids today! Twenty-five kids walked in here with cancer today, only five walking out! This ain't no sitcom! It don't wrap up all nice and tidy in thirty minutes! This is life! Welcome to the real world!"[11]

What Anthony Griffith says constitutes a much finer paraphrase of God's "gird up your loins like a man" speech than mine. A voice like Denzel has replaced the Lord speaking out of the whirlwind, but it amounts to the same theological experience of welcoming us to life, not life as we wish it to be but life as it is in all its mind-blowing and heartbreaking grandeur.

What we properly call God isn't just Zeus without Zeus's vices, as Job's friends and a lot of religious types seem to believe. Such a Zeus is well refuted by the Book of Job and the problem of evil. But this conception of God, however common, is superficial and hard to square with holy texts like the Book of Job. The nature of the universe outstrips our ability to understand it. Yet we demand, like Job, some sense of meaning. When God appears, it isn't to answer our demand but to clarify the paradox. If the universe is built of something as totally unacceptable as pointless suffering, perhaps it's impossible to believe in its comprehensive goodness or even intelligibility. But we should still commit ourselves to morality and understanding. God is the site of this problem, not its solution. Among other things, God is our way of talking about a complex set of things: the grand universe, our ability to seek meaning in it, our hope for goodness beyond what's given, the bitter existence of injustice. The anthropologist Clifford Geertz says, "As a religious problem, the problem of suffering is, paradoxically, not how to avoid suffering but how to suffer, how to make of physical pain, personal loss, worldly defeat, or the helpless contemplation of others' agony something bearable, supportable—something, as we say, sufferable."[12] To try to express the ultimate sacred reality in abstract terms, as I'm trying to do, is useful only up to a point. Very quickly these abstract terms fall short, and we begin to crave the mysterious poetry of a word like "God," something able to contain contradictions as well as to measure up to the profundity and personality of what we're trying to express, endure, and perhaps celebrate. Though we must use metaphors to talk about the experience of being welcomed to ultimate reality (the Lord, the Voice from the Whirlwind, I Am That I Am, Denzel), I find it hard to believe that mystical experiences—so common throughout human history, so strangely productive in people's lives—don't have something to them.

The last seven words that Job says—*Al ken em'as v'nihamti al afar v'efer*—have been translated in different ways. The Jewish Publication Society of America Version has it, "Therefore I recant and relent, being but dust and ashes." The King James Version says, "Wherefore I abhor myself and repent in dust and ashes." Stephen Mitchell, the noted contemporary translator, gives it a much less anguished feel: "Therefore I will be quiet, comforted that I am dust."[13] I rendered it "Now I truly know I'm human, and I'll shut up," which at least one Christian inmate felt compelled to say he didn't like as well as the King James Version's mention of repentance. I agree that the KJV can't be beat; still, I think it's important to emphasize that Job has discovered his humanity.

We sometimes think of "humanity" as simply a word to describe biological organisms like us. But it traditionally refers to a unique condition of in-between-ness, what Plato calls *metaxu*. "Humanity" means occupying the station where we exercise our unique power that elevates us above our fellow animals, but where we still look with awe and reverence on an order that far outstrips our power. The unique freedom of humanity is described with luminous words like "rationality," "mortality," "natality," "philosophy." Humanity is potential in all of us, but it can flicker on and off. Thus, we reasonably talk about actions as humane and inhumane, even deeply human and downright inhuman. The danger that perennially confronts us—described with dark words like "sin," "hubris," "dehumanization," "hate"—is to split ourselves into god and beast, ruler and subject, Frankenstein and Frankenstein's Monster, criminal and victim. Nowhere is this danger more apparent than in our relationship to suffering. Just as the term "God" contains the paradox of the universe's being at once meaningful as well as something that always outstrips our ability to understand it, so the term "humanity" contains the paradox of our capacity for understanding and our ultimate ignorance, our moral drive and our crooked timber. The theological idea of being made in the image of God seems about right: God and humanity are both an unstable, beautiful freedom, though one properly uses that freedom humbly, in dust and ashes. The conditions of this magnificent life where we get to have beautiful daughters and tell hilarious jokes on *The Tonight Show*—as well as discuss the Book of Job in prison—are suffering, injustice, and death. God and humanity are names for the sites of mysteries rather than the solutions to problems. Griffith names his heartbreaking story for the Moth "The Best of Times, the Worst of Times."

* * * * * * * * * * * *

Eventually the prisoners and I got onto the topic of the Book of Job's ending. I find it irritating, I grumbled, that Job has everything restored and then some. Job has lost all ten of his children, seven sons and three daughters. After his encounter with God, he gets ten new better-looking children. I'm sure new kids are a comfort and a blessing, but there's no replacing the loved ones we lose in our lives, let alone our own children. I'm not sure if Anthony Griffith had another child after the death of his girl, but I'm sure that even if he did have more children, they're no substitute for his daughter. He'll always be scarred by her loss. It's those scars, which we all have in one form or another, that make the concluding chapter of the Book of Job so hard for me to accept. If we wanted to be ungenerous in our reading of the Book of Job, we could accuse God of doing what abusive parents tend to do. After having smacked their kids around, they take them to an amusement park to make up for it. Don't get me wrong; I understand that there's something hard to take about a story that goes "A good man suffered horribly. His friends lied to him about why he was suffering. He never knew why he had to suffer so. The end." Or "America is built on the systematic plunder and abuse of its black citizens. Americans tell themselves lies about this reality. The end." The great moral philosophers tell us that we must struggle for the good even if these bleak tales are true. But doesn't something in us, some basic sense of the shape of a true story, cry out in protest?

The three new daughters of Job—"in all the land were no women found so fair"—are named Jemima, Kezia, and Kerenhappuch, which translate as Dove, Cinnamon, and Eyeshadow. A more generous reading of the Book of Job would suggest that these revivified daughters are symbols of spiritual awakening: Dove represents spiritual peace, Cinnamon spiritual riches, and Eyeshadow spiritual grace. In his drawings for the first scenes of the Book of Job, William Blake portrays a sleepy family gathered in prayer with books on the parents' laps; in the final scene, he portrays a bright-eyed family vigorously making music on their instruments. As Stephen Mitchell says, "There is something enormously satisfying about this prominence of the feminine at the end of Job. . . . It is as if, once Job has learned to surrender, his world too gives up the male compulsion to control."[14]

The macho inmates weren't all that taken with an allegory of the triumph of the feminine virtues. Even the most adamant Christian inmates found the ending of Job hard to swallow, though mostly everyone agreed that something in us longs powerfully for a happy ending. The most thoughtful said that Job's Hollywood ending should be taken as symbolically referring to the afterlife, the only possible place where a happy ending is believable. I looked around the room at the faces of the prisoners, some of whom were serving life without parole. I felt the ghostly presence of the victims of their crimes—the abused, the raped, the slain. My own wrongdoings and the pain they've caused washed over me. I could almost hear the source of the blues vibrating among us. To all of us a happy ending was crying out. At the same time, to all of us it seemed hard, if not vicious, to argue that things work out for those who suffer.

At this point the presiding guard, a beefy white guy, couldn't hold back any longer and boomed, "I just need to say something here. You know what your problem is?" He was pointing his finger at the prisoners. "You just can't take responsibility for yourselves. I know you're not bad guys, but the reason you're in here is because you couldn't say no. The guys you thought were your buddies said, 'Hey, come on, let's go do this thing,' and you just couldn't say no. Or maybe it was just a bad impulse you couldn't say no to. In any case, you just couldn't say, 'Hey, I'm responsible for myself.' Don't get me wrong. I could easily be in your shoes for stuff I did when I was young and stupid. But I've taken responsibility for myself." He went on in this vein for some time. Up to that point, the conversation had been lively and intense; the fact of prison had evaporated and left only free minds in search of what mattered. Maybe that very liberty had irked the guard. As he was weighing in, prison slowly and surely resolidified around us. By the end of his oration, I was an outsider, they were prisoners, he was the guard, and all around us was concrete. The inmates clammed up. Some even slouched down or hunched over, as if a weight had just been set on their shoulders.

Rather than YHWH, a prison guard had appeared at the finale of our reenactment of the Book of Job. Rather than God scolding false-speaking comforters, we got a low-level deity asserting the justice of a gray universe of punishment and reward. Thank God, I thought, that God transcends the categories of right and wrong, which had never appeared so puny to me as when they boomed out of the guard's mouth. Thank God for the unknown. Thank God for God!

* * * * * * * * * * *

One of the most significant details in the Book of Job generally goes overlooked. After Job suffers his major blows, his friends come to him and sit with him in silence for a week. "So they sat down with him upon the ground seven days and seven nights, and none spake a word unto him: for they saw that his grief was very great."[15] Job's friends get a bad rap, most of which is deserved, but here they come through with flying colors. They don't open their mouths. They comfort by their mere presence. It's a good lesson: it's much more important for us to show up to those in pain than it is for us to have something comforting or meaningful to say to them. Suffering whispers in our ear, "You're alone, you're cut off, you're all mine." The mere presence of others can rebuke that horrible message.

But I think that the significance of the presence of Job's friends goes beyond that important lesson, a lesson they unfortunately betray with their blathering accusations against their friend. I think that it helps us to see the Book of Job's ultimate message about how pointless suffering brings us to God—or, if you prefer, the peculiar, wondrous, awful personality of the universe.

Suffering threatens to cut us off not just from everyone but from everything. Who is Job? He's a father, a businessman, a lover, a friend, a religious practitioner, etc. But he loses his children. He loses his business. His disease imperils his ability to relate to others. Even his religion, as manifested by his friends, regards him as something of a pariah. What's left? For that matter, who is my friend Simon, this inmate who's had to give up the prime of his life to prison, who's sentenced to give up the rest of his life to prison? For that matter, who am I underneath the armor of civilization? What's left of us when we suffer pointlessly, as we all do in one way or another?

All that's left, in some ways, is everything. Stripped of all we think we are, we have the chance to see that we're not just the sum of our roles and accomplishments. Pointless suffering like Job's inevitably breaks us, but out of the broken pieces there's a chance of emerging as the surprising creatures we truly are. I don't say this to be comforting. I regard it as a hard, unforgiving truth. When the inmates discussed Job's wife's plea to "curse God and die," they unanimously took her to be talking about suicide. They all knew fellow inmates who had taken her advice. Many of them had spent nights in the shadow of that advice.

Moses Mendelssohn, the great Jewish philosopher of the Enlightenment, suffered a fate similar to Anthony Griffith's. After his daughter died when she was eleven months old, Mendelssohn wrote:

> The innocent child did not live in vain. . . . Her mind made astonishing progress in that short period. From a little animal that cried and slept she developed into a budding intelligent creature. One could see the blossoming of the passions like the sprouting of young grass when it pierces the hard crust of the earth in spring. She showed pity, hatred, love, admiration. She understood the language of those talking to her, and tried to make her own thoughts known to others.[16]

This is the kind of luminous language that comes to us only on the other side of grief. A life of eleven months, when examined without fantasies about how it should go, stops seeming like a tragedy and starts seeming like what it is: a gift—not a gift in the sentimental sense of the word, but in the true paradoxical sense. I think of how Simon has appeared to me in my own life as a gift. Here's someone who discusses Kant, Epictetus, and the Book of Job in a more philosophical, more human way than the majority of my colleagues at a philosophy conference. Here's also someone who has brought a unique grief into my life.

In the sense of embodying the powerful hope in us that things in the end will work out, the ending of the Book of Job makes sense. I get that. Neither Simon nor I can quite give up the idea that he might somehow get his sentence commuted. So why do I still find that Job's ending rings false? I suppose because it feels like everything valuable that has gone before, all the grief and questioning, has vanished in the new dispensation. Even after I grant the Book of Job the right to its fairy-tale logic, I still feel like the happy ending is just eyeshadow masking the bruises.

To make my point, let me contrast the happy ending of the Book of Job with another famous happy ending. A few days after their teacher is brutally tortured and murdered, some friends meet up and try to figure out how to go forward without the man who meant the most to them. Suddenly and miraculously their slain teacher appears among them in the flesh and instructs them what to do. A few days after that, the dazzled friends run into Thomas, a fellow student, and tell him about how they've seen their teacher alive and good as new.

> The other disciples therefore said unto him, We have seen the Lord. But he said unto them, Except I shall see in his hands the print of the nails, and put my finger into the print of the nails, and thrust my hand into his side, I will not believe. And after eight days again his disciples were within, and Thomas with them: then came Jesus, the doors being shut, and stood in the midst, and said, Peace be unto you. Then saith he to Thomas, Reach hither thy finger, and behold my hands; and reach hither thy hand, and thrust it into my side: and be not faithless, but believing. And Thomas answered and said unto him, My Lord and my God.[17]

Like Thomas, I have a tough time believing in a literal resurrection—or, for that matter, in the idea that the arc of history will someday issue in a final justice. I can understand the longing in us for something more than the Crucifixion as the total symbol of existence. I can understand that when we fight for justice and peace, even if we realize that we'll never see them realized in our lifetime, we nevertheless tend to work with the hopeful phrase "I have a dream" ringing in our ears. But I have not been blessed as those who "have not seen, and yet have believed." Like Thomas, I have the grim need, even in triumph, to finger the scarred cavities where the spikes were driven.

What I love about the resurrection story in the Gospel of John, whether it's taken literally or otherwise, is that Jesus still has his wounds. Whatever miraculous new life has been given to him, he's still marked by the suffering of his old life. He still has his scars and the stories associated with them. If we ever do find heaven on earth or in the sky, if we even simply make progress toward justice and happiness, if—God willing—Simon gets out of prison, we'll know the new condition as a good place not just because of its peace, riches, and freedom, but because our friends will still be able to touch our scars.

FIVE

POINTLESS SUFFERING

ATONES US WITH

NATURE

On Epictetus and the Gratitude for Existence

O while I live to be the ruler of life, not a slave . . .
No fumes, no ennui, no more complaints or scornful criticisms,
To these proud laws of the air, the water and the ground,
proving my interior soul impregnable,
And nothing exterior shall ever take command of me.

WALT WHITMAN

Though we don't have much to go on (we're not even certain of his real name), let's try to imagine what happened. The things we know for sure are, first, that as a boy he was a slave in the Roman Empire, and, second, that he had a bad leg. Why was his leg bad? The most probable explanation is that his master broke it. One story has it that as his master was abusing him, our boy said, "You're going to break my leg." When the master did indeed break it, the boy calmly replied, "Told you so." This anecdote can be traced back to Celsus, the second-century pagan philosopher who wrote a comprehensive rebuttal of

Christianity. It's reported in a Christian philosopher's book called *Against Celsus*. The pagan used the story to taunt his Christian audience: "What comparable statement did your god make while under punishment?" Early apologists for Christianity tried to cast doubt on the story of the broken leg. They argued that the kid was probably born a gimp. In other words, God broke it.

Nobody denies that Roman masters did things like breaking the bones of their slaves. Even if the Christian apologists are right about our boy, it certainly happened to many others like him. So let's go with Celsus's plausible story. Why did the master break the boy's leg? Probably in punishment. For what? Likely having failed to perform a task. Having spilled wine on a guest? Having refused a command? Or maybe breaking the bone wasn't a punishment; maybe the master did it for fun. The nature of the institution of slavery is such that the master class affirms and asserts its identity by arbitrarily inflicting its will on the bodies of the slave class. Even if the act was a punishment, it's not hard to imagine that the master enjoyed doing it: he certainly didn't stop when the boy told him that the leg was going to break. Celsus praises the boy for his equanimity in the face of suffering. But he was a kid, after all. If Celsus's story is true, I bet that the boy was trying to refuse his master any satisfaction, even as he fought back tears and the urge to cry out. Certainly there were sensations of pain coursing through his body—the leg twisting, the big bone trying to hold its shape under duress, the bone finally snapping, the nerve cells ripping, the marrow spilling, the jagged bone tearing through various tissues. No care was taken in setting the broken bone. The boy walked with a severe limp for the rest of his life.

He was eventually taken to Rome and sold to the secretary of Nero, a connoisseur of inflicting pointless suffering. After he'd lost control of the empire, Nero made an unsuccessful attempt at suicide. Finally, as menacing horsemen were approaching, the emperor forced his secretary to slit his throat. In the ensuing chaos, the boy—a man by now—got free and began to attend lectures on Stoicism, apprenticing himself to the great philosopher Musonius Rufus. Becoming a great philosopher in his own right, the greatest Rome ever produced, the limping ex-slave used to say to his students, "If I were a nightingale or a swan, I would sing the song either of them was born to sing. But I am a rational being, so I must sing the praise of God."[1] We know him simply as Epictetus, Greek for "the acquired."

* * * * * * * * * * * *

Stoicism is the name of one of the greatest traditions in Western philosophy. It's such a deep tradition that many, like the contemporary philosopher and intellectual historian Pierre Hadot, consider it simply the name the West gives to "one of the fundamental, permanent possibilities of human existence, when people search for wisdom."[2] In Chinese philosophy it generally goes by the name of Daoism, which means Devotion to the Way. Stoicism doesn't originally name anything so grand as Daoism. Zeno of Citium, who modeled himself on Socrates and Crates the Cynic, began teaching at the *Stoa Poikile* (the Painted Porch). Those who associated with him were called Stoics, which basically means Those Guys on the Porch. Though the ancient Greeks produced numerous masterpieces of Stoicism, their texts survive only in quotations and fragments. The main surviving sources date from the Roman period, like the *Meditations* of Marcus Aurelius and the various essays and letters of Seneca. The most eloquent and complete exposition of Stoicism is Epictetus's *Discourses,* the teachings written down and assembled by Epictetus's student Arrian at the beginning of the second century AD.

Where does the problem of pointless suffering lie? Simple: there's just too much death, pain, and misfortune in the universe—right? Totally wrong, according to Epictetus. The fact that we lament and object to death, pain, and misfortune is the true source of pointless suffering. Our lament is the cause, not the effect, of the world's misery. Death, pain, and even sin, if understood correctly, are beautiful facts of existence. We should all be singing like rational nightingales.

One of the central questions of philosophy is whether fate or chance rules the universe—in other words, whether our basic values are in harmony with the way things go, or whether the way things go is at odds with our basic values. As the Roman historian Tacitus puts it, "The wisest of philosophers disagree on this point. [Epicureans] insist that heaven is unconcerned with our birth and death—is unconcerned, in fact, with human beings generally—with the result that good people often suffer while wicked people thrive. [The Stoics] disagree."[3]

It's no coincidence that the Epicureans, who hold that the universe is the chancy combination of atoms, are probably the first in the Greek philosophical tradition to formulate the problem of evil. As Epicurus allegedly puts it, "Is God willing to prevent evil, but not able? Then he's not omnipotent. Is he able, but not willing? Then he's malevolent. Is he both able and willing? Then where does evil come from? Is he neither able nor willing? Then why call him God?"[4] When we believe that the world is the result of chance, what we value isn't always going to overlap with how things are. Epicurus's "gods" (we'd now probably call them "the laws of physics and biology") aren't particularly concerned with us. Yes, if we live right, we up the odds of finding some measure of well-being, but there's no guarantee that living right invariably leads to health and happiness. Bad things will sometimes happen to good people. Life's a gamble.

In traditional Christian theology the way out of the problem of evil is the view that the seemingly chancy misery of this world is the result of a fair punishment (say, for the primordial sin of Adam and Eve) and/or a place of soul-making where we must struggle with hardships in order to prepare ourselves for the heavenly kingdom to come. But the Stoics avoid the problem of evil in a different way altogether. They refuse to imagine a better world than the one that generates and sustains us. The secret of happiness—and not only happiness but freedom, and not only freedom but our very rationality—is to bring our mindset into accord with how things go. Heaven is available to us right now; in fact, it's only available to us right now. When we harmonize our minds with the zigzags of nature, the world appears to us as it truly is: the exact right place for us. Hell is simply our rebellion against nature.

"Stoicism," according to Pierre Hadot, "is a philosophy of self-coherence, based upon a remarkable intuition of the essence of life."[5] This remarkable intuition begins in the unremarkable insight that things try to persist, to survive. Life says yes to its own existence. But if we, as rational beings, think through the ramifications of life's self-affirmation, we come to see that we're part of a much larger, more remarkable order, what Epictetus generally calls "nature" or "Zeus," the whole universe in its unfolding. Nature is not a zillion units all chancily bumping into each other, though it can sometimes seem like that. Nature is a zillion units all depending on the singular self-affirming order that they help to form. When we begin to recognize our unique connection to the essence of life, a remarkable way of life emerges.

Take death, which at first glance appears to be completely at odds with our innate desire to live. If we consider the matter carefully, we see that the death of an organism is a condition of its life. There could be nothing of what we know as life without death. Cells must perish so that new cells can come into existence. Animals must expire so that other animals can live. People must die so that new generations can flourish. If we embrace life, we must accept the fact of mortality. It's a necessary rule of the only game in town.

In chapter 27 of the *Handbook*, the summation of Epictetus's philosophy, we read, "Just as a target is not set up to be missed, so evil is no natural part of the world's design."[6] The second clause is clear in its meaning: there's no pointless suffering in the setup of the universe. The first clause, which is more mysterious, is crucial to understanding the point. Epictetus isn't saying that we always hit the target. He's saying that the game of darts is set up just as it should be; likewise, the rules of the universe are set up just as they should be.

To vary the analogy slightly, consider the game of chess. To want chess to have different rules is not to want to play chess. I remember as a kid first playing chess with my dad. When I soon found myself with only a knight and a king, I ardently wished that I could make my knight move like a queen, zap all my father's many remaining pieces, and corner him into checkmate. If my father had been the indulgent sort (he wasn't), he would have let me do just that. I would have "won," but my victory would have meant the destruction of the very game that I wanted to win at. As it turns out, he checkmated me in a few deft moves. The game was not at fault.

For Epictetus, we're like chess pieces. We have limited moves that we can make, and we'll eventually be taken, but it's precisely these limits that make us who we are and the game what it is. We're like chess pieces with the crucial difference that we have inside us a *daimon*—a bit of divinity, our rationality—that connects us to the whole board. As Walt Whitman so marvelously puts it, this *daimon* is attached to the "mystic" meaning that makes all things move: "Only by law of you, your swell and ebb, enclosing me the same, / The brain that shapes, the voice that chants this song."[7] Even if we're taken in an early move by an opponent, even if our side loses, we know that the game goes on, and that we've contributed to its continuation. Epictetus says, "You might just as well say that the fall of leaves is ill-omened, or for a fresh fig to change into a dried one, and a bunch of grapes into raisins. . . . Yes, you will cease to be what you are, but become something else of which the universe then has need."[8] In fact, our life and death not only maintain the order, our shaping brains and chanting voices make a little more interesting this complex chessboard of tigers and tiger lilies, stars and starfish.

If I may switch my analogy again, this time from chess to basketball, consider the great rivalry between Magic Johnson and Larry Bird. If we think according to our non-Stoic categories, we'd be inclined to believe that the two must have hated each other, because each stood in the path of the other's triumph. But how did these great athletes see their rivalry? Larry Bird: "Everybody said there was a hate element. There wasn't hate. I just had so much respect. You never let your guard down because he was so good." Magic Johnson: "It made me feel good I was a thorn in his side. I'm supposed to be out there and go kick his butt. That's what my job was, and his job was to kick mine. I didn't want Larry to like me. He didn't have to like me. But we both respected each other."[9] What's true of Larry Bird should be true of suffering. Just as Bird was part of the magic of Magic, suffering is so interwoven into our nature that to remove it would be to unravel who we are. Without death, we wouldn't be able to have life, a process that depends on the metabolic exchange of matter. Without pain, we couldn't be animals, whose nature is to feel their desires. Without freedom, we couldn't be humans, whose nature is to stand back from the world and reflect on and redirect the ends of our actions. The attitude that Epictetus encourages when we face a hardship is "Bring it on: let's see what you got!"

For Epictetus there's a providence in all things, a connective tissue that holds things together and makes them what they are. If things were any different, we wouldn't be exactly who we are in exactly this situation. When something "evil" happens, it's no more than a violation of some local strategy. The overall order always flourishes, as do we insofar as we regard ourselves as part of that order. When my chess strategy comes to naught, the game of chess still goes on, as glorious as ever. Even in times of failure, I should remember that most of all I want to be playing chess, a game that requires some strategies to fail and others to pan out. My inner being as a chess player shouldn't be offended, should even celebrate, when I find myself in checkmate. The game never fails, even when we do. In this sense, failure is part of the success of the game. The target is not set up to be missed.

* * * * * * * * * * * *

According to Epictetus, if we tune up our souls, we should be able to be perfectly happy under any conditions, including those that involve failure by normal standards. Even if we find ourselves in prison, we should be able to say what Aleksandr Solzhenitsyn said about his eleven years in the Gulag, "I nourished my soul there, and I say without hesitation: 'Bless you, prison, for having been in my life!'"[10] Well, where better to test out the hypothesis than in an actual prison? So, for one of my sessions at Oakdale Prison, I taught the inmates Epictetus's Stoicism, spelling out to them how the secret of happiness is not to ask things to happen as we wish but to wish things to happen as they do; how there's nothing good or bad but thinking makes it so; how our mindsets are in our control; how if we undergo the right sort of mental discipline we can accept pain, death, and injustice; how we can work to fight against what appears to us as excessive pain, early death, and gross injustice, though we should ultimately accept these things as part of the greater order that sustains us; how our true happiness involves nothing more than reforming our souls; how, in short, we should be happy even in prison.

In my experience, one of the defining marks of great books, like Epictetus's *Discourses*, is that no matter who discusses them, whether erudite scholars or rough-and-tumble prisoners, the same fundamental human responses always emerge—though more slowly among the scholars. The prisoners, like contemporary Marxists, asked me hard questions about whether Stoicism leads to political quietism. They wondered, like ancient theologians, about the extent to which Stoicism is compatible with Christianity or Islam. They went back and forth, like Michel de Montaigne, about whether the Stoic ideal is humanly achievable. We got into an interesting debate, reminiscent of Albert Camus's play *The Just Assassins*, about if it's possible for Stoics to be revolutionaries, or if it's necessary for revolutionaries to be Stoics—a debate that seemed to unsettle the presiding guard.

As I was attempting to defend Epictetus, a prisoner stood up threateningly and launched into how Stoicism is a loser's philosophy, sour grapes for people who can't get ahead. I challenged him, "What really does it mean to be a loser? Was Jesus on the cross a loser? Was Martin Luther King Jr., who never reached the mountaintop, a loser? Were the famous three hundred Spartans who died at Thermopylae losers?" I was trying to find examples of people whose inner virtue could be easily seen through the veil of their worldly defeats. Retorting that *300* wasn't real, he refused to believe me that the core of that over-the-top movie is historical fact. I brought up Marcus Aurelius, anything but a loser, whose Stoicism helped empower him to do his duty as the emperor of Rome. The prisoner just got angrier. Mention of an emperor seemed to make him suspect me of being part of a prison-wide conspiracy to make the inmates docile.

Coming to my rescue, one of his fellow inmates stood up and pointed a finger at him. "Do you know where you are? Guess what? You're a *loser*! We're all losers. Why do you think we're in here?" The enraged prisoner responded, "Fine, I'm a loser, just like the rest of you. But I'm not a true loser, and I'll never become one. A true loser is someone who accepts being a loser, and I don't accept being in here. I refuse to accept that I'm a prisoner!" He turned to the guard and growled, "I can't stand this anymore. Take me back to my cell."

The irony that someone who refused to accept his status as a prisoner was demanding to go back to his cell was not lost on those who remained in our dingy academy. In the stunned wake of his departure, one of my students piped up, "Epictetus's point is that real freedom comes from within, from acceptance of things—right? Wasn't he always telling people who balked at Stoicism that they were just going back to their cells, whether or not they were actually in prison like us?" I'd never felt so much like I'd been part of a Socratic dialogue, the kind that works its way past a hothead like Callicles or Thrasymachus into a genuine exploration of the truth among thoughtful interlocutors.

The angry prisoner's objection, that Stoicism is a philosophy of inaction, is based on a common misunderstanding of Stoicism. According to Epictetus, the choice is not between action and inaction, between rebellion and sour grapes; it's between doing your duty and acting like a fool. Go back to my chess analogy. If you're committed to the game of chess, you don't stop playing it! Just the opposite, you respect the rules and try your best to win. To do any less is to be a spoilsport. What you shouldn't do is cheat or whine, much less knock the board over when you're losing. It's the same with life. Do your duty—in other words, don't try to cheat the laws of nature (news flash: you can't), but do your best at whatever activities you engage in. If you enter into politics, do your best as a political agent, but remember that the game of politics is possible only on the conditions of disagreement, compromise, loss, and so on. If you become a parent, remember that kids don't come out exactly how you expect, will get sick, may even die before you, will challenge you, and so on; once you've accepted the fact that you're having mortal children and not little gods, you're going to be in a better position to be a good parent.

The attitude that Epictetus encourages is exactly the paradoxical lesson we try to teach our children when they're playing games. On the one hand, we say to them, "Try your best." On the other hand, we say to them, "It's just a game." It's immature, even by children's standards, to hold that these two injunctions cancel each other out. As parents, we rightly try to get our kids to have a double mind about games. We want them to see that the fun of the game depends on someone winning and someone losing ("it's just a game"); but the fun—as well as the character-building—also depends on the players giving it their all ("try your best"). This same double mind is the essence of Epictetus's Stoicism. To use the language of one contemporary scholar of Stoicism, we must learn to take the same things seriously and not seriously at the same time.[11]

If you're unjustly imprisoned, you should certainly try to appeal your sentence, but you should do so in full realization that your appeal may or may not be granted. In the meantime, you'll have to deal with other hardships. I recently heard a talk by an ex-con who'd attended Grinnell College's liberal-arts-in-prison program. He told of how inmates would mock each other for any perceived weakness—for instance, attending a course about philosophy. One of his classmates in prison had endured just this kind of insult, one that escalated to physical abuse. But the inmate knew that if he fought back, he'd be thrown into solitary confinement and not allowed to attend any more classes. "He had to take some punches for that class," the ex-con said. This is what Epictetus would call doing your duty.

* * * * * * * * * * * *

But isn't it unfair that the inmate had to take those punches? Isn't this proof that Epicurus is right and Epictetus is wrong? Don't such common occurrences show that bad things do indeed happen to good people, that the universe isn't a great orderly whole? Wouldn't the world be better if children didn't die young, if unjustly imprisoned inmates never died in prison, if suffering could somehow be minimized or eliminated? Shouldn't we refuse to accept nature? Isn't "nature" just a word for what we don't yet have the power to modify? This objection, much more powerful than the passivity objection, is the one that's central to this book.

When neo-Stoicism had taken hold in the early modern period, Gottfried Leibniz, one of its exponents, argued that the current universe was the "best of all possible worlds." In *Candide* Voltaire famously ridiculed such metaphysical optimism in the figure of Dr. Pangloss, who in the face of rape, earthquakes, slavery, torture, and tragic choices blithely asserts that everything happens for the best. At one point in *Candide* we meet an old woman who tells a particularly horrible tale. During a siege she was trapped in a castle. When its defenders began to go hungry, they procured food by cutting off one buttock from every woman, including her. She concludes, "If there be one of [you] all, that has not cursed his life many a time, that has not frequently looked upon himself as the unhappiest of mortals, I give you leave to throw me headforemost into the sea."[12]

But let's not forget that Epictetus, whose leg was snapped by his master in the midst of the brutal Roman Empire, was no stranger to the kinds of suffering that seem like such a no-brainer refutation of Stoicism to the likes of a Voltaire. What gives? Epictetus emphatically does not hold that everything is working toward some happy end, that every bit of suffering is heading for a great payoff. The payoff is right now. As we speak, the order is perfect. Before you right now, according to Stoic wisdom, is everything you need to be happy and free—in fact, probably much more than you need, whether you're unjustly imprisoned or not. I think of something William James says in his discussion of Walt Whitman's poetry:

> The indisputable fact [is] that this world never did anywhere or at any time contain more of essential divinity, or of eternal meaning, than is embodied in the fields of vision over which [our] eyes so carelessly

pass. There is life; and there, a step away, is death. There is the only kind of beauty there ever was. There is the old human struggle and its fruits together. There is the text and the sermon, the real and the ideal in one.[13]

Life itself is the gift. It's a hard, mysterious gift, like some gift out of a fairy tale that appears like a curse but is just what our salvation depends on. Our fundamental duty is gratitude. Be grateful that you can struggle, suffer, and find out things about what you're truly committed to, things you could never have found out otherwise. You're a rational, free human being who's been given the chance to express your rationality and freedom. Magic Johnson, meet Larry Bird.

But what of those who face terrible misery, who suffer from extreme pain, whose lives are surrounded and overtaken by the butcheries of the world? The Stoics have often been ridiculed for holding the view that one could be happy even while being tortured. Here especially we must be careful not to associate the Stoics with a fragile vision of happiness. It's not impossible that the story of Epictetus's intentionally broken leg was, in fact, a euphemism for much worse abuses. Moreover, Epictetus served in the court of Nero, whose achievements included lighting Rome at night by dipping Christians in oil and lighting them on fire. The Stoics knew all about the kinds of suffering that we might throw in their faces as proof that life isn't happy. What's the kind of happiness that Epictetus has in mind for those subjected to torture and injustice? They're blessed with being human. They're blessed with a challenge, an extreme challenge, that puts our humanity to the test. In the face of the most difficult tests of pain, injustice, and death, their attitude should be "Bring it on."

What's our other option? We should fight against misery and injustice, but they're not going away. What do we do with that fact? At those who rail against the inevitable unfairness of life Epictetus snaps: "The chief thing to remember is that the door is open. Don't be a greater coward than children, who are ready to announce, 'I won't play anymore.' Say, 'I won't play anymore,' when you grow weary of

the game, and be done with it. But if you stay, don't carp."[14] If you refuse to accept your suffering or the suffering of the world, you don't
need to participate in existence. The Stoics ask us to be courageous
and embrace life, but they have a deep understanding of those who
commit suicide. What they find irritating is those who complain. Life
may be a prison, but the door to your cell is unlocked.

In my book *The Deepest Human Life,* I tell the story of James Stockdale, a navy pilot who was brutally tortured over the course of eight
years by the Viet Cong. Stockdale had studied Epictetus in college
and used what he remembered of Stoic wisdom to maintain and even
enhance his humanity in a pit of depravity. He didn't always live up
to Stoic principles. He was sometimes broken—as we all are in this
life, usually by less dire circumstances than his. But after he was released, he was able to say, "Bless you, prison, for having been part of
my life." From a local perspective, Stockdale suffered terrible injustices. He gave his all in combatting them. From the perspective of the
universe, the great mind of which our minds are little parts, he was
participating in the magnificent game of being human, a game that
involves freedom and hence the abuse of freedom. The prison taught
him the meaning of gratitude.

* * * * * * * * * * *

Another stumbling block for us moderns is the Stoic view that the
universe has a soul and a purpose. The contemporary French philosopher Luc Ferry dismisses Stoicism with a wave of his hand: "If anyone
claimed today that the world is alive, animate—that it possesses a soul
and is endowed with reason—he would be considered crazy."[15] Modern physics and evolutionary biology, in Ferry's view, clearly rule out
the idea that the universe is alive.

The Stoics were perfectly aware of the possibility of a physical
universe made of atoms and governed by chance; it was the view of
the Epicureans. Though the Stoics rejected it, they seemed to think
that even if chance rather than providence governed the universe we

should still be Stoics. If it's not the case that we lovingly submit to the will of Zeus, then we should proudly affirm our own rationality in opposition to chance. If we can't be Stoics fitting into a rational universe, we should be Stoics rebelling against a meaningless universe.

That said, I'm not so sure that the aliveness of the universe is such a crazy idea. It's certainly true that most physics textbooks paint a universe of randomly bouncing dead atoms. But the Cartesian view of the universe, which puts the human mind on one side and a mechanical universe on the other, has long been considered problematic, if not fatally flawed. The great mystery it generates is a rather embarrassing one for us. How, where, and why does our own consciousness originate? Contemporary philosophers and scientists seem to be totally at sea in answering this question. Our best science seems to be able to account for everything but us!

The theory of evolution, in the popular mind, pits randomly bouncing organisms against each other in a chaotic battle for survival. But, in fact, the theory weaves organisms deeply into their environments, so much so that we can't fully distinguish the one from the other. Though the actual scientific theory doesn't require a belief in a living order, I don't see that it rules it out. The Stoic view of providence is not some Pollyanna view of life "evolving" to nicer and nicer states. It's simply that there is an order, much bigger than our usual conceptions, which our lives depend on for their very existence, and which we can tap into to increase our joy. In what sense is such a view ruled out by the study of fruit flies or the view that humans are related to other mammals? In fact, can't our biological science lend support to Stoicism's piety toward nature? We might be able to learn something from "crazy" thinkers like the philosopher Hans Jonas or the architect Christopher Alexander, each of whom has written an arresting book called *The Phenomenon of Life* arguing that the Cartesian legacy has run its course and that a richer conception of life is necessary. Perhaps we should think seriously about the fact that most people throughout history have been animists, believing that everything is invested with soul. Though certain Stoic views about the physical universe would need updating to be reconciled with science, perhaps Epictetus's overall sense of a living universe is not behind the times but rather ahead of them.

When I present on Stoicism to professional philosophers, many of them gripe at the idea that we must accept what's given to us. They think that "nature" is just a word used to impede progress. As moderns who have benefited extensively from overcoming things that we once thought were God's will, they balk at the Stoic concept of nature as a fundamental limit. Philosophers are willing to take the modern ideal to the extreme and question even the necessity of death. It's disturbing that I find myself saying to those paid to pursue wisdom, "I'm going to go out on a limb here and assert that we all have to die."

Admittedly, the ancient Stoics didn't envision just how extensive is the human power to modify what's given. But I think that their concept of nature can still be relevant to our technological age. In fact, given the environmental devastation that threatens the order of life itself, it may be vital for us to revive something like the old idea of nature. As long as we regard nature as fundamentally flawed, our technological destruction of it will proceed apace. Rather than think of nature as a set of known limits, perhaps we should see it as a set of limits that we learn ever more deeply through our challenges. Let me repeat that I think death is indeed a known limit (moreover, it would be a nightmare if it were possible for us to overcome it). I also think that sickness and injustice, in the general sense, are known limits (and it would be a nightmare to overcome them as well, I'm guessing). But the extent to which death, sickness, and injustice can be rolled back is an open question. I don't think there's anything in Stoicism that forestalls our efforts to fight a disease or prolong a life. But the Stoics insist we must appreciate that nature is an order transcending our efforts, and that disease and death (and trees and tigers) are to be respected, even in our frequent opposition to them. It's fine to be fighters, but we need to learn how to bow after our bouts.

* * * * * * * * * * *

There's a Zen-like passage in the *Discourses* where Epictetus gives the following version of a Stoic conversation:

"His ship sank."

"What happened?"

"His ship sank."[16]

The idea, I take it, is that we should divest ourselves of value judgments when describing or thinking about something. Our usual conversations go something like "'His ship sank.' 'What happened?' 'There was a terrible storm, and he tragically died.'" We add misery to a world that doesn't ultimately contain it. His ship sank, period. Evil disappears precisely when our minds refrain from supplying it. In what's maybe the shortest and sweetest version of the problem of evil and its solution, Epictetus offers the following exchange, "'But my nose is running!' What do you have hands for, if not to wipe it? 'But how is it right that there be running noses in the first place?' Instead of thinking up protests, wouldn't it be easier just to wipe your nose?"[17]

Though this practice of judgment-free description can seem like an emotionally colorless vision of reality, when carried out it leads to the opposite of a drab inner life. If anything, the shipwreck of the world suddenly appears in heightened colors and intensified lines. The Stoic practice is a kind of painterly technique—painterly in the sense of the greatest painters, like Caravaggio or Rembrandt, who cut through our impediments and show the world in its startling textures. One of the things I love most about van Gogh is that his shoes aren't gussied-up footwear or an indictment of the plight of the poor but shoes that you actually wear; his chair isn't a throne but the chair you sit in to put on your shoes; his crows aren't symbols of something foreboding or promising but the crows that happen to be flying over the field. And yet this world of beat-up old shoes and creaky chairs and dirty crows is utterly luminous, charged and swirling with holiness. My point is that when we bring our minds to reality, not reality as we prejudge it, but reality as it is in its rough actuality, our vision is not at all diminished—quite the contrary. Let me again quote Walt Whitman:

> In my periods of trouble—when I am sleepless—lie awake thinking, thinking, of things I ought not to think about at all—am flustrated—worried. Then I recover by centering all attention on the starry system—the orbs, globes—the vast spaces—the perpetual, perpetual, perpetual flux and flow-method, inevitability, dependability of the cosmos. It excites wonder, reverence, composure—I am always rendered back to myself.[18]

I adore that neologism "flustrated."

The practice of judgment-free observation is particularly ennobling when practiced in relationship to our fellow humans. Though Epictetus counsels us to hold ourselves to the highest standards, he says that we should be endlessly forgiving toward others. The worst moralists go around judging others and forgiving themselves. The true moralists judge themselves and forgive others. As Epictetus says, "So when someone assents to a false proposition, be sure that they did not want to give their assent, since, as Plato says, 'Every soul is deprived of the truth against its will.' They simply mistook for true something false."[19] Our job is to remove hatred of and anger at others. Our job is to let be. Epictetus advises us to follow the ancient Cynics: "You are going to be beaten like a donkey, and must love your tormentors as if you were their father or brother."[20]

We're all living parts of one great organism, all citizens of the cosmos. We should act in service of the whole. Though the Stoics aren't enemies of the social order, they nevertheless see through our superficial hierarchies into the wondrous humanity underneath. When a master asked Epictetus how to treat a clumsy slave, he replied, "My friend, it's a matter of bearing with your own brother, who has Zeus as his ancestor and is a son born of the same seed as yourself, with the same high lineage. . . . Remember who you are and whom you govern—that they are kinsmen, brothers by nature, fellow descendants of Zeus."[21] It's one of the first times in history the idea of the universal fraternity of humankind is clearly expressed.

* * * * * * * * * * * *

One of the most enjoyable scenes in the movies occurs near the end of *Limelight*, a Charlie Chaplin talkie. He plays a washed-up, aging vaude-ville comic named Calvero, a version of what Chaplin could have be-come had he not made it big in cinema. It's "the story of a clown who has lost his funny-bone," to use Chaplin's own description of the plot. I'm interested in the scene in *Limelight* where Calvero rediscovers his funny-bone. Calvero has finally scored a big comeback performance and enlisted for support an old vaudeville colleague, played by Buster Keaton. With great seriousness the two giants of silent comedy stroll onstage in the exaggerated duds of a concert violinist and a concert pianist. They are to play a duet. But everything around them begins to conspire against their concert. The simplest task of setting sheets of music on the piano stand proves again and again impossible for Keaton. In the meantime, one of Calvero's legs somehow begins to shorten. It simply disappears up into his pants—in a masterpiece of physical comedy on Chaplin's part. When Keaton tries to give Cal-vero a note by which to tune the violin, the piano develops a strange disease that makes its notes rise ever higher. Eventually both instru-ments are irreparably broken. As Robert Warshow says, "The difficul-ties that confront Calvero and Keaton in their gentle attempt to give a concert are beyond satire. The universe stands in their way, and not because the universe is imperfect, either, but just because it exists; God himself could not conceive a universe in which these two could accomplish the simplest thing without mishap."[22]

Yet Calvero and Keaton accept the recalcitrant universe with infi-nite patience. Over and over they deal with the tasks at hands (trying to bring a leg back to a normal length, trying to fix the strings of a piano that tighten and pop for mysterious reasons). Finally, as if by magic, Calvero whips a violin out from behind his back, Keaton starts pounding on the cured piano, and they deliver a hilarious, satisfying number—one that rocks back and forth between a sad adagio (where Calvero weepingly talks to his violin) and a frenzied presto (which carries Keaton right off his piano bench).

The scene embodies Stoicism—not the morose Stoicism that many imagine, but Stoicism in its lived reality. In fact, I imagine if we were truly Stoic sages, we wouldn't even laugh at it, for it would read like the most transparent realism. It's part of our nature—our fate—that the universe pushes back against our designs (this is what most of us regard as pointless suffering). But each of these pushbacks is part of a grand comic design, without which the scene itself would lose its interest and meaning. What's so marvelous about Calvero and Keaton is that they come across exactly like Charlie Chaplin and Buster Keaton, two wise old comics who understand life and have given up their silly protests against it, who understand that in the end the only truly pointless suffering is our belief in pointless suffering. To use Stoic terms, they have become one with nature; they're acting rationally. When Calvero is emoting, alternating between tragic weeping and comic frenzy, he's simply playing the appropriate part for the time. He's doing his duty, to use Epictetus's term. The triumph of Calvero and Keaton is dramatically expressed by the resolution of the scene, which, as Warshow says,

> comes to us out of that profundity where art, having become perfect, seems no longer to have any implications. The scene is unendurably funny, but the analogies that occur to me are tragic: Lear's "Never, never, never, never, never!" or Kafka's "It is enough that the arrows fit exactly in the wounds they have made."[23]

In other words, it goes beyond comedy and tragedy to the pure reality that generates them in the human mind.

Epictetus understood full well the problem of having your leg inexplicably altered. In the absurdities and tumult of the Roman Empire he found, like the wise old comics, order and peace. Stoicism is often thought to be a recipe for dourness and emotional frigidity. What did Epictetus do when he finally retired from the life of a teacher? Tradition has it that he adopted an orphan, maybe even a boy who'd have otherwise been given over to slavery—in any case, a child without parents. He devoted himself to giving the child a good upbringing. Doesn't an orphan deserve the same kind of devotion as is commonly given to our own flesh and blood? Isn't an orphan also a child of Zeus? As the classicist Robert Dobbin says, "That he had absented himself from family life for so long shows that he regarded philosophy as a jealous mistress who demanded practically all his time and attention, which family life would not allow. That this renunciation of family life represented a real sacrifice is suggested by the fact that he took to it immediately upon retiring."[24] I like to imagine the aging Epictetus horsing around with his boy.

It's no accident that throughout this chapter I've been slipping in quotations from Walt Whitman. America's most ebullient poet was deeply indebted to Epictetus and drew insight and comfort from Stoicism throughout his life. A few years before his death Whitman wrote a friend, "Epictetus is the one of all my old cronies who has lasted to this day without cutting a diminished figure in my perspective. He belongs with the best of the great teachers—is a universe in himself. He sets me free in a flood of light—of life, of vista."[25] About Epictetus's *Handbook* Whitman told Horace Traubel, "This book has become in a sense sacred, precious, to me: I have had it about me so long— lived with it in terms of such familiarity."[26] (Deep as Whitman's Stoic influence was, we shouldn't reduce the poet to a philosophy; Whitman also said, "I guess I have a good deal of the feeling of Epictetus & stoicism—or tried to have. . . . But I am clear that I include & allow & probably teach some things stoicism would frown upon & discard. One's pulses & marrow are not democratic & natural for nothing."[27]) Someone like Whitman reminds us that Stoicism should conjure intensified vision and joyful environmentalism rather than dourness and emotional remove. Our poet heartily knew that when the half-gods of happiness go, the real gods just might arrive.

INTERLUDE ON HEAVEN
AND HELL

After humans had placed all pains and torments in hell, there was
nothing left for heaven but boredom.

ARTHUR SCHOPENHAUER

One of the fundamentally weird things about being human is that we
have a sense of time. Though the present moment is our only real hab-
itation, we commonly project ourselves into a nonexistent zone called
the future and wander around in a made-up land called the past. Because we delineate yesterday and tomorrow, we also recognize now as
now, generally wishing to slow it down or speed it up, though we occasionally enjoy it as it crumbles away. Other animals—infants too—
seem capable of surfing on the eternity of experience, though once in
a while beasts and babies appear to have a rudimentary sense of time
that locks them in their own cages.

Which came first: the consciousness of time or the consciousness
of suffering? One theory is that we were hurt into time. As we became aware of a vague dissatisfaction with the givenness of our condition, we began to think of how things could be different. Our sense of
hunger as an affront evoked past moments of satiety. Our sense of the
insufficiency of nature and the possibility of tools nudged us to blueprint a future. Thus, suffering gave birth to time. Come to think of it,

this theory is probably wrong, because it seems already to presume a past and a future for suffering to force us into. There's a wonderful essay by Jorge Luis Borges called "A New Refutation of Time," the title of which is a sly refutation of its own thesis. So, maybe it's the other way around, and time is the mother of suffering. Because we think of past and future, we judge the present to be inadequate. Or maybe it's just that human consciousness gives birth to identical twins, time and suffering. Simone Weil says, "Two things cannot be reduced to any rationalizing: time and beauty. One must begin from them."[1] Three things, really: time, beauty, and suffering.

In any case, humanity has concocted marvelous variations on its invention of time: heaven and hell. Since our moral principles and deepest longings war with reality, heaven and hell are elsewhere: up among the stars, somewhere below the earth, or in another metaphysical locale altogether. They're often imaginative incarnations of the ideals that guide us through life. For example, the Mormons believe that couples are married forever in the afterlife. Marriage is not immediately given in reality: among other things, it's a shaping of our sexual and emotional drives into a human creation that never sits perfectly with who we are. The Mormon belief about heaven is, among other things, a way of saying that marriage is really, really important. The ancient Norse belief that the souls of warriors slain in battle will be served mead by Valkyries in Valhalla until they tragically do battle against a giant wolf expresses a somewhat different view of what's most valuable in this world.

I'm not saying that heaven and hell aren't real. Just because something is an invention doesn't mean that it isn't also a discovery. Just because the past is a product of the imagination doesn't mean that things didn't actually happen yesterday. Just because the future is a fantasy doesn't mean that what we predict never comes true. And just because heaven and hell are inventions doesn't necessarily mean that it's all over for us when we sputter our last breath. Admittedly, I'll be somewhat surprised if the Mormons or the Norse are right, and my soul is stuck in a marriage or a mead hall when my bones are left to the courtesy of worms. But I won't be totally surprised, given the wondrousness of this cosmos.

Plus, the belief in heaven makes a lot of psychological sense. The world is full of pointless suffering, which we try desperately to understand and alleviate. Isn't it understandable that we should hope and strive for a condition free of misery? The complex dream-architecture of heaven and hell originates in the "God damn it!" we yell at the world's mishaps. As I said in the chapter on Job, the very shape of a story runs counter to pointless suffering. It's extremely hard to tell a story that goes "The hero was born, suffered pointlessly, and died. The end." Not impossible (I'm thinking here of certain French films), but extremely hard. A story—even a tragedy, in fact especially a tragedy—naturally endows suffering with meaning. Plus, our greatest tragic tales tend to have some measure of a happy ending. As awful as Oedipus's fate is, his punishment is what cures Thebes of its plagues.

A distinction can be drawn between heaven and paradise. Paradise—sometimes called earthly paradise—is our attempt to imagine human life without any suffering whatsoever. It can be charming but is ultimately crass, a product of the humble part of the soul that wants no more than pleasure and the avoidance of pain. By contrast, heaven, properly speaking, is our attempt to imagine human life free of the pathologies that generate pointless suffering. It can be profound in a way that Paradise can't. When the hobo-songwriter Harry McClintock sings, "In the Big Rock Candy Mountain you never change your socks/ And little streams of alcohol come trickling down the rocks," he's envisioning paradise. When Martin Luther King Jr. launches into "I Have a Dream," what follows is heaven.

* * * * * * * * * * *

The blueprint for paradise seems easy enough to draw up: just remove all the thorns from existence. Don't want to grow old and die? Let's have two fountains, one of youth and one of immortality. Don't want to feel pain? Let's exile natural disasters, illness, and any other bit of suffering. What about the misery we inflict on each other? With hypnotic music let's enchant all the citizens of our earthly paradise so that they never think of harming each other. Basically, we're imagining the life of the Hyperboreans, as described by the ancient Greek poet Pindar:

> The Muse never leaves that land,
> For this is their life:
> Everywhere the girls are dancing,
> And the sound of the harps is loud,
> And the noise of the flutes.
> They bind their hair with bay leaves of gold.
> They feast and are glad.
> And sickness never, nor cursed old age
> Touches their holy bodies:
> Without toil, without war
> They dwell, and do not trouble
> The stern scales of Nemesis.[2]

This peaceful, tranquil vision is common to many cultures, but is it the best we can do in imagining paradise?

In my view, an even better construction of paradise can be found in the cartoons of Warner Bros. and Hanna-Barbera: Sylvester and Tweety, Bugs and Elmer Fudd, Tom and Jerry, and all their other marvelous creations. Wouldn't you rather run eternally with the Road Runner and Wile E. Coyote than twirl endlessly with Pindar's Hyperboreans? Seriously, how long could you put up with "the noise of flutes"?

The beauty of the Saturday-morning cartoons of my youth is that they tap into the weirdness of our most basic desires—out of necessity, for their original purpose was to capture the attention of children, and children's desires have a laserlike purity and intensity. The issue is not so much that the license of Pindar's enchanted isle would reintroduce the kind of abuses of freedom we want to eliminate in paradise. It's that the very sexiness of paradise depends on our being allowed to violate the norms we must suffer in our current life. Prohibition and risk, up to a point, generate and enhance pleasure. The nature of desire is that we want to have our cake and eat it too. Eden should be governed by laws and taboos, but they should exist only to enhance—and in some sense—create our pleasure. Kids understand this.

The elastic cartoon body, which pops immediately back into shape after being flattened or crushed, is a brilliant solution to our childish desire to have risk and fun without pain and injury. In cartoons, pain is a purely visual phenomenon: little lines and stars that emanate from your butt after the bull sends you flying, or imaginary birdies that chirp around your lump-sprouting head after it's been flattened by a steel weight. But with a shake of the head and a wiggle of the hind end, you're restored to perfect shape and back in the game.

Classical versions of paradise tend to be vegetarian: the wolf lies down with the lamb. As a cook and a lover of food, that's not exactly what I want to do with lamb! There's a childish part of me that wants to have shepherd's pie for dinner but doesn't want any lambies to die. Thus, cartoons are at once carnivorous and vegetarian: no animal is ever fully digested, even though cartoon animals are always hungry and dreaming of eating. The wolf never fully eats the lamb, but doesn't lie down with the lamb either. The wolf dreams of eating the lamb, chases the lamb all over, occasionally swallows the lamb, but the lamb is always delivered, like Jonah from the whale. In an ingenious solution to the problem of desire, we are forever hungry and forever eating.

The cartoonists' solution to the problem of shame and guilt is also ingenious. An important part of their minidramas involves a presiding authority figure denuded of real power. There's a dutiful bulldog or brow-beating granny, as in the Sylvester and Tweety cartoons, to chastise the predator just enough to make eating the prey a little naughty. But the moral prohibition is ineffective in preventing the predators' commission of the crime. When he's caught, Sylvester's guilt is always a put-on. The charade of prohibition functions much as in kinky fantasies.

The great cartoonists' vision of the ideal relationship is so ingenious as to be virtually impossible to describe to anyone who hasn't watched their shows. All the great relationships of the classic cartoons have a strong sexual (and sometimes homosexual) undercurrent. Yet they also blend friendship and deep rivalry. Think of Sylvester and Tweety, Wile E. Coyote and the Road Runner, Tom and Jerry. They've found a miraculous way of mixing the joys of desire, friendship, and animosity—a mixture that mirrors and exults the deep but undefined bonds formed by children.

The best example is Bugs Bunny and Elmer Fudd. In "What's Opera, Doc?" Bugs dresses in Norse drag to escape from being hunted by his nemesis Elmer Fudd ("Kill da wabbit!"), who then falls in love with the feminine version of Bugs. They reenact the romance of the demigod Siegfried for Brünnhilde. At some point, Bugs's tucked-in ears accidentally unfurl and reveal who he really is. Enraged and humiliated, Elmer Fudd responds by hunting down and killing Bugs ("Stwike da wabbit!"). But after Bugs's demise, Elmer Fudd becomes morose, as if he's lost his real lover, and carries off the dead body of Bugs into the sunset. He's lost the object of infinite desire! Naturally, Bugs perks up at the very end to say, "What did you expect—a happy ending?" By introducing death, the episode takes us just beyond the limits of paradise and then pulls marvelously back at the final moment to remind us that death isn't really real.

We take such satisfaction in Bugs, as in that wonderfully ironic last line, because Bugs is in on the game. Most cartoon characters don't know they're in paradise. They pursue like they need the food; they flee like their lives depend on escape. But not Bugs. While everyone else is obsessed with the hunt, Bugs nibbles away at his carrot and concocts bizarre situations to enjoy his wisdom and power. In one sense, he embodies the power of art itself: the ability to be above the world and yet simultaneously to participate in its crazy affairs with style. In another sense, he prefigures the allure of video games: the ability to enact violence and "die" over and over without ever putting anything real at risk.

As brilliant as are the cartoons of Chuck Jones, Friz Freleng, William Hanna, and Joseph Barbera (we should be proud of our great democratic artists, even when their art is used to hawk sugar cereal), I don't think that these masters have successfully imagined Paradise. And if they haven't done it, it's impossible! Take Bugs. Doesn't he suffer from a deep boredom? The answer to his incessant question "What's up, Doc?" is, I'm afraid, "Nothing." The problem is that in removing the thorns of death, pain, and freedom, we remove the resources of overcoming meaninglessness. Once the evils of life have been removed, what can we do, after heaving a sigh of relief, but wonder, "What now?" Part of what it means to have a self is to have a story, and part of what it means to have a story is to have evil, and another part of what it means to have a story is to have an ending, happy or unhappy. Bugs is forced to be revived forever in the next episode. He's forever parasitic on real stories. As his final quip in "What's Opera, Doc?" makes clear, Bugs's story never ends. TV, like any other Paradise, turns out to be hell. The gods eventually long to be mortals. I don't mean to be macabre, but I get the sense that if Bugs could come clean, he'd repeat the plea of the Sibyl of Cumae, whom Apollo granted as many years of life as grains in a handful of dust. Eventually she cried out, "I want to die." Maybe "What's up, Doc?" is just Bugs's way of softening the blow.

In his essay "Can the Devil Be Saved?" Leszek Kołakowski puts my point this way:

> The spectacle of man perfectly united with himself and with his social and natural environments is as incomprehensible as the concept of heaven. The inconsistency is basically the same: an earthly paradise must combine satisfaction with creativity, a heavenly paradise must combine satisfaction with love. Both combinations are inconceivable, since without dissatisfaction—without some form of suffering—there can be no creativity, no love. Complete satisfaction is death; partial dissatisfaction entails pain.[3]

In the beloved poem "Birches" Robert Frost describes his longing to get away from our confusing, painful world. But he qualifies his escape wish: "May no fate willfully misunderstand me/ And half grant what I wish and snatch me away/ Not to return. Earth's the right place for love:/ I don't know where it's likely to go better."[4] He longs to escape by climbing a pliant birch tree that will eventually bend with his weight and gently set him back on earth again. We need our Looney Tunes and Hyperborean Isles. But may no fate willfully misunderstand our purpose. We should rejoice that the flute music comes to an end. We should be glad that Mom turns off the cartoons and makes us go outside to play.

* * * * * * * * * * *

Our imagination of heaven often contains a strong element of paradise. Heaven is generally conceived to be free of death and pain. Insofar as it is, Kołakowski is right: it would destroy the creativity and love essential to being human. But heaven, properly conceived, outstrips the contradictions of paradise and can be used to illuminate the possibilities of our nature and its higher callings. Even if you don't believe in an afterlife, you can still have faith in heaven.

I've already mentioned Martin Luther King Jr.'s "I Have a Dream" speech. Toward its beginning, King describes the promise of American ideals as a bank check that hasn't yet been cashed, but he says, "We refuse to believe that the bank of justice is bankrupt." The desire for heaven is always an expression of the virtue of hope, the committed belief against all evidence that justice is never bankrupt and will pay out in the end. In this sense, heaven isn't exactly another metaphysical locale; it's about what's possible and best in us. Martin Luther King Jr. gives voice to a version of the American heaven, the possibility of living without racist pathology, an ideal that can inspire and guide us insofar as we believe in what our dream-energies can realize. King is a homegrown bodhisattva, an enlightened one who commits to the endless work of saving suffering beings.

One of my favorite scenes in the *Paradiso* is when Dante, in the heavenly circle of the sun, comes across a bunch of theologians, many of whom argued for competing theories in their earthly existence. Thomas Aquinas, a member of the Dominican order, begins to sing the praises of St. Francis, the founder of the Dominicans' rival order. When he's done, Bonaventure, a Franciscan theologian, begins to celebrate Dominic. Now that's heaven! To update Dante's vision, imagine a circle of the sun where evolutionists speak passionately of how much wisdom is contained in the Bible's creation story and creationists celebrate the virtues and insights of Charles Darwin. Imagine Republicans and Democrats, atheists and believers, Kantians and Hegelians, communists and capitalists, all praising what is best and brightest in their opponent's legacy. Each group has some splinter of truth and is driven by some good impulses. It's heaven when we're able to get out of our ego and recognize both our own shortcomings and the magnanimity lurking even in our enemies. As Dante says, "It's right that where one is, the other enters,/ In that as they warred for a common goal/ So now together does their glory glisten."[5]

It's totally rational to look at the history and practice of American life and conclude that our country will go to its grave as a racist nation, just as it's totally rational to conclude that human nature will always be marked by faction and sin. I don't think such conclusions make the belief in heaven irrational, for it's possible to undo injustice in flashes, and if it's possible for a few moments, it's possible more generally. Isn't it possible that "on the red hills of Georgia the sons of former slaves and the sons of former slave owners will be able to sit down together at the table of brotherhood"? Isn't it possible that we act in accord with justice, temperance, courage, prudence, hope, faith, or love? Plus, to believe in these possibilities is to make them more possible. The essential thing to say about heaven is just what Jesus says: "The Kingdom of God is within you."[6]

* * * * * * * * * * *

It's telling that we've always imagined hell with more gusto than heaven. Let's face it: a lot of hell is simply our longing to torture others. Nietzsche calls Dante "the hyena which *poetizes* on graves."[7] That's unfair to the author of the *Comedy*, but it's not totally unfair. The great Christian poet does seem to relish imagining one of his former pals carrying around his own severed head like a lantern in the basement of Hell, to select just one example from an embarrassment of riches.

But our imagination of hell isn't exclusively sadistic. Sometimes a righteous desire for hell can be overwhelming. I remember when I first read of Jerry Sandusky's arrest for fifty-two counts of the sexual abuse of young boys. As you probably recall, Sandusky was a popular assistant football coach at Penn State, the author of several books about football, the founder of a charity for underprivileged boys, and a family man. But it came out that he used his coaching position and charity organization to prey sexually on at-risk youths. As I learned of his crimes, I was overcome by a vivid feeling, almost a waking dream, of all the child molesters who never get caught, who go to their graves as "pillars of their communities," while their victims suffer from their poorly tended psychological scars and die without justice. I found myself desperately longing for hell, so that the balance would be righted, so that the ultimate story of the universe was not one of blessing the wrongdoers and cursing their victims.

This desire for hell isn't all bad, but it isn't all good, either. It's easy for us Americans to wish hell on Hitler, but it's tougher for us to wish it on our own cowboys, politicians, and settlers whose successful genocide of native peoples Hitler admired and strove to emulate. It's satisfying to wish hell on Jerry Sandusky, but I find it hard to wish hell on myself. The fact is that it's not only easy for me to resist molesting children, it would be impossible for me to molest them. However, when I am strongly tempted by wrongdoing (luckily, less egregious wrongdoing than child abuse), my record isn't spotless. Earthly justice hasn't caught up with all my sins. I can easily imagine that some of those people whom I've wronged wouldn't mind seeing me spend some time in the Devil's laboratory.

I don't want hell for myself, but I do sometimes wish for purgatory. Don't we have to believe in some outpost of good in us, something worth saving? As C. S. Lewis says:

> Our souls *demand* Purgatory, don't they? Would it not break the heart if God said to us, "It is true, my son, that your breath smells and your rags drip with mud and slime, but we are charitable here and no one will upbraid you with these things, nor draw away from you. Enter into the joy"? Should we not reply, "With submission, sir, and if there is no objection, I'd *rather* be cleaned first." "It may hurt, you know"—"Even so, sir."[8]

Admittedly, sometimes my soul demands to be in the land where little streams of alcohol come trickling down the rocks! But when I'm reflecting on myself in the light of truth and justice, my soul demands purgatory, just as Lewis says. I don't simply want to get the reward. I want to be worthy of it. Or at least almost worthy of it—a little grace is surely going to be necessary with me!

Maybe we should wish purgatory for everyone? Aren't we all in need of gussying up before entering the grand ballroom? Or, to put it in non-otherworldly terms, shouldn't we want to reckon honestly with our problems rather than have them magically solved for us? For instance, I tend to think that many of our attempts to remedy racial injustice—body cameras on the police, affirmative action, and so on—are often done in the wrong spirit of simply wanting to poof away our very deep-seated problems, of wanting to avoid the reckoning. What I primarily wish for America today is not the immediate heaven of justice but the purgatory that would make us worthy of justice.

A common problem with hell is that eternity seems a bit much for the length of punishment. Does anyone merit being tortured forever? It's hard to see how. Retributive justice is limited by the principle of an eye for an eye. Shouldn't even Hitler have a chance of parole after six million or so life sentences? If Hell is conceived as a penalty inflicted by God for our sins, I don't see how we can resist the heretical hope of those religious groups that deny the concept of eternal punishment altogether.

But there's another way of conceiving of hell, one that perhaps escapes the charge of unfairness. Maybe hell isn't simply God's torture chamber for sinners but rather the state of a soul in rebellion against justice and love. Maybe after several million life sentences, Hitler would still stand by *Mein Kampf.* Maybe he still wouldn't want to enter heaven. The mystery of the soul's conversion requires, among other things, the mind's consent. In short, the belief in the eternity of hell conceals a laudable commitment to human freedom and dignity. In Dante's *Inferno*, there's a charming scene in the pit of hell where Farinata, the proud Ghibelline aristocrat, turns upward and, with both hands, flips off God. He doesn't want to be in heaven. If God were to force him there against his will, it would be crueler than leaving him in his fiery tomb. Better a chosen hell than a coerced heaven.

* * * * * * * * * * *

My personal favorite vision of the afterlife is found at the end of the *Mahabharata*, the infinite Hindu epic that narrates the fratricidal war between the Pandavas and the Kauravas. After the great Pandava king Yudhishthira, his four brothers, and their wife, Draupadi (theirs is an interesting case of polyandry), have finally won the war and returned peace and prosperity to the land, they renounce their wealth and kingdom and take a final journey together into the mountains, taking with them nothing that they don't already carry in themselves. The small exception is that a stray dog attaches itself to them on the trip. One by one, the Pandavas begin to fall. First Draupadi dies, then each of Yudhishthira's brothers. The journey is complete.

Finally, Indra, the king of the gods, appears in a chariot before Yudhishthira and offers to give him a ride to heaven. All he must do is renounce the world. "I've already renounced everything," Yudhishthira declares. Indra points at the stray dog and says, "There's still that dog. You can't take it with you." The king looks down at the whimpering dog and says, "I can't do it. It would be wrong to turn my back on such a devoted creature for no more than my selfish desire to go to heaven."[9] The god and the king argue for a bit, but Yudhishthira holds his ground. At last it's revealed that the dog is Dharma himself, the god of righteousness. In refusing to renounce Dharma, Yudhishthira has passed Indra's test and earned the right to enter heaven.

Yudhishthira finds heaven to be the most beautiful place imaginable. But to his surprise its population includes his archenemies the Kauravas. His brothers and wife are nowhere to be found. "Don't worry, they're fine," Indra says, "Just enjoy heaven with us. There's no enmity here." But Yudhishthira insists on visiting his family. When a celestial messenger takes him to them, he finds that they're in a hole reeking of decomposing, maggot-ridden bodies. "There they are," the messenger says, "Now, let's go back to heaven." But Yudhishthira refuses to return. Despite the stench, he's going to stay with them in hell. Soon Indra appears again and turns hell into heaven, saying, "This was just another test. You can experience heaven only once you've truly experienced hell."

Though the Pandavas all end up in heaven, the overwhelming feeling the *Mahabharata* leaves you with is that of the eerie provisionality of all things, something like the feeling you get when you wake up from a dream and then wake up again. Could this too be another test, another illusion?

Nobody's perfect, especially in the *Mahabharata*. Yudhishthira, though generally a paragon of virtue, has a particularly low moment, one that ends up precipitating the war. In the throes of gambling addiction, he loses his entire kingdom to the Kauravas. Unable to stop, he bets his brothers and finally his wife, Draupadi. He loses them all. The beautiful Draupadi is called in to be raped by the family who has won her. She makes an impassioned, lawyerly plea that it's invalid to gamble with human lives, but the Kauravas are unimpressed. They order her sari to be ripped off. But the god Krishna is on Draupadi's side, and his magic makes her sari endless. As they unspool it, it just keeps piling higher and higher on the floor.

Just as the Kauravas are unable ever to know Draupadi in her nakedness, we're unable to know life in its perfectly clarified state. The ending of the *Mahabharata*, where test is rewarded with test, feels like a version of pulling at the sari. The takeaway seems to be that heaven will always be deferred—or at best will appear in momentary, confusing glimmers. Nevertheless, we must strive to be worthy of heaven, even when God appears to be putting us in hell. It's all a test! My advice: no matter what you're promised, don't renounce whatever that dog stands for.

SIX

POINTLESS SUFFERING
EVOKES OUR HUMANITY

On Confucius and the Rituals of Compassion

> For out of acceptance of this truth: that the pleasures and joys of life
> are fleeting and rare, that life contains a larger measure of hurt and
> misery, suffering and despair—must come not the bitter frustration
> and anger of self-pity, but love and concern for the human condition.
>
> DAVE HEATH

After reading the first ten books of the *Analects*, we've developed a picture of Confucius that resembles how he's portrayed in paintings and sculptures: a bemused, unflappable, twinkling teacher. Then we get to book 11. It begins serenely enough. Confucius says that when it comes to observing the rules of propriety and playing music, he generally prefers the ways of peasants to the ways of the nobility. According to the random-seeming arrangement of the *Analects*, we're reminded of his favorite student, Yan Hui, a young gentleman with boundless intellectual and moral promise, someone who could have been Aristotle to Confucius's Plato. With teasing humor, the Master says, "Yan Hui is of no help to me. There is nothing that I say that he doesn't like." Then we learn "there was one Yan Hui who truly loved learning. Unfortunately, he was to die young. Nowadays, there is no one." Suddenly, in sharp contrast to that flat reportage of tragedy, Confucius is thrown into wild grief. He begins to cry out, "Heaven is the ruin of me! Heaven is the ruin of me!" His usually deferent students chastise him for grieving with abandon. Confucius rages back, "I grieve with abandon? If I don't grieve with abandon for him, then for whom?" It's one of the most remarkable moments in literature: the sage comes unglued.

We're used to everyday people grieving with ferocity when a loved one dies, but we expect the wise to transport us to a higher plane of consciousness. Particularly in the face of death, sages are supposed to unveil a jewel of wisdom, something that gleams with our cosmic fate. Why do we read the *Analects*? Isn't it because Confucius responds to the soul's wonderings with authoritative answers, even when—especially when!—they're riddling answers? But in the face of Yan Hui's death, Confucius offers us nothing more than our usual untutored, raw grief at mortality. We don't even get a cryptic saying. What good is Confucius if he cries the same tears as the rest of us?

After getting over my shock at his commonplace grief, I've come to find both comfort and wisdom in Confucius's discomforting and unwise sobbing. The space of pure grief he occupies in his lament over pointless suffering is the very space of being human, the very space out of which his whole philosophy—and civilization itself—is born. He refuses to refine tragedy into anything but tragedy, and there's something profoundly right about that.

* * * * * * * * * * *

To get a taste of Confucius's world, consider one of his contemporaries, Wu Zixu (526–484 BC), a government official whose father was held hostage and murdered by the king. In search of revenge, Wu Zixu was disappointed to find that the murderous king had already been killed. So he dug up the royal body and whipped the corpse three hundred times. He then allied himself with the king of Wu, who was warring with the neighboring province of Yue. The king soon turned on Wu Zixu and forced him to commit suicide. His last words were "Be sure to plant catalpa on my grave, so that they can be made into instruments for coffins, and pluck out my eyes and hang them above the eastern gate of Wu, so that I can watch the Yue invaders when they enter and destroy it." The king stuffed Wu Zixu's corpse into a wineskin and ignominiously drowned it in the river, though, obligingly, he first gouged out the eyes and hung them above the province's gate. As luck would have it, Wu Zixu's bloody eyes did get to oversee the destruction of Wu by Yue invaders.[1]

Such exponentially increasing brutality was common at the end of the Spring and Autumn period (771–476 BC) and eventually led to what's known as the Warring States period (475–221 BC). That the powerful were gouging out the jelly of one another's eyes was a symbol and a symptom of the entire society's breakdown. The central quandary of classical Chinese philosophy was essentially the question of Rodney King, whose beating by the LAPD in 1991 was captured on videotape and led to widespread rioting: "Can we all just get along?" Confucianism—like all the Hundred Schools of Thought, as the competing philosophical movements of the time came to be known—is largely about solving the problem of unjust suffering insofar as unjust suffering is inflicted by us. Philosophy, born of wonder, is often fathered by collapse.

Confucius, the Latinized name of Kong Fuzi (Master Kong), was born around 551 and died around 479 BC. In a sense, his life was a failure. He believed that he was destined to reestablish out of his society's moral and political breakdown what his hero the Duke of Zhou had established five hundred years earlier in the Middle Kingdom: a peaceful, civilized order. Confucius wandered from state to state in hopes that he would persuade various rulers to employ him and enact his vision. It was only at the beginning of his life that Confucius ever held an official position, a minor one. The various dukes and rulers would generally listen politely to Master Kong and then send him on his way, occasionally with the threat of violence. To anyone who has not achieved worldly success and recognition, Confucius offers the following consolation: "It is a disgrace to remain poor and without rank when the way prevails in the state; it is a disgrace to be wealthy and of noble rank when it does not."[2]

Though he's the legendary author or editor of many classics, we don't have any writings that can be reliably attributed to Confucius. Our sense of his personality and philosophy comes primarily from the *Analects*, the luminous spiritual portrait of the Master. Not only do we witness him interacting with his students with humor and insight, we learn other touching details from the *Analects*, like that Confucius was an avid sportsman, hunter, and archer, and that he loved music so intensely that hearing a rare ancient song once made him forget the taste of meat for three months.

Despite its dismissal by the hardheaded dukes and rulers of the late Spring and Autumn period, Confucianism is one of the most practical philosophies for dealing with pointless suffering, in broad outline as useful now as ever. Suffering and our response to it underlie the essential Confucian virtues. Unlike most practical philosophies, Confucianism doesn't really give us any principles or guidelines, other than a gentle version of the Golden Rule: "Do not impose on others what you yourself do not want."[3] More than any other philosopher Confucius is interested in evoking what it means to be genuinely, richly, and humanely human, for he believes that any order not grounded in our humanity is both fragile and undesirable. Alan Watts says:

> It was a basic Confucian principle that "it is man who makes truth great, not truth which makes man great." For this reason, "humanness" or "human-heartedness" was always felt to be superior to "righteousness," since man himself is greater than any idea he may invent. There are times when men's passions are much more trustworthy than their principles. . . . Reasonable—that is, human—men will always be capable of compromise, but men who have dehumanized themselves by becoming the blind worshipers of an idea or an ideal are fanatics whose devotion to abstractions makes them the enemies of life.[4]

The word Confucius uses to denote this state in which all our cramping and damaging energies have been smoothed out is *ren*, which is translated in various ways: not just, as Watts mentions, "humanness" and "human-heartedness" but also "benevolence," "love," "goodness," "authoritative conduct." I think of these English equivalents like darts thrown by skilled players at a target. Maybe none of them squarely hits the bull's-eye, but together the darts are suggestive of where it is.

The Chinese graph of *ren* has two elements: that of a person and what's either the number two or a character suggesting transcendence. Both etymologies are suggestive. Person-times-two resonates with the Confucian idea that it's only in relationships we discover and prove who we are. As the scholar Herbert Fingarette wonderfully puts it, "For Confucius, unless there are at least two human beings, there can be no human beings."[5] Person-times-transcendence, the alternative etymology, is evocative of the way that our biological impulses can be exulted to noble proportions. As Confucius himself wonderfully puts it, "Those authoritative in their conduct (*ren*) enjoy mountains."[6]

* * * * * * * * * * *

One common way of dealing with chaos—whether in the form of civil war, rioting, crime, or simply our children's acting up—is to impose order with rules backed up by the threat of punishment. In Western political philosophy, the position is best expressed by Thomas Hobbes. In classical Chinese philosophy, it's given voice by Mozi and Han Feizi, the latter of whom advised the Qin in the conquest of the state that still bears their name.

Confucius holds the opposite view. Rules and punishments are the wrong way of generating order out of breakdown. He says:

> Lead people with administrative injunctions and keep them orderly with penal law, and they will avoid punishments but will be without a sense of shame. Lead them with [moral] excellence and keep them orderly through observing ritual propriety and they will develop a sense of shame, and moreover, will order themselves.[7]

Penal law, for Confucius, is a losing game. A little punishment is perhaps necessary in the context of an already established order. But in creating and maintaining a civilized society, penal law at best creates the semblance of order; at worst it exacerbates the very tendencies that provoke its implementation. As the Master says, "What we must strive to do is to rid the courts of cases altogether."[8]

Consider a law that criminalizes the abuse of a child. If the main thing keeping parents, teachers, and neighbors from abusing children is fear of punishment at the hands of the state, then something's desperately wrong with our community. We shouldn't want to abuse our children! If we do feel the occasional impulse to do so, it should be reined in by a sense of shame, a sense of our humanity. If compliance with the law crowds out that sense of humanity, society will always be fighting in vain to reestablish the bonds, like those of parent and child, that give order to our lives and make them worth living.

In place of penal law Confucius proposes *li*. At this concept, translators have thrown words like "ritual," "rites," "customs," "etiquette," "propriety," "morals," "rules of proper behavior," and "worship." I'm partial to the translation of the *Analects* by the important contemporary Confucians Roger T. Ames and Henry Rosemont Jr., who translate *li* as "ritual propriety" or "observing ritual propriety." They note:

> *Li* are those meaning-invested roles, relationships, and institutions which facilitate communication, and which foster a sense of community. The compass is broad: all formal conduct, from table manners to patters of greeting and leave-taking, to graduations, weddings, funerals, from gestures of deference to ancestral sacrifices. . . . They are a social grammar.[9]

Let's start with a little example. As you absentmindedly stroll down the street, you run into me. My first impulse is to be hostile. If you say nothing and keep on walking, I might hurl obscenities at you. One thing could lead to another, and it's not impossible we come to blows. But if, after running into me, you simply say, "Excuse me! I'm so sorry," my aggression instantly evaporates. I brush the incident off: "No problem." We've gone from competition to harmony. We've stepped out of hostility into *ren*, all because of a tiny act of etiquette. *Li* has orchestrated a relationship and dignified our common humanity (person-times-two.) Even if a little hostility remains, and I grumble, "Watch where you're going next time," at least your act of ritual propriety has averted violence.

Saying "excuse me" and other little acts of observing ritual propriety turn out to be crucial for a functioning society. Much of being a parent is tirelessly reminding children to say "please," "thank you," and "excuse me." These "magic words" really are miraculous. They harmonize us with other people and allow us to navigate the human world successfully and respectfully. If I bark at you, "Give me that book on the table," you're liable to feel like a mere tool of my desires and either resent or refuse me. If I soften my tone and add the magic word, "Would you *please* bring me that book on the table?" your humanity is recognized, and you happily hand me the book.

The failure to observe these little acts of ritual propriety unleashes violence, chaos, and inhumanity. In the great tragic works of the Western tradition, we think of suffering as being written in the stars, the result of an ancient curse or original sin or biology. But a Confucian reading of our tragedies would regard many of them as the straightforward consequences of ignoring ritual propriety. Imagine the story of King Lear if he hadn't made the graceless command to be complimented by his children, or if Cordelia had just spoken a little more politely to her father. Hamlet and Ophelia might have married and lived out regal years if his mother and uncle hadn't engaged in the impropriety of marrying so soon after his father's death that "the funeral bak'd meats/ Did coldly furnish forth the marriage tables." How many plays by Sophocles would be exceedingly boring if the antagonists had simply let the protagonists practice the fundamental ritual of burying their loved ones? The whole stomach-turning tragedy of Oedipus could have been averted had he simply said, "Excuse me," and made way when he bumped into an elder on the road.

Oedipus's unwitting murder of his father is, to my knowledge, the first documented example of road rage. Driving on the cluttered freeway, with all its frustrations and dangers, is a useful example of what life is like with a bare minimum of ritual propriety. It's hard for us when we're isolated in our cars to communicate "please" and "excuse me." Admittedly, there are some rituals on the road, often unique to the locale, but mostly order is kept, especially in big cities with bad traffic, through the internalization of rules and the fear of the police. If the Confucian concept of *ren* means two people in relationship, it's hard to find it on the freeway, because we're all lonely competitors encased in steel.

When for graduate school I moved from Grinnell, Iowa, to Atlanta, Georgia, I was an extremely polite driver, accustomed to the easygoing midwestern proprieties of taking turns, waving people in, blinking my headlights to indicate dangers, driving reticently. Suddenly, in what *Forbes* magazine once proved to be the worst traffic in America, I found myself, after waving one car in, watching thirty cars take advantage of my politeness. Full of small-town calm, I flattered myself that my sterling character put me above all the big-city mental cases white-knuckling their steering wheels. After a few years of dealing with nobody taking turns, nobody giving an inch, road rage began to seethe in me. I too stopped giving an inch and integrated a running commentary of cursing into my daily commute. Figuring my car was old and beat-up anyway, I swerved at vehicles I suspected of the least aggression. I finally woke to what I'd become when a left-turner failed to yield to my oncoming traffic, and I slammed on the brakes and screamed something less than Confucian out the window. The car stopped, and the driver screamed back at me. Five years of idiots on the road, and my honor had been impugned enough. I got out of the car ready to fight. The other driver must have had an even worse history, because he got out of his car and flipped open a switchblade. Having read *Oedipus*, I scurried back into my car and, as my tires squealed, reflected that my character was less sterling and more socially constructed than I'd hitherto imagined.

Road rage is, to use a term from literary criticism, a synecdoche for social fraying—a part of the thing that can stand for the whole thing. The more we feel encased in our steely egos, and the less our lives are orchestrated in terms of ritual propriety, the more likely we are to become both agent and victim of brutality, like Wu Zixu. Even when violence is averted by self-interest or the fear of penal law, and the traffic is flowing along nicely, we're still stressed out, still shaken in our humanity. To use Confucius's terms, we become petty people, more concerned with profit and self-interest than our own humanity and society at large.

I've dwelt on relatively small but crucial observances of ritual propriety, but *li* extends much further than "excuse me" and "thank you." In the *Analects*, we're instructed in when and how to eat rice, when and how to drink wine, when and how to talk, what to wear, how to get into a chariot, how to hold gifts when we're presenting them. Human life is an artwork, the elevation of our presence in the world into a more graceful way of being. Not only are virtuosos of ritual propriety unlikely to offend their neighbors, their lives glow with beauty.

* * * * * * * * * * *

My students in prison, when they studied Confucius, were taken by the importance of ritual and humanness and wondered why something like Confucianism didn't play a bigger role in our own educational systems. However, as much as they were charmed by the idea of getting rid of law and punishment, they were skeptical of the workability of Confucianism on this point. Can we manage without penal law? Is ritual propriety up to the task of maintaining order in society? What are we supposed to do, these serious criminals wondered, when people commit serious crimes? At least some of them shared the skepticism of Han Feizi, who mocks the Confucian ideal by saying that if order depends on a virtuous leader to inspire ritual propriety throughout the kingdom, then we're going to be waiting a mighty long time for peace and stability.

What is crime? A standard answer is that it's a violation of a law. What is justice? The corresponding answer is that we should figure out who's guilty and give the convict what he or she deserves and thereby restore balance to the legal system. But a new movement in the criminal justice system, called "restorative justice," gives very different answers to these questions. Though I don't know of any direct influence, restorative justice suggests that the Confucian ideal of allowing ritual and humanity to maintain order isn't so farfetched, even in contemporary America. So, after our study of the *Analects*, the guys and I did a brief interlude on restorative justice to see just how far the Master is right about trying to empty the court of cases altogether.

When you think about it, it's weird that the two parties generally overlooked by all the hoopla of our penal system are the victim and the offender. According to those in the restorative justice movement, crime is a harm to people, relationships, and communities. What needs restoration isn't the law but human connection. Criminals need to be reintegrated into respectful social relationships, and victims need to have their wounds healed. The first task of justice involves figuring out who's been hurt by whom, what the victim's needs are, what the causes of the crime are, and who has a stake in the situation. The next job is to involve the major stakeholders, particularly the offender and the victim, in the restoration of balance to the community, in mending the broken relationships associated with the crime. Essentially, restorative justice involves a ritual (*li*) meant to restore our humanness (*ren*), sort of like when the teacher makes a kid on the playground apologize for hitting the other kid so that play can resume. Basically, the relevant parties encounter each other through honest attempts to describe reality, telling and listening to each other's emotionally frank stories. If the encounter works, the criminal party apologizes, makes amends for the harm, and even engages in generosity that extends beyond restitution.

I've learned a lot about restorative justice from Jerry Partridge, a longtime prosecuting attorney in Washington County, Iowa, where I grew up. As a teenager in the 1960s, Jerry was arrested for armed robbery. A judge gave him a choice of going to prison or shipping off to Vietnam. He joined the navy, got his act together, went to law school after the war, and became a county attorney. When he found that most of the temporary foster care in his area was provided by Mennonites, he decided it was his duty to see what they were all about and, after an intense foot-washing session, ended up converting. His new faith led him to an article on victim-offender reconciliation, a technique he tried out of desperation and found to work miraculously well. His version of restorative justice is straightforward: get the victim and offender in a room together, have them commit to being honest, and let the magic happen.

One of Jerry's favorite stories of restorative justice, practically a parable of its beauty, starts with a guy named A.J. breaking into a house under the PCP-fueled illusion that it was his. The actual owners were extremely disturbed, and A.J. was too, each seeing the other as the intruding menace. A.J. began screaming over and over, "I'm gonna kill you!" The police finally arrived and, in the nick of time, stopped the drug-crazed A.J. from fulfilling his vow. As the county prosecutor, Jerry had the guy dead to rights on two counts of attempted murder, each carrying twenty-five years of prison with it.

In the wake of the crime the victims found themselves unable to feel safe. Their traumatization spread even to their poodles, who'd bark like crazy whenever a car drove by. When they told Jerry that they were thinking of moving to another state in hopes of finding normalcy, he replied, "They still have cars and drugs in Indiana. Believe it or not, I think your best bet is to confront the guy who did this to you." The wife, though not the husband, eventually agreed, as did A.J.

Jerry asked them, as they sat awkwardly close in a circle, simply to be as honest as possible. So the wife stood up and began to berate A.J., detailing the multiple ways her and her husband's lives had been devastated. Her tirade concluded, "This is the worst thing that's ever happened to me in my life." After a pause, she added, "In some ways, it's also been the best thing, because I've found God." Then A.J. arose and launched into how his life had also been devastated. He was looking at fifty years in prison, which meant no more wife, no more job, tenuous connections with his own children, and dreary routine in exchange for liberty. He added that, after having heard what she had to say, he lamented most of all that he'd ruined their lives. "This is the worst thing that's ever happened to me too," he sighed and then confessed, like his victim, that it was also the best, because he too had found God. Both parties felt the primordial road rage of humanity evaporate and wept cathartically.

When A.J. came up for trial, he freely admitted his guilt. At the sentencing several weeks later, he asked the judge to throw the book at him, explaining that he was prepared for whatever he deserved. Though the husband testified that A.J. should be given the maximum sentence, the prosecutor, at the behest of the wife, asked for merciful justice. The judge was flummoxed. What are you supposed to do when the defense asks for justice and the prosecution for mercy? He retreated into his chambers. An hour ticked by. Finally, he emerged and issued his ruling: "I sentence you to fifty years in prison. But I will suspend the sentence, if for five years you can abide by this list of conditions." He produced an extensive list of requirements, right down to never touching booze and always showing up to work on time. "I don't think you'll be able to meet all these requirements, and if your parole officer finds that you fail to meet even one, you're going to prison for fifty years. But you'll be a free man if you can live squeaky clean for five years." And that's what A.J. did.

When I asked Jerry the limits of what restorative justice can accomplish, he said that, except in the rare case of sociopaths, the sky's the limit, at least as a starting point in criminal cases. Even if progressives could enact all the best social policies, and conservatives could uphold a healthy culture of morality and personal responsibility, it's still inevitable that crimes will be committed. We're not angels. But we're also not monsters—well, very few of us are. A healthy dose of honesty can go a long way toward helping criminals to get their act together and, as a wonderful bonus, easing the suffering of their victims. The truth really does set us free. I pushed him, "What about rape? Are you really willing to put a rape victim in the same room with the rapist?" He responded that restorative justice could be particularly important in rape cases, because, in his experience, many rape victims suffer from a potentially lifelong wound that only a direct confrontation with the truth can heal. This wound, he said, is kept fresh by a lie victims tell themselves: that they're somehow to blame for what happened to them. The most effective way to dispel this self-lie is for the rapist to take full responsibility for his actions to the victim's face. Though he admitted that rape, especially in the case of child victims, presents difficulties for restorative justice, Jerry insisted that we need much more of its honest, merciful spirit in our criminal justice system.

Whether restorative justice can replace the system of laws and punishments, as Confucius dreams, is a thorny question. Perhaps we need retribution as backup, the guys reasonably argued, for those times when offenders are unwilling to take responsibility for their crimes. Perhaps we also need it as a threat. But I can't tell you how hungry those prisoners were, quite independent of the length of their sentences, for a restorative encounter with their victims. Almost to a person, they pined for reconnection with community, for a spiritual transformation that wasn't bound by the solitude of a penitentiary, for a chance to make amends with those who'd suffered from the worst thing they'd done and to share their own awakenings with others. As Simon exclaimed, "Restorative justice is so practical! I would love to be able to confront the family of the victim of my case—to cleanse my heart and soul by letting the family hear me say how sorry I am for having played a role in the death of their loved one!" Restorative justice is the work of seeing others not primarily as black or white, male or female, criminal or victim, rich or poor, good or evil, but fundamentally as suffering, thinking individuals with a complex story. Buried under our systems of rules and punishments is a profound human drama that can be accessed only when we're honest with each other about the suffering we've inflicted and endured.

* * * * * * * * * * * *

Rather than emphasize equality, as we tend to do in Western civilization, Confucius happily embraces the hierarchies that characterize almost all social relationships. Like Nietzsche, he recognizes that power dynamics are a big part of human life. Unlike Nietzsche, Confucius would never counsel cruelty, even in sport. The whole point is to find ways of managing our natural power dynamics in ways that overcome unnecessary suffering and enhance all parties' well-being. There are various important Confucian relationships: ruler/minister, ruler/subject, husband/wife, elder brother/younger brother, teacher/student, friend/friend. These relationships all involve power imbalances—with the exception of friendship, a relationship of natural equality (which is why it looms so large in Western philosophy). Though friendship is certainly important to Confucius, he gives the lion's share of his attention to the other relationships of power imbalance.

Our Western sensibilities incline us to think of hierarchies as oppressive. The very idea of a ruler rankles us, as does the idea that the husband should command the wife in the family, or vice versa. Many of my students, failing to see any purpose in calling me "Dr. Samuelson" or "Professor Samuelson" or even "Mr. Samuelson," address me, "Hey Scott!" One reason that hierarchies strike us as oppressive is that we tend to see power as vested in individuals, and our sense of equality rebels at the idea of one person being intrinsically above another. But is there an individuality that exists outside our roles? For Confucius, we are who we are only by being a subject of a certain state, a child of certain parents, a parent of certain children, a friend of certain friends, and so on. Power is vested in relationships rather than individuals. Any one of us inevitably occupies various power positions in hierarchical roles. If I'm your teacher, I have power over you. If you invite me to your house for dinner, now you as host are in the position of power. It's not that I have power over you, or you over me, in any ultimate sense. We're never completely equal or unequal. Everything depends on the shifting roles of the situation.

Hierarchies, according to Confucius, are natural and far from inherently oppressive. (Listen up, students!) Though he has no concept of freedom, Confucius also has no concept of slavery. To help make sense of his positive vision of hierarchy, it might be helpful to consider one relationship where Westerners still generally see things in Confucian terms: the parent-child relationship. Though even here there's some traction to the idea that parents and children should be friends (that is, should be equals), for the most part we agree that parents have power over their children, and that children should respect and obey their parents. It's possible for parents to abuse this power, but it's not at all inevitable. In fact, the power wielded by parents is generally exercised for the benefit of children—"eat your vegetables," "look both ways before crossing the street," "do your homework." In respecting their parents, children aren't simply stroking the ego of Mom or Dad; they're furthering their own development into healthy, decent, safe human beings.

Rather than freedom and individuality, Confucius places loyalty and empathy at the foundation of his philosophy. He says that the one unifying thread to his whole vision is "nothing more than loyalty (*zhong*) tempered by sympathetic understanding (*shu*)."[10] The idea is that our social relationships, governed by ritual propriety, are best maintained with a sense of doing our utmost in our roles and an ability to put ourselves imaginatively in another's shoes so as not to abuse whatever power we wield.

Loyalty, for Confucius, means fidelity to our roles. It's not a my-country-right-or-wrong sort of loyalty. Though Confucians are generally careful about criticizing authorities (a big exception is Mencius, who gleefully lays into potentates), loyalty sometimes requires us to remonstrate with superiors. Consider the case of Hai Rui, a Confucian in the Ming dynasty, who had to figure out what to do about the abusive Jiajing Emperor. The Confucian's impeccable loyalty led him to issue stern criticisms of the emperor—and to bring his coffin along with him. Both the coffin and the criticism show what loyalty really means.

When asked if there's a single principle that can always be employed, Confucius says, "There is empathy [*shu*]: do not impose on others what you yourself do not want."[11] Empathy—or "sympathetic understanding"—is a virtue more likely to be developed by those who have suffered, but it's a virtue, according to Confucius, that really should be cultivated by the powerful. The fundamental principle of Confucianism is rooted in our shared experience of suffering. We find the vulnerable, hurting part of ourselves and use it as a sympathetic guide to how to treat others and manage the imbalances built into our nature. When we're in a position of power over others, whether as parents, teachers, or especially politicians, it's crucial for us to put ourselves in the place of our subordinates; otherwise our power can blind us to their humanity. If subordinates should be reluctant to criticize leaders, leaders should be reluctant to impose on subordinates.

Though there isn't any explicit emphasis on the concept of individuality in the *Analects*, there's a distinct feeling for uniqueness in Confucius. We have no selves outside our roles as parent, child, teacher, student, sibling, spouse, friend, and so on, but part of the point of our cultivation of these roles is for a distinctive style to emerge. It's like playing Schubert. At first you try to play the notes correctly—loyally. Then you try to play those notes with feeling—with empathy. Finally, mastery involves playing those notes with a unique touch—like Sviatoslav Richter playing Piano Sonata no. 21 in B Flat. As a performer he emerges through Schubert, not despite him. As humans, we emerge through the loyal and empathetic performance of our roles, not despite them.

* * * * * * * * * * * *

Confucius has the belief that authoritative conduct tends to humanize whoever is touched by it. Order naturally spreads outward. As he puts it, "The excellence of the exemplary person is the wind, while that of the petty person is the grass. As the wind blows, the grass is sure to bend."[12] We intuitively recognize and bow to genuine expressions of our humanity, just as the grass bows to the wind. This is particularly true, according to Confucius, when exemplary people hold power. Virtuous bosses, teachers, parents, county attorneys, and political leaders don't have to micromanage us: we naturally want to live up to their example.

In fact, Confucius believes that real leadership is mostly about setting a good example. At one point he says that government is about providing military protection, making sure everyone gets enough to eat, and setting a good example so that the people trust their leaders. He then says that if one of these must be sacrificed, it should be the military. If yet another must be sacrificed, it should be the food: "Death has been with us from ancient times, but if the common people do not have confidence in their leaders, community will not endure."[13] If our leaders set a good example and have our trust, we can bear even the fundamental suffering of hunger and death!

Clearly, it's not enough just to encourage people to be kind and polite. The cultivation of our humanness involves a strong commitment to education in the arts and humanities. We should study poetry, because it makes articulate "the tones given off by the heart," to use Ezra Pound's resonant phrase.[14] We should study history, because it makes us broad-minded and sharpens our judgment. We should study art and music, because they cheer us and give us a sense of grace. We should study rituals, because they make us respectful and humble. We should study philosophy, because it makes us thoughtful and gentle. Any of these subjects presents certain dangers: poetry can make us indulgent; history can make us despair about progress; art and music can make us dissolute; rituals can make us too haughty; philosophy can make us cold and remote. But these dangers can be averted if our study is directed by the best examples of the arts and humanities and motivated by the intrinsic good in them. Notice that the humane arts Confucius asks us to study—poetry, music, history, ritual, philosophy—all confront human suffering. They don't necessarily fix it, though we can learn important lessons from these subjects about how to overcome our worst tendencies. But the arts and humanities do help us to relate to suffering with dignity and understanding.

They're what Kenneth Burke calls "equipment for living," the very soul of restorative justice.[15]

* * * * * * * * * * *

It was both sad and fortuitous. As I was writing this essay, Caitlinn came into my office and burst into tears. Caitlinn is an endangered species: a real reader. Based on her wide-ranging comments, I suspect that she reads all the assigned books at the beginning of the semester and then, as the semester unfolds, rereads them with the rest of her classmates. If you recommend three books to her on Friday, she returns on Monday wanting to talk about each of them. Knowing my fondness for Daoism, especially Zhuangzi, she stood in my office, tears bubbling up in her eyes, and said, "I've been reading and rereading what Zhuangzi says about death, and it isn't working." Before continuing, she wiped at the tears now streaming down her cheeks. "My aunt just died. I loved her so much."

I knew just the passage to which Caitlinn was referring. Huizi comes to see Zhuangzi expecting to find his friend in mourning for his just-deceased wife. Zhuangzi is playing drums and singing jubilantly. The horrified Huizi says, "You lived with this person, raised children, and grew old together. Not to cry when she died would be bad enough. But to beat on a tub singing! Isn't that too much?" Zhuangzi replies:

> No. When she first died, don't you think I was like everyone else? But then I considered her beginning, before she was alive. Not only before she had life, but before she had form. Not only before she had form, but before she had *qi* [energy]. In all the mixed-up bustle and confusion, something changed and there was *qi*. The *qi* changed and there was form. The form changed and she had life. Today there was another change and she died. It's just like the round of the four seasons: spring, summer, fall, and winter. She was resting quietly, perfectly at home, and I followed her crying "Wah-hah!" It seemed like I hadn't comprehended fate. So I stopped.[16]

Everything Zhuangzi says makes logical sense. Epictetus would nod in approval at every word. Having achieved harmony with the cosmic order, he celebrates his wife's miraculous existence, from before her unlikely origin through the many springs and autumns of her life to the absolute winter of her dissolution. Why couldn't Caitlinn find a similar delight in the seasons of her beloved aunt's life? It wasn't that Caitlinn didn't understand Zhuangzi's philosophy. Trust me, she's up to it. Maybe she just hasn't risen to the highest level of understanding that involves not only a sensitive account of a philosophy but the ability to embody it? She herself wondered as much in my office. But she also wondered if there wasn't something fundamentally missing in Zhuangzi's connection to the Way. It was at this point we began to discuss Confucius and his grief over his beloved Yan Hui.

Simon Leys, one of Confucius's contemporary translators, notes, "In the short essay he wrote on Confucius Elias Canetti made a point that had escaped most scholars. He observed that the *Analects* is a book which is important not only for what it says, but also for what it does not say."[17] I've read Canetti's essay on Confucius, and it's a gem. But I can't find where he makes this point. I guess Canetti's essay is also important for what it doesn't say![18]

In any case, Leys is dead on: the unsaid in the *Analects* is crucial. It's exactly what Caitlinn and I talked about: how Confucius doesn't say anything remotely philosophical about Yan Hui's death. He cries out in misery, but he remains theoretically silent. In fact, Confucius gives us no account of death at all. In book 11, right after Yan Hui's death and funeral, a student asks Confucius about death. The Master replies, "Not yet understanding life, how could you understand death?"[19] There are other important silences in the *Analects*—for instance, "The Master had nothing to say about strange happenings, the use of force, disorder, or the spirits." These silences are all connected to his fundamental silence about death. Ghostly happenings, force, disorder, the supernatural: Aren't these all tied to our deep-rooted difficulty with confronting death?

Up to now this chapter has been about the elimination of pointless suffering in society, about how humanness can rise above pointless suffering and even eliminate the vengefulness of punishment itself. I've tried to evoke the parts of Confucianism that make Max Weber observe, "Completely absent in Confucian ethics was any tension between nature and deity, between ethical demand and human shortcoming, consciousness of sin and need for salvation, conduct on earth and compensation in the beyond, religious duty and socio-political reality."[20] But Weber is not totally right. There is a tension in the *Analects*, and it's only when we get to this tension, those stubborn moments of pointless suffering, that our humanity is fully realized. I'd go so far as to say that the silence about pointless suffering is an essential feature of Confucius's whole philosophy.

Even when we raise our nature into a state of loyalty, empathy, and humanity, there will still be occasional transgressions; moreover, there will still be the problems of extreme natural pain and early death—Yan Hui's death, for instance. Here was a young man of towering promise, Confucius's best student, who "could go for months without departing from authoritative thoughts and feelings," someone with whom Confucius had an intuitive connection, someone who could have had an impact equal to or even greater than Confucius on the world—and he was cut down in his prime, well before he realized his full potential. Why? The text simply says that he died young, presumably of natural causes. At one point in the *Analects* Yan Hui heartbreakingly says, "While the Master is alive, how could I dare to die?"[21]

What do we do in the face of such inevitable losses and pains? If we can't prevent them, we lament them. But we often don't just lament them. We also imaginatively flee from them. We say something like "Yan Hui is in a better place now." Or, if we refuse to cover our grief with the veils of superstition, we say something like "Everything has a reason." Or, if our minds are expansive enough, we adopt a cosmic attitude, like Zhuangzi, and beat our drums in celebration. Confucius simply stands in the lamentation. At the core of all his ritual and righteousness there's a remainder of suffering that can't be overcome, at least not without leaving behind our humanness. Pointless suffering just is. Confucius refuses consolation, explanation, imaginative vision. He mourns. He sits down by us and cries with abandon. This wordless grief clears the space in which his whole compassionate philosophy appears. It's a deep act of restorative justice, a fundamental act of *ren*, in which our honest lament in the face of suffering reestablishes our humanity.

His example makes for practical advice. A common anxiety about going to a wake or a funeral, or visiting the sick and the suffering, is not knowing what to say. We're skittish about the horror of it. We want to comfort, to help, to say something profound. But what in the world is helpful in such situations? Without any useful equipment for living, we often want to turn around and go home so as not to confront the agony, the corpse, the grieving. The Confucian advice is simple. Show up and grieve. No need to say a helpful word at all. If you do say something, cry out, "Heaven has abandoned us!" or, in more contemporary terms, "It hurts like hell!" Don't run from our humanness into superstition (false even if well-intentioned) or some kind of rationale (bogus even if true). If these superstitions and rationales have any value, it's simply that they help us to show up; at best they're like the meaningless "ums" and "likes" you mumble while you wait on your mind to supply your sentence's next word. Be there for those who suffer. Be there for yourself when you suffer. Be honest about what outstrips our limited minds. Our humanity appears in full when we stand, and maybe hug, in the center of our ignorance and let the river of pointless suffering pound us.

Confucius embodies a paradox with regards to *tian*, which is often translated as "heaven," though the term is more down-to-earth than the Judeo-Christian idea of heaven. Ames and Rosemont, who leave the word untranslated, say, "*Tian* is both what our world is and how it is."[22] On the one hand, Confucius worships heaven and believes in its justice.[23] On the other hand, he suggests that heaven is amoral.[24] In the case of Yan Hui's death, he comes close to suggesting that heaven is wicked. If we think of philosophy as the logically tidy resolution of problems about what and how the world is, Confucius fails desperately as a philosopher. How can nature be simultaneously moral, amoral, and immoral? But if we think of philosophy as the enlargement of our humanness, and we believe that our humanness contains a contradiction, the Master is scrupulously philosophical.

Confucius worships and trusts heaven because nature is what sustains us in every possible way. It's the very ground on which we stand. Much of what seems like built-in pointless suffering is, in fact, the result of human failures. For example, a lot of Hurricane Katrina's devastation could be chalked up to us: our unwillingness to protect the poor, our failure at various levels of government to act compassionately and decisively, the decades-long breakdown of social trust that caused many not to heed the warnings of the authorities, our poor investments in levees, our bad city planning. The weather was just doing what it does to maintain the ecosystems of the earth. Xunzi, one of Confucianism's most articulate exponents, says that we should pay attention to human omens rather than natural omens. When people suffer from a hurricane, we shouldn't be asking heaven, "Why us?" We should be asking ourselves, "Why didn't we protect the vulnerable among us?"

Even though the practice of good government and humane society would eliminate much of the devastation of nature, the young and innocent will still occasionally die, and people will still suffer in ways that boggle the mind. Thus, Confucius regards heaven as having an amoral quality. I've been trying to argue that the stubborn fact of pointless suffering is constitutive of being human. Confucius doesn't argue the point. He simply embodies it. When pointless suffering comes, he cries out. Most fundamentally, this experience of suffering is what launches his whole philosophy: it generates the sympathetic understanding and the ritual propriety that exult human life. The very definition of humanness (*ren*) is our ability to rise above the amoral, if not immoral, energies of nature and create a society where power operates without oppression, where who we are emerges fully in the graceful performance of our relationships to one another. But this humanness can appear and grow only against a backdrop of suffering that overwhelms us. In a sense, Confucius is more Daoist than the Daoists, more Stoic than the Stoics. He doesn't imaginatively transform pointless suffering into something else; he lets it be just what it presents itself to be. Is that any help at all, Caitlinn?

Do you need a reminder of the good of being human with all its attendant suffering? Book 11 of the *Analects* culminates with a lovely flash of grace. Confucius asks his students what they would do if their worth was recognized. One after the other boasts of how they'd enact their Confucian values and bring peace and prosperity to the people. The last of the bunch takes a different tack: "At the end of spring . . . I would like, in the company of five or six young men and six or seven children, to cleanse ourselves in the Yi River, to revel in the cool breezes at the Altar for Rain, and then return home singing." Confucius sighs and responds, "I'm with you."[25] Book 11, which begins with the simplicity of ritual and climaxes with the tragedy of Yan Hui's death, concludes with Confucius splashing joyfully in nature with friends.

SEVEN

POINTLESS SUFFERING

INSPIRES ART

On Sidney Bechet and the Music of
Blues-Understanding

Do the Sorrow Songs sing true?

W. E. B. DU BOIS

Because I listen to a lot of music, much of it rooted in the blues, my kids—Irene and Billy—have grown up with Mississippi John Hurt, Slim Harpo, Dinah Washington, and Etta James ringing in their ears. When Billy was about four, at the prompting of a tune on our stereo, he asked me, "Where does the blues come from?" Seizing the opportunity to give my kids a lecture on American history, I told the story of slavery, work songs, Sorrow Songs, New Orleans, W. C. Handy, Jim Crow, Robert Johnson's pact with the Devil, Louis Armstrong's trip up the Mississippi, Saturday night, Sunday morning, the Chitlin' Circuit, and civil rights. I waxed on about how our country has given the world one of its most beautiful musical forms. A natural-born philosopher, Irene—five or six at the time—chimed in. Ignoring all my fine points, she cut to the heart of the matter: "So, if we hadn't had slavery, we wouldn't have the blues?" I tried to regain the upper hand: "Well, honey, I suppose we wouldn't. We'd have lots of other great music, but probably not a music quite like the blues." (All parents will instantly recognize my phony wise-sounding back-pedaling way of trying to answer a child's penetrating question.) But now my children's minds were hot on the logical trail. "So, is it good," innocent-eyed Billy mused, "that there was slavery so that a great music was invented?" I snapped back, "No, it's not good—of course not. But, well . . . you see, great things often come out of evil things." In other words, I shrugged and said, "That's just how it is," which is generally the unsatisfactory answer we give to our children's questions.

I've been thinking about the gist of their question for about a decade now. For the last few years I've been working on a book about it. Does profound art that arises out of suffering redeem suffering? How does suffering relate to creativity? How should we think about slavery in light of the blues? What does music have to tell us about pointless suffering? How should we raise our children in light of the death, pain, and injustice that characterize the world into which we've thrown them? I think I now have something of an answer. Though it pertains to the blues, a mostly twentieth-century phenomenon, it reaches back into the most ancient kind of human response to suffering, the wisdom of our oldest songs and sagas. It begins with a dream and a dance.

* * * * * * * * * * *

When in the early 1950s the jazz lover Joan Reid arrived in France with the hope of taking down Sidney Bechet's story, she didn't need to twist his arm. The New Orleans jazz master declared, "I want to tell you about this music before I go. A man don't have all the time in the world, and there's things he has to do before he can go happy."[1] After making numerous tape-recordings, Miss Reid gave the material to Desmond Flower, who arranged it and showed it to Bechet for his approval shortly before his death in 1959. In other words, *Treat It Gentle*, the autobiography that emerged from these sessions, is itself a kind of jazz, made in the same improvisational manner as Bechet's shimmering recordings on the clarinet and soprano saxophone.

"My grandfather—that's about the furthest I can remember back," Bechet says at the beginning of the second chapter of *Treat It Gentle*.[2] He goes on to tell of how his grandfather Omar has a dream about losing his right arm at the elbow. Omar begins to practice various activities with his left hand, because he takes the sinister nightmare— rightfully, we soon discover—as an omen of things to come.

The dance occurs in Congo Square, the open area in New Orleans where slaves were allowed to congregate and celebrate on Sundays. According to Bechet, because slaves were denied spaces of free expression, they became adept at musical communication: "[The slave] had no house, he had no telegram, no newspaper. But he had a drum, and he had a rhythm he could speak into the drum, and he could send it out through all the air to the rest of his people. . . . That chant, that memory, got mixed up in a kind of melody that had a crying inside itself."[3] In part because he has a lenient master and is permitted to practice his music whenever he wants, Omar becomes a leader of Congo Square's festivities. One Sunday afternoon, Omar sees and falls in love with a fourteen-year-old slave girl. Already the center of attention, he begins to solicit the girl's love with his drumming. When the girl's master catches on to the seduction, he sees the slave girl in a whole new light and begins to covet her for himself. The master becomes obsessed with her.

A few days later, after having sent the girl a covert message, Omar makes his way through the bayou to a ball at the mansion where she works. Late at night she slips out from under the master's obsessive gaze and meets Omar in a hidden spot. Though they've never said a word to each other, they're already "a tribe" and take full carnal and spiritual advantage of their moment of privacy. The master, having secretly tracked her there, catches them in the act. Desire-crazed, he grabs the girl and fires his rifle at Omar, hitting him in the right arm. The girl screams for Omar to flee, and he does, eventually finding shelter with some sympathetic slaves who are forced to realize his nightmare and amputate his wounded arm at the elbow.

Listen to how Sidney Bechet describes the man responsible for his grandfather's agony:

> The master was mad, in a frenzy—my grandfather gone, the girl gone, everything he'd thought about himself happening between them happening right there and him coming on it, finished before he had a chance to do anything, and all that lust he'd had for the girl, someone else turning it all bitter—not the lust, but all that pleasure from thinking about it, all that pleasure he'd had warming inside himself all these weeks. Maybe it's hard to blame him, even. People can't help feeling something when a pretty woman or someone passionate passes by right in front of them; maybe you try to tell yourself something different, but you know that's the truth. If you're a human person, it's just a natural thing to feel something that way.[4]

It's a remarkable moment, though totally in line with Bechet's way of "remembering back." We could easily imagine him portraying the master as evil. Instead Bechet says, "Maybe it's hard to blame him, even." Bechet's particular virtue is something deeper than pity or empathy. I'll call it "blues-understanding" and try to explain it momentarily.

The gunshots attract attention. The master, to justify his extreme agitation, declares that his own daughter has just been raped by Omar, even as he covers and cuddles the slave girl. "His lust had made him forget all about what colour she was," as Bechet puts it. "All he could remember was her eyes, all warm, all melody like when she was dancing—her hips, like sides to a moon, moving, swaying; her body, all about to topple over because of that love feeling she'd had when she was dancing."[5]

The master returns to his mansion and tells his wife that in his anger and confusion he identified a raped slave girl as his daughter. He orders that his lie be upheld by the family lest he lose face. The slave girl is sequestered in one room, his daughter in another, and his wife goes between the two, slowly unraveling the truth of the situation and the tangled emotions of her husband. A blues-understanding begins to dawn on the wife, whose thoughts Bechet "remembers back":

> She sat there thinking about her life, about the kind of child she had raised, about all the things she had done. . . . And underneath all that she was feeling what kind of a man her husband was. Beginning to know for certain, and wishing life could give you a time to be young all over again so you could have it different. And when the girl came to, when she stopped rambling inside herself from the shock and began to cry and to call my grandfather's name—not hateful like but in a kind of pain, crying his name like she was saying she had lost something, like everything had become unbearable . . . it was then the mistress knew she couldn't doubt any more. . . . She heard it all in a kind of tenderness for the girl. This feeling she had, that they were losing something together, it filled her with a softness, a pity. That feeling, it's got no touch with how things are in the day. It was a night kind of knowing, like when you wake up in the dark and hear your own name, your own voice—and then when you get beyond that, when you get to calling a name that's not your own, but that's got even more of what's you in it, more what's got your heart, . . . "You love him?" That was what the woman asked.[6]

Much of New Orleans starts hunting for Omar to get the substantial reward the master has placed on his head. After hiding out in the bayou for a few days, the proud Omar can't take it anymore and returns to the plantation to see his beloved. Because the white men of the house are all out looking for him, he's able to waltz in the front door. The girl and Omar embrace and fill each other in. Marie (that's the girl's name: Omar hasn't known it until now!) is forced once more to tell him to flee. Once more he does, barely in time, for a fellow slave has betrayed him to the master.

Though various opportunists have him in range and take their shots, Omar makes a narrow escape and finds shelter in a friend's shack. Since he hasn't slept much in days, he decides to take a short nap. His friend, thinking about how the posse has just been shooting at Omar, stands over the sleeping runaway and mulls over his options: "And hearing that shot before, knowing it was shooting for my grandfather, it didn't make him so much alive somehow. As if that bullet was his death. . . . Somehow, even without hitting him, that shot had made a dead man of him. The friend sat there in the dark thinking, *He's dead . . . as good as dead . . . that shot already killed him.*"[7] Following out his twisted logic, Omar's friend decides to murder him in his sleep and drags the dead body back to the mansion for the reward.

When the master's wife sees the corpse, she can bear it no longer. Finally her "night way of knowing" demands to be brought into the light: she makes her husband unburden the truth. The black community, raging and grieving, demands a proper burial for Omar. In a moment of contrition, the master says that he has to be the one to bury the slave. The friend receives no reward. The master and his wife invite Marie, now pregnant with Omar's child, to live with them in their house, almost like their own daughter. When she gives birth, she has no surname to give the baby, so they ask her to give the child their own: Bechet.

＊ ＊ ＊ ＊ ＊ ＊ ＊ ＊ ＊ ＊ ＊

One of the founders of jazz, particularly but not exclusively the type we think of as Dixieland, Sidney Bechet was born in 1897 to a New Orleans Creole family with the legacy of slavery and the name of a master. At the age of six, without formal lessons, he began playing a clarinet to the marching band going by outside his house. The crowd, thrilled by his inventive accompaniment, called him out and was shocked by his tender years. Soon he was improvising in the groundbreaking early ensembles of jazz—with Freddie Keppard, Bunk Johnson, King Oliver. As a teenage big shot, Bechet even threw a few coins to the street-performing, slightly-younger Louis Armstrong. He blazed what would become a common path for jazz musicians, going from New Orleans to Chicago, then New York, and eventually Europe in search of a musical home.

Sidney Bechet's playing, with its melodic genius and unique tremolo, was a favorite of artists like Duke Ellington and John Coltrane, both of whom composed songs in his honor. The British poet and jazz critic Philip Larkin compares Bechet's broad vibrato to the city lights of New Orleans reflected on rippling water. Larkin also says, "On me your voice falls as they say love should/ Like an enormous yes."[8] Bechet's musicianship inspires these rhapsodies in part because of how personal it is. "I'm going to give you one note today," Sidney Bechet once told a student. "See how many ways you can play that note—growl it, smear it, flat it, sharp it, do anything you want to it. That's how you express your feelings in this music. It's like talking."[9] He insisted on treating his music gentle, though he could be fierce when he set down his instrument. He once got in a fight with a fellow musician over the subject of chord changes, challenged him to a duel in the afternoon traffic of Paris, and ended up shooting by accident a passing mademoiselle.

In one episode of *Treat It Gentle* Bechet runs into a Mexican in New Orleans. Despite the language barrier, they hit it off, because "he'd got the kind of laugh about him you can't help wanting to see happen."[10] The Mexican has no money or home, so, after some deep drinking, they try to sneak into Bechet's brother's house. A policeman mistakenly believes they're trying to break in and arrests them both. At the jail, the police savagely attack the Mexican, beating him just this side of death. Bechet later finds out that one of the policemen once had some trouble in a border town and now insists on brutalizing any Latino he finds. But Bechet doesn't know this at the time and fears he's next.

They take the jazz master to a cell with other prisoners in it. Since he has his clarinet with him, they all start in on some blues. One of the inmates sings, "Got a life full of so much punishment, got me a feeling. Come down, Jesus./ Oh, why don't they put God on this earth where you can find him easier?" Though Bechet is already a virtuoso, he be-gins to understand his music more deeply: "Oh my God, that was a blues. The way they sang it there, it was something you would send down to earth if it had been given to you to be God. What you'd send to your son in trouble if he was on earth and you was in Heaven."[11]

Among musicians the blues refers first and foremost to a form: a generally twelve-bar structure with a chord pattern based on the I-IV-V chords of a key, though musicians often add or subtract bars from the twelve-bar structure at will, and jazz musicians sometimes so thoroughly reenvision the structure that the blues progression is sketched with any number of bars. A significant feature of the blues is "blue notes," which come from flatting or bending the third or the seventh interval of the scale, sometimes even the fifth or the sixth. In general, blue notes fall in between the cracks of the piano keys. These semitones and quartertones ring with a wide variety of mixed emo-tions. Blue notes keep the scale honest, so to speak. They remind us of the notes suppressed for its orderliness.

More fundamentally, the blues form is the vehicle for a certain powerful spirit, which also goes by the name of the blues. The blues in this sense refers to an emotional state of low spirits, the "blue devils," a close-to-suicidal kind of hurt ("I'm going to lay my head on some lone-some railroad line/ And let the two-nineteen pacify my mind"), which musical art transfigures into a celebration and often a revelation.

The music of the blues requires distance from the experience of the blues. We need a Congo Square, a juke joint, a guitar and a street corner, a living room with a stereo, a pair of Beats, or even a jail cell of congenial souls, where it's possible to regroup from the blue devils' as-sault. The blues isn't a way of immediately coping with suffering. It's a way of integrating painful experience into the rest of our psyches. It's a way of going on—and not just going on, but going on whole or almost-whole. The blues represents the basic triumph of meaning over chaos.

What's magical about the blues is that, for all its structure-breaking and musical impudence, it's beautiful. It's not some discordant twelve-tone protest. Though in life the blues is associated with low spirits, in art it's strangely pleasant, often downright celebratory. One of the insistent themes of Albert Murray's classic *Stomping the Blues* is that the blues is life-affirming:

> But as preoccupied with human vulnerability as so many of its memorable lyrics have always been, and as suggestive of pain as some of its instrumentation sometimes seems to be, blues music can hardly be said to be synonymous with lamentation and commiseration. Not when the atmosphere of earthiness and the disposition to positive action it engenders are considered. And besides, sometimes the lyrics mock and signify even as they pretend to weep, and as all the finger snapping, foot tapping, and hip cocking indicate, the instrumentation may be far less concerned with agony than with ecstasy.[12]

The buoyancy of the blues, in my view, is that it musically reconciles a great deal of humanity, good and bad. It's eloquent of the deep conflicts in us. We enjoy expert expressions of the blues, because it's satisfying to put into play both halves of who we are, victim and victimizer, seeker of justice and doer of injustice, faller-down and getter-up, fixer and facer of suffering. The complex balancing act of the blues can tilt toward agony or ecstasy, sympathy or accusation, carnality or spirituality, comedy or tragedy, hope or despair, but it strives to maintain the essential truths of both sides of these fundamental dualities and so makes us all free and equal. At its worst it puffs up our self-pity, reinforces our pathologies, protests that it can't get no satisfaction, and distorts the truth. At its best the blues is humanity-expanding, a means of asserting our basic nature, screwed up perhaps, but rich in meaning. What I'm calling "blues-understanding" registers injustice and yet extends real sympathy, not understanding all and thus forgiving all, but in the charitable way that regards everybody as in it together, however bad we can be to each other.

"Blues-understanding" is very close to what we normally call "compassion." The contemporary French thinker André Comte-Sponville says, "To have compassion is to commune in suffering, and this incalculably vast community imposes on us, or rather proposes to us, its own law, which is gentleness: 'Do your good with the least possible harm to others.'"[13] This is very close to blues-understanding. Comte-Sponville's principle of compassion is basically "treat it gentle." But there's something rowdier and lovelier about blues-understanding: it recognizes that the power to inflict suffering isn't separate from the self. Thus, it's less a question of minimizing harm than a question of maximizing dignity. In fact, sometimes harm can't or even shouldn't be avoided, but the dignity of our humanness should always be maintained and celebrated.

The blues can be profoundly unifying, for it delves under religion and philosophy into what generates them. In *The Souls of Black Folks* W. E. B. Du Bois illustrates the power of what he calls the "Sorrow Songs" with a story of a soldier working for the Freedmen's Bureau, the federal agency designed to help ex-slaves during Reconstruction: "When, struck with a sudden poverty, the United States refused to fulfil its promises of land to the freedmen, a brigadier-general went down to the Sea Islands to carry the news. An old woman on the outskirts of the throng began singing this song ["Nobody Knows the Trouble I've Seen"]; all the mass joined with her, swaying. And the soldier wept."[14] The unfilled promise of land was, by extension, an unfulfilled expectation of food, home, and the other equipment of dignity. The soldier's weeping, therefore, was hardly compensatory. But it was a start. The Sorrow Song constructed a common space in which weeping might lead to awakening.

In her essay "The *Iliad*, or the Poem of Force," the twentieth-century mystic and philosopher Simone Weil provides a philosophical expression of blues-understanding, though she doesn't call it that. The great mystery of human existence, according to Weil, isn't that people abuse their freedom or that the physical body suffers from disease and death. The great enigma is what she calls "affliction" (*le malheur*), the fact that victims of suffering can be sullied by their suffering, that those who have been abused feel self-contempt and even guilt. "The man who does not wear the armor of the lie," she says, "cannot experience force without being touched by it to the very soul. Grace can prevent this touch from corrupting him, but it cannot spare him the wound."[15] Suffering doesn't just hurt; it has the potential to disfigure who we are. This disfiguration is precisely the chaos opposed by the blues. The usual formulation of the problem of evil— why does God allow pain, injustice, and death?—doesn't bother Weil. What she finds shocking is that "God should have given affliction the power to seize the very soul of the innocent and to possess them as sovereign master."[16] Slavery is her prime example of a social institution dedicated to afflicting others.

Weil's answer to why God would send us not just pain and death but affliction speaks directly to the question of why Bechet says he would send the blues from heaven to his troubled child on earth. Think of the blues as a long-lost friend who returns and embraces you so hard it hurts. The hurt is love, the most intense kind of love. To be able to feel that affliction, that breaking down of the self, according to Weil, as the violent love of God is to be fully human. The ability to express affliction with grace is, according to Weil, part of the "Greek genius," first seen in Homer, continuing through Aeschylus and Sophocles, and culminating in the Gospels, though more or less of it persists in Villon, Shakespeare, Cervantes, and Molière. She ends her essay on a note of hope: "Perhaps [the peoples of Europe] will yet rediscover the epic genius, when they learn that there is no refuge from fate, learn not to admire force, not to hate the enemy, nor to scorn the unfortunate."[17] It turns out that the artists of our epoch most intimate with the tragic muse are a people not of Europe but of America.

* * * * * * * * * * *

In 1944 Sidney Bechet returned to New Orleans to visit his brother Leonard, a dentist, who fitted him with some dentures. After a stint in Springfield, Illinois, Bechet then went to New York to record with the fledgling record company Blue Note. He'd already recorded Blue Note's first big hit, his version of "Summertime," backed by boogie-woogie pianist Meade Lux Lewis and Big Sid Catlett, among others. Now, with Sidney de Paris on trumpet, Vic Dickenson on trombone, Art Hodes on piano, Pops Foster on bass, and Manzie Johnson on drums, Sidney Bechet picked up his clarinet and gave his new dentures a workout on what is generally regarded as his magnum opus, "Blue Horizon."

"Blue Horizon" is a perfectly negotiated series of blues choruses, which begins with a statement of the noble melody and then ventures through five fugal variations on it. Maybe "fugal" is the wrong word; the subsequent choruses are *centripetal* variations, because rather than inventively flee from the melody, they inventively bore deeper into it, bringing us closer and closer to a hard truth. I don't know for sure what motivated the song's title, but I imagine Bechet was thinking about a musical landscape-painting of six mountains, a majestic blues horizon; for each chorus originates in the lower registers, rises jaggedly up to various peaks, and then scoops back into a valley.

It's common for a blues solo to lather itself up into increasingly powerful emotions. "Blue Horizon" is a more nuanced drama. After Bechet's statement of the melody, he gives us three choruses of increasing attack, then pulls back in the next chorus, as a hint of doubt momentarily restrains his propulsion, and then in the last chorus we have a final assault, which ends not in grand triumph but pious acceptance—on its knee, as it were. Perhaps rather than a musical mountain-scape we should think of "Blue Horizon" as the cardiogram of a hero's journey to something almost unbearable.

What's the dragon at the center of Bechet's musical odyssey? It's tempting to say that it's slavery, affliction in America, Omar's biography. Bechet himself lends some credence to that idea: "All the music I play is from what was finding itself in my grandfather's time. It was like water moving around a stone, all silent, waiting for the stone to wear away."[18] But the story of "Blue Horizon" taps into an even more universal story. In the *Rhetoric* Aristotle outlines the main causes of tragic compassion: death, injustice, injury, sickness, old age, extreme hunger, loneliness, separation from loved ones, deformity, the inability to enjoy good things, getting bad things when you expect good. The beauty of great music is that it's like a math equation into which you can insert any of those tragic variables, and it always adds up to joyousness.

The story of the blues isn't the one we normally associate with progress, especially political progress, even though I hope it's compatible with progress. It's not, in the end, the story of conquering the problem. It's the story of confronting suffering, living in relation to it, doing battle against it, and ultimately coming to terms with it. The feeling "Blue Horizon" leaves us with is the peace that passeth understanding. The point to draw is not that injustice must be tolerated. The point is that political and private life will always be enacted by "human persons," souls embroiled in the excesses of love and jealousy. Our heroism involves doing battle with injustice while maintaining piety toward the jagged human condition. What Martha Nussbaum says of ancient Athenian tragedy applies to the best of the blues:

> [It] produced a critical ferment in which people ask themselves how much of the suffering they see is indeed the result of things that cannot be changed, and how much the result of bad human conduct. Tragedy does convey the limits of human ambition, but not in a way that leads to paralysis of the will, and not in a way that silences difficult questions about blame, responsibility, and the possibility of change.[19]

It's understandable, though not justifiable, for those inflicting the blues to tell stories that dehumanize their victims. It's understandable, and somewhat justifiable, for those suffering from the blues to lament their condition and angrily lash out at the enemy. In "Blue Horizon," as in all great tragedies, we transcend the categories of victim and enemy and perceive the world around us from a humanizing skyline. We don't give up on justice, but we grapple with the blue horizon against which justice must be pursued.

When we consider the highest examples of tragedy, we find something deeper than self-pity, discontentment, macho aggression, or mockery; we find a uniquely dignified way of relating to suffering, one that confronts our own pathology and pain and extends sympathy toward others, toward even the enemy. Following Simone Weil's lead, we can partially capture this spirit in a Pentalogue of Blues-Understanding:

Thou shalt not admire force.
Thou shalt not hate thy enemy.
Thou shalt not scorn the unfortunate.
Thou shalt face thy suffering with style.
There is no refuge from the human condition.

The ennobling spirit of tragedy, of the blues, recognizes violence and suffering in oneself and others in a way that doesn't dehumanize either the abuser or the abused; it embodies the paradox of accepting and combatting pointless suffering in a way that is ultimately joyful, even as it registers our lamentation at injustice, misery, and death. At the outset of *Treat It Gentle*, Bechet declares, "Oh, I can be mean—I know that. But not to the music." Throughout his autobiography he's at pains to emphasize how his experiences of force and his personal and historical memories of suffering and inflicting suffering are at the heart of his jazz. "That man there in the grocery store, the Mexican, the jail, they're all in the music," he says in his concluding remarks:

Whatever kind of thing it was, whenever it happened, the music put it together. . . . What it is that takes you out of being just a kid and thinking it's all adventure, and you find there's a lesson underneath all that adventure—that lesson, it's the music. You come into life alone and you go out of it alone, and you're going to be alone a lot of time when you're on this earth—and what tells it all, it's the music. You tell it to the music and the music tells it to you. And then you know about it. You know what it was happened to you.[20]

* * * * * * * * * * *

Irene and Billy, you asked me a deep, hard question several years ago, "How should we think about slavery and white supremacy in light of the fact that it has helped to give birth to the musical tradition of the blues?" And, by extension, "How should we think about pointless suffering in light of the fact that it sometimes inspires our greatest art?" And, by further extension, "How should our own art of living relate to pain, injustice, and death?" I apologize that it's taken me almost a decade to give you something approaching a serious answer.

Remember that scene in Homer where Odysseus washes up on an island and is taken to its king, who, following the ancient protocols of how to treat a guest, feeds and entertains Odysseus before he asks him his name? The blind bard Demodocus starts in on his recent crowd-pleaser, the song of the Trojan War. But hearing about Greek death after Greek death hits too close to home for Odysseus. He can't help but weep. The king stops Demodocus and rebukes his guest. Doesn't he understand that "the gods . . . sent [humans] their misfortunes in order that future generations might have something to sing about"?[21] The king doesn't yet know that his unknown visitor is Odysseus, one of the tragic protagonists of the tale.

It's striking, maybe even disconcerting, how often theologians and philosophers have answered your question by saying that we suffer for the sake of a beautiful song. St. Augustine writes that God "would never have created any men, much less angels, whose future wickedness He foreknew, unless He had equally known to what uses He could put them on behalf of the good, thereby adorning the course of the ages like a most beautiful poem set off with antitheses."[22] Could we possibly talk about the affliction of slavery as merely an "antithesis" that adds zest to the harmonious poem of our country's history? One of my heroes, the Polish philosopher Leszek Kołakowski, ridicules such an idea by comparing it to the entertainment favored by the Sicilian tyrant Phalaris, who had a method of roasting his enemies alive inside a big copper bull in such a way that their screams of pain were transformed by special nostril-flutes into charming melodies.[23]

If our idea of singing is simply taking a break from real life and making some pretty noise, then the idea that we suffer so we can sing is guilty of a fiddling-while-Rome-burns sort of heartlessness. But you and I know that making music is more than hitting a few nice notes. Real music is the sound we make when we're touched to the core by the universe. It's the sound—to mention some of our favorites—of Louis Armstrong, Johnny Cash, Mahalia Jackson, Brittany Howard. It's the sound of being human. Remember our friend Michael's brother Steve? At his funeral his wife, Diane, who suffers as he did from mental illness, began singing. In a warbling otherworldly voice, to the extremely slowed-down tune of the U.S. Air Force song (the one that begins, "Off we go into the wild blue yonder"—recall that Steve had attended the Air Force Academy), she improvised lyrics to her husband in heaven—the kind of made-up, half-silly, heartfelt, intimate lyrics that we privately sing to our lovers or our children. The gist of her song was that she missed him, that she loved him, that she'd be with him soon. Not long before, the congregation had sung a carefully composed hymn from the Methodist hymnal, just as directed. Whose song had the real singing in it?

Is reality better for the sound of singing like Diane's? Is the universe more satisfying with or without Sidney Bechet's "Blue Horizon" or Billie Holiday's song about lynching? If our answer is that the universe is better for our blues, better off with us and all our accompanying contradictions, we should remember that we and our music are impossible without the horror of pointless suffering. The music doesn't for one moment make up for all the pain and injustice! It wouldn't be the blues but for its mournfulness about the suffering and its desire to be delivered. We must live with the wish to be freed from suffering *and* the beauty of what it means to sing out of it. Blues music can be incredibly joyful, but it's permeated by lament. Think of the story from the *Odyssey*. What's beautiful about it, as well as noble, is that it contains not just the king's theodicy but the hero's weeping. It contains the beautiful song and the reality that the pain behind the beautiful song is too much to bear in its raw state. As Sidney Bechet puts it, the music is like rushing water, and suffering is the hard stone being ground imperceptibly at the center of the stream.

The blues in no way justifies slavery, but perhaps the blues does justify humanity, the same humanity that, among many other things, inflicts and suffers terrible injustices like slavery. That's what I find so powerful, and genuinely moral, about the kind of blues-understanding in Sidney Bechet's stories and music. He sees injustice very clearly, and he knows that it's woven into all of us. But he ultimately doesn't see Omar's master as simply a slaveholder, much less Omar as simply a slave. He sees them as "human persons," infinite grab bags of good and evil—sometimes so mixed up that you can't tell one from the other. His vision doesn't at all excuse slavery; on the contrary, he condemns it to the core. But his vision makes it understandable to the mind and heart of humanity. Here I think about an important point that Ralph Ellison makes in his review of LeRoi Jones's (Amiri Baraka's) *Blues People*:

> "A slave," writes Jones, "cannot be a man." But what, one might ask, of those moments when he feels his metabolism aroused by the rising of the sap in spring? What of his identity among other slaves? With his wife? And isn't it closer to the truth that far from considering themselves only in terms of that abstraction, "a slave," the enslaved really thought of themselves as *men* who had been unjustly enslaved? And isn't the true answer to Mr. Jones's question, "What are you going to be when you grow up," not, as he gives it, "a slave" but most probably a coachman, a teamster, a cook, the best damned steward on the Mississippi, the best jockey in Kentucky, a butler, a farmer, a stud, or, hopefully, a free man! Slavery was a most vicious system, but it was *not* (and this is important for Negroes to remember for the sake of their own sense of who and what their grandparents were) a state of absolute repression.[24]

It's hard to recognize our continuity with the past, a heritage always marked but never totally defined by injustice. It's hard to "remember back."

When it comes to our country and its relationship to evil, I have two worries about our attempts to tell our story, to "remember back."

The first worry is that our country will remain unable to face up to what we've done and what we do. Too many people whose ancestors weren't slaves suffer from a moral amnesia, inculcated by schools and popular culture, that passes itself off as history. The deluded memory goes something like this: "Once upon a time white Americans had slaves, and it was really bad. (Of course, my ancestors never owned slaves, or, if they did, they treated their slaves well.) Then the U.S. fought the Civil War and abolished slavery. There were still a few minor problems, which were solved by Martin Luther King Jr. in the 1960s. Now, but for the occasional racist jerk, we live in a fair society. Just look at who was the forty-fourth president!" This account, which contains just enough truth to make it believable, leaves out the horror of using people as mere tools in order to build a democratic society, the centuries-long systematic violence, the forcible removal of children from parents and spouses from spouses and friends from friends, the endless sexual violence, the constant insults, the crushing of the aspirations of black citizens during Reconstruction, the lynchings, the relentless humiliations of Jim Crow, the ongoing theft of black political and economic power by subtle and not-so-subtle means, the biases built into even progressive political achievements like the New Deal and the GI Bill, the practice of "redlining," the incarceration of blacks many times more than whites guilty of the same infractions, the lingering condescension in those with "a friend who's black," the constant pressure on black Americans to be twice as good in order to get half as much, the enormous transfer of intergenerational wealth from blacks to whites, the benign-seeming puzzlement about why blacks don't do as well as whites, the seriously considered theory that blacks must naturally have lower IQs, and so on, and so on—in short, the poverty of spirit that creates poverty. White Americans often suffer, as James Baldwin warns, from needing the category "nigger" to feel whole. The inability to remember the past or face its legacy in the present dooms people to an acute form of injustice. It also makes our culture meager and unsatisfying by keeping us from ourselves. To be under the spell of the official line renders us unable to sing the blues.

My second worry concerns the inability to hear the blues as the blues. The backlash against injustice can sometimes make us forget that injustice is an inevitable part of humanity, especially when it comes to politics. The most famous instance is Communism, which was a response to horrid social and economic problems, especially in Russia. When sins are so profound as serfdom or white supremacy, there's a tendency to want to bend all parts of the human spirit to remedy them—to believe that thought and expression have to be policed in order to expunge all traces of the injustice down to the finest microaggressions, to demand that works of reason and imagination need to be subject to political tests for inclusion in a curriculum, to define people primarily as victimizers and victims rather than the admixtures that Bechet calls "human persons," to listen to Bechet or to read Baldwin because they're black rather than because they're great, or not to perform Bach or Shakespeare because they're white, to believe one's own side is beyond criticism, to interpret the blues as simply an accommodation to a past injustice and not a coming-to-terms with humanity itself.

One of the central themes of this book is that we shouldn't think of our relationship to suffering in terms of war, for it can never be eradicated, and when we do try to eradicate it, we generate whole new forms of evil. I've tried to explore different ways of relating to suffering, ones that involve a paradoxical combination of facing and fighting it. This paradox could be approached through the metaphor of the martial arts. Martial artists simultaneously fight and respect their opponents. Though our humanity is opposed to suffering, pain and death are part and parcel of us, and injustice is fundamental to our freedom and the institutions that sustain our humanity. The point should be less about winning than about learning through sparring. Martial artists fight with all their wiliness and strength but do so without rancor, bowing to their rivals at the beginning and end of their bouts. We should fight against injustice, especially the concrete instances of injustice in front of us. At the same time, we should channel our artistic instincts into accepting disease, injustice, and death. In other words, we should be forgiving, tolerant, and deep. Let's not shy away from laughing at ourselves. And when the time comes for us to bow out altogether, may we do so with respect for suffering, the teacher who is also our sparring partner.

Deeper than the metaphor of us as martial artists is that of us as blues musicians. The martial artist blends fight and respect; the blues musician blends sorrow and joy. When Sidney Bechet says, "You come into life alone and you go out of it alone, and you're going to be alone a lot of time when you're on this earth—and what tells it all, it's the music," he's trying to put words to the blues-understanding we hear in his music and in all profound music. The wisdom of the martial artist is that we should work vehemently against injustices, even as we respect the infinite interplay of justice and injustice, win and loss. But we're all defeated in the end. We need the blues, which makes a joyful noise even when we're soaked with sorrow.[25] It doesn't all add up into our categories. The closer you get to the heart of things, the more you recognize how gigantic the paradox there is. When I hear the blues, I'm glad it's a mystery rather than a cut-and-dried logical problem. When our music embodies this mystery, it's as good as it gets on this earth. Do the Sorrow Songs sing true? That's up to us.

The greatest philosophers assert that music shapes the character more fundamentally than preaching and philosophizing. Irene and Billy, you've been raised with the music of Sidney Bechet and Billie Holiday ringing in your ears. I can't tell you how happy I am that you have ears for the blues. I hope a fringe benefit is that this music has nudged you to confront life with honesty, compassion, and panache. Treat it gentle, kids.

THE WAY OF

SUFFERING HUMANLY

In the prison of his days
Teach the free man how to praise.

W. H. AUDEN

A queen dreams of a white elephant with six tusks (to use the legend's wonderful expression for having sex). She "wakes up" pregnant and in due course gives birth to a son. Warned by a prophet that the boy will abandon his royal station if he learns of old age, sickness, and death, the king and queen order the construction of a suite of palaces to shield the prince from suffering. The boy's education includes nothing more than archery, calligraphy, swimming, and luxury. As a teenager, he's married to a beautiful princess. He's also given a harem of eighty-four thousand concubines—just in case.

One day the prince demands to take a ride in his coach, which his parents make sure has its curtains tightly drawn. But he peeps out anyway and glimpses a novel sight: a wrinkled, bald, stooping animal— a parody of the lovely humanity he's exclusively known. Asking the coachman who or what the thing is, he learns for the first time about old age. On his next ride, he catches sight of a pasty, coughing creature with features otherwise like himself. Again he asks the coachman about the novelty and learns for the first time about sickness. On his third ride, he sees a stiff, colorless body and finally learns about the fate of death. Shaken by a mix of compassion and fear, he takes a fourth ride, sees a monk, and learns of religious people who forsake this world for a better life. Much to the chagrin of his parents, Prince Siddhartha Gautama renounces his royal station and becomes a monk.

Though not without its satisfactions, ascetic discipline doesn't restore him. Siddhartha comes to realize that renunciation doesn't free you from the illusions of the suffering world: think of how anorexia is still a perverse obsession with food. Even as a pious monk, he's without relief from the miseries glimpsed on the road. So Siddhartha sits under a big tree and ponders the mystery. After eighty days (to use the legend's way of saying "a really long time"), without the interruption of food or water, four noble truths dawn on him. First, life is suffused with suffering. Second, the cause of suffering is desire and ignorance. Third, there's a cure to suffering. Fourth, the cure is to follow the Middle Way, the basis for what we've come to call Buddhism.

Ancient myths have a way of being eerily intuitive of the present age. When the story of the Buddha first took shape in India, old age, sickness, and death were ubiquitous. Doesn't it seem like the real meaning of this myth—a myth about the ultimately fruitless attempt to shield humanity from suffering altogether—has been waiting patiently, century after century, for our technological epoch? Nowadays many parents do indeed try their damnedest to shelter their little princes and princesses from the elderly, the tragic, and the dead. When my kids were little, and *Finding Nemo* was popular, I met a parent who refused to let her child see the Pixar masterpiece because it dealt with loss (ironic, because the movie is in part about how our attempt to shelter children is misguided). Our scientists work furiously to extend life and root out the sources of sickness. When pills and surgeries reach their limits, we hide away the sick and the old in places euphemistically named to veil the horror of what the residents have lost. My grandmother, who suffers from Alzheimer's, resides in Legacy Gardens. The rest of us ensconce ourselves in virtual palaces, which our flat-screen TVs and smart phones magically generate around us. We have atheists trying to shout down religion in the name of technological science. We have religious types preaching of the need to withdraw from our luxurious culture. Eighty-four thousand concubines: that seems like a low number when you consider how many nubile temptresses are available to any teenage boy with internet access.

The great stories seem up-to-date because they ring down the grooves of being human. The myth of Siddhartha isn't just for our mediated, medicated world. If there's anything unique about our flight from suffering, it's that we happen to live in a time when the great debate is whether we should deny suffering through science, religion, or politics. No matter what age we're living in, we peep out the curtains of our preconceptions and glimpse the contorted bodies of those who suffer—sometimes in the mirror. We're always tempted to overindulge in the two great responses to suffering: ignoring it or dreaming of eliminating it. The Middle Way is ever a struggle to walk. The Age of Terror, such a fitting appellation for our own time, describes pretty much every other time as well.

Our temptation is to build a wall. On the one side, those of the First World who believe that they can fight wars without casualties. On the other, those of the Third World on whom the bombs fall with more or less precision. On the one side, the well-heeled with near-boundless access to health care. On the other, the destitute who lack clean water. On the one side, parents who ensure the internet is filtered on their toddlers' iPhones. On the other, parents for whom a screen, any screen, is the only affordable babysitter. John Berger, imagining the hotel in which various intellectuals drafted and signed a document about just war in support of the War on Terror, says, "What really happened in history and what is happening today beyond the walls of the hotel is unadmitted and unknown. Isolated De Luxe Tourist Ethics."[1] Inside the hotel, comfort and soullessness. Outside, misery and meaning. Inside, those for whom the idea of prison is remote. Outside, those for whom it is an all-too-distinct reality. Both sides of the wall constitute a kind of prison. We never live exclusively on one side of the divide, for we build the wall right through our hearts. We all find ourselves in the presence of the old hard gods of unexpected pain, injustice, and death. We all risk what Heidegger calls "the forgetting of Being."

Where's the Middle Way?

The chapters of this book have examined different philosophical attempts at increasing our humanity by living in light of pointless suffering. It's what inspires real music. It's what reveals our deepest humanity. It's what plugs us into the network of nature. It's what brings us to God. It sharpens the dignity of work, action, and thought. It increases our power. It stirs our moral sense and inspires political effort. Our profound reliance on technology generates the illusion that suffering can be fixed in the way an engine can be fixed. Yes, we should and will fight suffering, for there's something about us that's stubbornly opposed to it. But if that's our only relationship to suffering, something fundamental has been lost. Throughout the book I've been trying to examine how we should accept suffering even as we struggle against it. This is a paradox. If you approach it from the logical assumptions of Bentham's utilitarianism, it makes no sense. But if you approach it from the perspective of, say, blues music, it makes all the sense in the world. We must embody a mystery or else our song suffers.

* * * * * * * * * * * *

An up-and-coming neurosurgeon, Paul Kalanithi was diagnosed with severe lung cancer in his late thirties. With his little remaining time, he did two significant things: have a child with his wife, their first and only, and write *When Breath Becomes Air*, a profound memoir about his final days as a doctor and a patient. Wondering if they should have a baby in the face of his imminent demise, his wife, Lucy, bluntly asked him, "Will having a newborn distract from the time we have together? Don't you think saying goodbye to your child will make your death more painful?" He responded, "Wouldn't it be great if it did?"[2] Here I wish we could just be silent for a minute as the beauty of that question sinks in.

Except for our moments of relaxation, we should be spending our time loving, making, working, thinking, playing, praying, dreaming, pitching in, doing good—certainly never trying to suffer! However, the avoidance of suffering threatens to hollow out the value of our lives. I've met tremendous resistance among academic audiences whenever I've argued for the importance of accepting suffering, which strikes certain ears as complaisant if not downright cruel. To be blunt, this resistance—compounded though it is of lots of genuine goodheartedness—strikes me as fundamentally inhumane. There's a whole set of virtues that just don't exist without the ability to say, "People are like that sometimes" or "*C'est la vie*"—forgiveness, compassion, awe, belly laughter. All the fundamental positive human activities open us up to suffering. Insofar as we're governed by the principle of maximizing pleasure and minimizing pain, of eliminating suffering as much as possible, we dry up the sources of meaning. Work becomes a chore for getting money rather than a sphere of soul-making. Play becomes downtime from work rather than a challenging arena of self-delight. Education becomes the facilitation of information transfer or the flattering of personal identity rather than the difficult, rewarding initiation into the best of the human inheritance. Nature becomes a product to be reengineered rather than the ground of our being. Politics becomes the management of prosperity and security rather than the exercise of freedom and rights. Leadership slumps into management. Republics decline into empires. Democracies become tyrannies. We dwell in the virtual rather than the actual world. We trash the planet. Love starts to seem like one big nuisance, a gamble not worth the bother. Life becomes a deluxe despair.

In some sense, my paradoxical call to fight and accept suffering is common sense. Think of raising children. On the one hand, you want to keep them safe. On the other hand, you don't want to keep them safe at all costs: you want them to take risks, have adventures, and be challenged. While there are better and worse ways of striking the balance between keeping kids safe (preventing suffering) and giving kids freedom (accepting and even soliciting some inevitable suffering), there's no perfect theory about that balance; nor is there a philosophical or political line that will ever perfectly delineate good and bad suffering. In fact, character development requires a bit of imbalance, a bit of excessive unwilled suffering. Raising children requires judgment but also a lot of luck; there was certainly nothing morally wrong with Matt Kaufman's parents letting him pop wheelies after school.

But there's more to the great paradox than common sense. Or, to put it more accurately, if we follow the thread of common sense, we're led to an uncommon way of living, where we see nature and each other as connected, where we escape over the wall into the world of compassion and adventure, healing and praise. The question for Paul Kalanithi was not if having a daughter would make his life less painful or more pleasurable. Having a child, our fundamental act of saying yes to life, is a value that transcends by a whole other dimension the figures on the spreadsheet of pleasure and pain, no matter what that child's fate is. Because the boy who grew up to write *When Breath Becomes Air* died too soon, the memoir is technically unfinished; in this way, the book resembles the tragedy of most lives, which usually end with a careless comma rather than a confident period. But its last words, penned right before he died, are a fitting conclusion, better perhaps for being a semicolon.

> I had thought I could leave her [his daughter, eight months old at the time] a series of letters—but what would they say? I don't know what this girl will be like when she is fifteen; I don't even know if she'll take to the nickname we've given her. There is perhaps only one thing to say to this infant, who is all future, overlapping briefly with me, whose life, barring the improbable, is all but past. That message is simple: When you come to one of the many moments in life where you must give an account of yourself, provide a ledger of what you have been, and done, and meant to the world, do not, I pray, discount that you filled a dying man's days with a sated joy, a joy unknown to me in all my prior years, a joy that does not hunger for more and more but rests, satisfied. In this time, right now, that is an enormous thing.[3]

As he says earlier in the book, his daughter's birth made his death more painful and his life more joyful. "Lucy and I both felt that life wasn't about avoiding suffering."[4]

* * * * * * * * * * *

In her important history *From the War on Poverty to the War on Crime: The Making of Mass Incarceration in America*, Elizabeth Hinton writes, "Arguably the most important question facing American society today is why, in the land of the free, one in thirty-one people is under some form of penal control."[5] Her answer goes beyond, even as it contains, the widely accepted theory that the situation is generated by the overzealous War on Drugs. In response to the moral triumph of the 1964 Civil Rights Act, the American government began to fear the prospect of urban rebellion. Politicians grew worried about how the country could maintain control of blacks without Jim Crow. Though violent crime was decreasing, the fear of crime spiked. President Johnson compounded his War on Poverty with the War on Crime. Criminality was understood to be innate to poor black neighborhoods. The new idea was that police weren't just to deal with crime, as they always had, but to weed it out altogether, to deter it before it happened. The steep increase in the number of arrests started a vicious circle of making crime appear to be on the rise, which meant that the War on Crime needed to escalate, which meant that more citizens needed to be incarcerated. When we mixed in the War on Drugs (in which drugs are deemed the underlying cause of crime) and the increased ability of businesses to profit off prisons (such that more "customers" is good for business), our incarceration rates soared to the highest in the world. "And," as Hinton says, "assuming punitive programs continue in their present form, African Americans born after 1965 and lacking a high school diploma are more likely to eventually go to prison than not."[6]

Some argue that the War on Crime has worked because the crime rate has gone down. Even if we accept the highly disputed claim that the War on Crime is the cause of the downturn, and even if we adopt the utilitarian principle of calculating how many people are positively and negatively affected, it seems like a stretch to think that the price of housing roughly 25 percent of the world's prisoners in a country with less than 5 percent of the world's population is worth a slightly more secure society for those fortunate enough not to be behind bars or have a friend or family member behind bars. But I'm inclined to think that the problem runs much deeper than a cost-benefit analysis. Even if it could be shown that a sufficient majority benefits from the War on Crime, isn't it still unjust insofar as it treats thousands of people like my friend Simon unfairly? Would you want yourself or your children to spend extra time in prison for the feeling of security in others? Doesn't the Golden Rule tip us off to the fact that our penal system needs first and foremost to be humane? Isn't it a depressing failure of the moral imagination that it's generally only when the War on Crime begins to affect affluent white families that judges are inclined toward leniency, the general citizenry is awakened to the moral problem, and politicians are pressured to ease sentencing laws and explore rehabilitation as an alternative to punishment?

Without the ability to accept suffering as part of our humanity, we inflict dehumanizing kinds of injustice, like the War on Crime, by seeing any threat to our security and tranquility as monstrous. Evil must be bravely confronted. Crime needs to be punished. We need boundaries and borders. We should be extremely grateful to those who take on the fraught responsibility of defending us. Moreover, we need to be more understanding of the profound difficulties faced by law enforcement officers. But evil cannot be eradicated; there's no human society without crime. Reasonable limits should be maintained and respected throughout any system that confronts it. To apply the Golden Rule requires blues-understanding, the ability to see others as not wholly alien from ourselves. This is no easy task with lawbreakers under the best of circumstances, for it's natural to feel alienated from those who commit serious crimes against our community. But it's especially hard when our culture commonly soft-serves or sentimentalizes slavery and Jim Crow, stigmatizes those from the other side of town, and portrays people behind bars as a different beast. At least in America, a lot of this walling off, though not all of it, has to do with the absurdity of racism. But the charge of racism, regardless how accurate, has never been very useful. Racism and other forms of often-unconscious injustice, including certain forms of backlash against injustice, are animated by the conscious fear of suffering, especially the fear of crime, violence, loss, or humiliation. The bitter irony is that this fear blinds people to their own injustices and rationalizes their own forms of violence and intimidation. I like what Hafiz, the Persian poet, says: "Fear is the cheapest room in the house./ I would like to see you living/ In better conditions."[7]

As I've taught incarcerated students, it's dawned on me how much the history and practice of philosophy is bound up with prison. Philosophers, though they dream of being monarchs, generally find themselves in chains. Socrates has some of his most famous conversations under lock and key. Prior to his execution, Boethius composes the *Consolation of Philosophy* under house arrest. Giordano Bruno spends seven years locked up in the Tower of Nona before he's burned at the stake for heresy after having an iron spike driven through his tongue because the authorities feared his eloquence at the moment of death. Something about prison puts inmates in a philosophical mood, and something about philosophy tends to land its practitioners in the clink!

Philosophers often use prison as a symbol of the condition most of us find ourselves in. We carry prison inside ourselves. A few unexamined concepts wall us off from our flourishing. The symbolic prison of the mind has the power to put others inside literal prisons. Though it's a perennial duty for us to enact laws that reduce the odds of our building these dangerous mental prisons, the issue runs deeper than policy. The author of the seminal book *The New Jim Crow* and an important crusader for criminal justice reform, Michelle Alexander says:

> I don't view mass incarceration as just a problem of politics or policy,
> I view it as a profound moral and spiritual crisis as well. I think that

racial justice in this country will remain a distant dream as long as we think that it can be achieved simply through rational policy discussions. If we take a purely technocratic approach to these issues and strip them of their moral and spiritual dimensions, I think we'll just keep tinkering and tinkering and fail to realize that all of these issues really have more to do with who we are individually and collectively, and what we believe we owe one another, and how we ought to treat one another as human beings. These are philosophical questions, moral questions, theological questions, as much as they are questions about the costs and benefits of using one system of punishment or policing practice over another.[8]

These moral and spiritual dimensions have a lot to do with our relationship to suffering, which is arduous to confront, and which at some level can't be totally fathomed by the human mind. It's hard to face our history and fears. It's hard to face the injustices we individually and collectively inflict. It's easy to drown out our griefs and ignore our sins with trivial distractions. It's easy to lapse into the belief that our identity is separate from suffering, separate from evil, separate from history, separate from nature. Yet by ignoring suffering we all suffer. By waging wars on crime, terror, imperfection, sickness, and death, we lock ourselves out of "the place where in the end/ We find our happiness or not at all."[9]

* * * * * * * * * * *

The theologian John Hick, in his magisterial *Evil and the God of Love*, uses the concept of "soul-making" to describe what he thinks is the only humane way of making sense of suffering while believing in a good God. He plucks the idea from a marvelously rambling letter written in 1819 by John Keats.

I will call the world a School instituted for the purpose of teaching little children to read—I will call the human heart the horn Book used in that School—and I will call the Child able to read, the Soul made from that school and its hornbook. Do you not see how necessary a World of Pains and troubles is to school an Intelligence and make it a soul? A Place where the heart must feel and suffer in a thousand diverse ways! . . . Call the world if you Please "The vale of Soul-making."[10]

It's a parable that connects education, reading, suffering, soul-making, and life itself, and does so with the panache of how the young Keats, doomed to die the following year of tuberculosis, was making a soul by reading the textbook of his heart. We often think of education as giving us what we already want or what someone else has figured out that we'll need down the road. But for Keats we go to school to figure out what we want and even who we are. Life is a transformative reading practice.

Hick claims that we can't give a positive theodicy. There's no way to complete the sentence "The reason that people suffer so much is . . ." But we can give something of a negative theodicy. In other words, we can realize that when we try conceptually to remove the possibility of pain, death, and wrongdoing from the world, we destroy the possibility of character development, of Keats's "soul-making." This world, Hick claims on behalf of Christian theology, isn't supposed to be a paradise; it's supposed to be a testing ground. The process of creation is ongoing, and "God bears with us the pains of the creative process."[11]

But, the critic counters, isn't there more suffering, much more suffering, than is required for the cultivation of virtues? Here Hick's negative theodicy gives a somewhat tricky answer. First, there must be too much suffering, or else we wouldn't be sufficiently challenged: "It may be that the very mysteriousness of this life is an important aspect of its character as a sphere of soul-making."[12] Second, the excess of suffering, in light of God's goodness, means that there must be an idyllic world beyond this one, a Celestial City beyond our imagining, where we are so alive that suffering is no longer a problem. But Hick admits that there's no earthly way of understanding how the end justifies the means, which we know to be extremely harsh. He cites the famous conversation in Dostoyevsky's *The Brothers Karamazov* where Ivan asks Alyosha if he would be willing to make all human beings genuinely and truly happy if all he had to do was torture a baby to death, and Alyosha murmurs that he wouldn't. Hick even admits that he can understand the refusal to believe in God's goodness: "And if I had myself experienced some deep and engulfing personal tragedy, drawing me down into black despair and a horrified rejection of life, I might well share that negative response."[13]

I've tried to show in the preceding chapters that Hick's idea of suffering as soul-making isn't exclusive to the Christian tradition. Great thinkers from various backgrounds understand that suffering is integral to human growth. Not only do we need challenges and risks, we need some of them not to make sense. We're primordially opposed to suffering. There's always a gap between the world as it is and the world as we think it should be. Ivan's challenge and Alyosha's refusal will always haunt us. The most important concepts we use to confront that gap—God, nature, humanity, art—contain a fundamental paradox, the mystery that there's something beyond our reckoning. The concept of God, in our great holy books, actualizes that mystery by placing ultimate value beyond this world. The concept of nature, in thinkers like the Stoics or the Daoists, actualizes that mystery by making the harshness of reality worthy of our utmost respect. The concept of humanity, especially in a thinker like Confucius, actualizes that mystery by founding civilization on grief. The concept of art, in our best artists, actualizes that mystery by converting injustice and heartbreak into genuine beauty. Our fundamental words run the perennial risk of being hollowed out, cheapened, degraded to their worst versions. But they never totally lose their value, and they contain in their semantic DNA a memory that's capable of refreshing them indefinitely. In the American vernacular, we describe certain pieces of music as having soul. I love this way of talking. "Soul" here doesn't mean a ghostly metaphysical entity, as it does in theoretical treatises. It refers to an original, stirring, and ultimately joyful way of expressing suffering, half-earned and half-graced. This kind of soul-making characterizes the purpose of all the best human activities, especially philosophy.

I want to emphasize one last time that the idea of soul-making doesn't justify or explain all, or even most, suffering. Part of having soul involves lamentation. "There's something about the gospel blues," Sister Rosetta Tharpe says, "that's so deep the world can't stand it."[14] We philosophers like to bring up the likes of Auschwitz and Hiroshima as stumbling blocks for any attempt to justify suffering. But my former next-door neighbor Ashley is more than sufficient, as I'm sure are some of the tragedies you've witnessed or endured. As long as one poor caterpillar is being eaten alive by a baby wasp, this is not a moral world. The primary danger I've been warning against in the preceding pages is our attempt to see suffering merely through the utilitarian-colored lens that makes everything appear as a problem to be solved. But my warning, which involves the recognition of the soul-making power of suffering, doesn't at all imply that every instance of death, misery, and injustice can be adequately fathomed, let alone justified or forgiven, by the human mind. Even the Stoics, who deny the existence of evil altogether, recognize that a natural grief sometimes pours from us when our limited standpoints are challenged by the twists and turns of the universe.[15] We shall always run through the universe crying out in protest. Suffering throws some people into the arms of God. Others it drives permanently away from the divine. Either way, suffering opens us to an infinite mystery. There will always be space for God in the human imagination. To sum up our situation in twenty words or fewer, I don't think I could do better than George Herbert in his poem "Bitter-sweet":

> I will complain, yet praise;
> I will bewail, approve:
> And all my sowre-sweet dayes
> I will lament, and love.[16]

* * * * * * * * * * *

Michel de Montaigne spent August 24, 1581, from morning to night, trying to pass a kidney stone in La Villa, a picturesque town in the Dolomites. At dinnertime, after enduring pains often compared to childbirth, he finally expelled a pellet "as big and long as a pine nut, but as thick as a bean at one end, and having, to tell the truth, exactly the shape of a prick."[17] He'd been journeying through Italy in search of a cure for his kidney stones, drinking and bathing in supposedly curative waters—as well as taking in the sights, trying out new wines, perfecting his Italian, and immersing himself in curious expressions of common life. He even got around to arranging a beauty pageant of Italian ladies, judging them not simply on their prettiness but on "the carriage and grace and charm and elegance of the whole person."[18]

After he'd expelled his kidney stone in La Villa and cleaned up all the blood, Montaigne sat down at his journal and wrote:

> There would be too much weakness and cowardice on my part if, finding myself every day in a position to die in this manner, and with every hour bringing death nearer, I did not make every effort toward being able to bear death lightly as soon as it surprises me. And in the meantime it will be wise to accept joyously the good that it pleases God to send us. There is no other medicine, no other rule or science, for avoiding the ills, whatever they may be and however great, that besiege men from all sides and at every hour, than to make up our minds to suffer them humanly.[19]

The master of French prose wrote this entry in Italian, because he liked the beauty of the language and was trying to become a more fluent traveler. Even in the face of death, it makes good sense to work on your Italian!

We're lucky to live in an age that has found better ways to deal with kidney stones than a mineral-water bath. But our successes have exacerbated the temptation to see ourselves as separate from pain, death, and injustice, to imagine that our true destiny involves a reengineering of our suffering selves. Insofar as we succumb to this temptation, you and I run the risk of suffering inhumanly—in other words, demeaning ourselves and, ironically, generating new kinds of suffering. Just when they're most embattled, we find ourselves in need of the strongest forms of art, music, literature, history, science, religion, and philosophy to give us ways of looking honestly at our inherent vulnerability.

Montaigne tells us to suffer "humanly"—*umanamente*, to use the musical Tuscan adverb. What does this mean? It has something to do with being able to live with our fragilities, both our physical weaknesses and our philosophical ignorance. It means that we must oppose wrongdoing and yet accept that wrongdoing is an intrinsic part of us. It means that we face up to the barbarism and monstrosity in ourselves and so refuse to dismiss others as barbarous and monstrous. It means that we strive to ease suffering and yet also somehow accept that suffering is so dissolved into certain goods of life that it can't and shouldn't be totally separated out. As Montaigne puts it, "Our being is cemented with sickly qualities. . . . Whoever should remove the seeds of these qualities from man would destroy the fundamental conditions of our life."[20] Try the curative waters. Just remember there's no final fix. Evil is fundamentally a mystery rather than a problem. Montaigne tries not to add to his physical pains the mental misery of regarding them as a conspiracy against him or a flaw of life itself, though he also refuses to mock up a phony myth or theory about how they're deserved. Suffering has something to do with the carriage and grace and charm and elegance of the whole person, precisely because it never adds up.

A SAD POSTLUDE

I wish I could show you when you are lonely or in darkness
the astonishing light of your own being.

HAFIZ

I thought I was doing a good thing. Though for several months I'd taken a hiatus from volunteering at the prison to have time to finish this book, I'd kept in touch with Simon through correspondence. He'd been so generous with his time and wisdom that I decided at Christmas to give him some money. He could purchase yummy food, continue to pay for his correspondence, or even rent a TV for a few months. I vowed not to brag about the gift. I wouldn't tell anybody but Simon, lest my morality be for show over substance. Though it wasn't a huge sum of money, I puffed up at the thought of my good character.

When I checked in with Simon after the holidays, he told me that my gift had been frozen, as the prison authorities suspected him of acquiring the money illicitly. No problem: I'd assure the authorities that it was a gift freely given. Suddenly I found myself in hot water for violating a policy that prohibits volunteers from giving anything to inmates. They informed me that I was now banned from volunteering.

Full of American pragmatism, I thought if I explained that I'd forgotten the policy, and that I was thinking of myself as a friend rather than a volunteer when I gave the gift (I hadn't been volunteering for months), I'd be reinstated right away or, if necessary, after a grace period. Maybe I'd even get an apology. My letters of explanation scaled the chain of command and eventually reached the warden, who responded—addressing me "Ms. Samuelson"—that I was indefinitely suspended from volunteering. If I still wanted to volunteer after Simon was no longer incarcerated, they would reconsider my case at that time. Recall that Simon, who's in his late fifties, is serving a life sentence without parole. My subsequent requests have been met with silence.

In his poem "The Shield of Achilles" W. H. Auden reimagines what Hephaestus carves on the great warrior's armor. Rather than the orderly microcosm of civilization we find in Homer's *Iliad*, the modern poet's god chisels a depiction of a behaviorist society, in which we've lost the ability to see the preciousness and generosity of human life. The Crucifixion is no longer recognized as the murder of God's child and the last-second salvation of two thieves but simply as three anonymous figures being executed while "ordinary decent folk" go about their business. In imagining the mindset of an urchin in this nightmare society, Auden says

> That girls are raped, that two boys knife a third,
> Were axioms to him, who'd never heard
> Of any world where promises were kept,
> Or one could weep because another wept.[1]

Simon speaks often of "the noble struggle," by which he basically means the attempt to maintain dignity and humanity under difficult conditions. More precisely, the noble struggle involves refusing Auden's vision of a society where unjust suffering is ignored by the lucky and is axiomatic to the unlucky, where compassion and generosity vanish for everyone, where we become statistics in a multitude, where Simon is subsumed into Offender #0803380. Michel Foucault horrifyingly asks, "Is it surprising that prisons resemble factories, schools, barracks, hospitals, which all resemble prisons?"[2]

The prison officials were enforcing rules they understand better than I do. I'm grateful for the hard, necessary job they do. I'm also grateful that they granted my requests to unfreeze the money. But I felt that my generosity, in the machine of their bureaucracy, had become invisible. Simon must have been grifting. I must have been scammed by him, or maybe "Ms. Samuelson" was trying to scam them. In their vigilance to prevent abuses of power, they'd negated a small but potent space of goodness. The many classes I'd freely taught over several years, with their immense value for me and the guys, were now over. Because of an action I was foolish enough to have been proud of, my privileges have been revoked. I'm now locked out of prison, without parole.

ACKNOWLEDGMENTS

All one has cared about has been a few women, and they have
worried one more than falling empires.

HENRY ADAMS

In the middle of an insomniac's night, there's one minute of truth that begins at 2:59 a.m. Prior to that is an excruciating interval of self-doubt, in which past decisions torture the tosser and turner. A spell of self-hate commences promptly at 3:00 a.m., which can inspire suicidal thoughts in even a well-adjusted, employed insomniac. However, for the sixty seconds between 2:59 and 3:00 the shambles of existence are unveiled. One night, a few years back, when my alarm clock began blinking 3:00, I decided to get out of bed and write down my vision rather than transition immediately into self-loathing. By the time my kids came down for eggs and toast, I'd composed much of this book's introduction and a chunk of my interlude on the problem of evil.

Along with my insomnia, let me thank my divorce. One main theme of this book is that modernity is fundamentally good but poses huge problems. Well, divorce is practically synonymous with modernity. The foundation of the modern world involves breaking up with the past—for instance, Martin Luther's protest or Galileo's astronomy. Indeed, one of the most important moments of modernity involves a string of literal divorces, those of Henry VIII; and one of modernity's earliest and noblest defenders of freedom, John Milton, writes four pamphlets arguing on behalf of no-fault divorce. The English republican declares, "In God's intention a meet and happy conversation is the chiefest and noblest end of marriage."[1] I'm grateful for the hard-won liberty to pursue a meet and happy conversation beyond the vows we make in our youth. But it must be admitted that to break a vow, especially a sacred vow, is an awful thing. Even if a divorce ultimately reduces suffering in the long run and enhances the pursuit of happier conversations, it does so only by scarring everyone involved, including the children. As "Protestant" as I am on the issue, I pray that there will always be solid "Catholic" opposition to divorce: that side of the equation needs eloquent defense as we hurtle into an increasingly irreverent society.

Another main theme of this book is that we should have a double mind about suffering, seeing it simultaneously as a good and a bad thing. One of the many challenging things about a divorce, or a breakup of any kind, is the human tendency to see things in one way only: exclusively terrible or predominately good. It's hard to understand things as both. It's hard to remember that a relationship can be bad enough to justify divorce and yet still be worthy of our utmost gratitude. As I was writing my chapter on Nietzsche, the challenge of the eternal return haunted me. The answer I give is yes, I would do it all over again. I wouldn't have my kids otherwise. I wouldn't have been shaped by the same, often lovely, memories otherwise. But that doesn't mean I'm not sorry. I've come to see that the inability to talk openly of suffering was at the root of my marriage's breakdown. Forgiveness is necessary all round. I'm in especial need of it.

Let me also give thanks for my time in prison. I'm not sure that this book would have found its inner orientation if Mike Cervantes hadn't invited me to run seminars at the Iowa Medical and Classification Center. I realized in prison that the pathologies of private minds are tied to the pathologies of public matters, and vice versa. I remembered that philosophy isn't simply an enjoyable pastime but a way for us to wake up and get our act together. The classical response to the theological problem of evil, going back at least as far as Augustine, is that human freedom, a great blessing, is the ultimate source of evil, and thus God is not to blame for suffering. It was in prison that I came to understand freedom in ways more vivid than any legal definition or medieval abstraction. My thanks to Mike Cervantes and the guys at the Iowa Medical and Classification Center who participated in our philosophy seminars. In my correspondence with my friend Simon Tunstall (a.k.a. Nefer Em Ra), who's unfairly serving a life sentence, I've begun to fathom what he calls "the noble struggle," the hard-fought attempt to win freedom behind the mental and physical walls that cut through our lives. I'm so grateful for this lesson from Simon, even as I wish that the occasion for his ability to teach it to me had never arisen. He often reminds me to utilize and enjoy my liberties. I'm trying, my friend.

Certain contributions to this book are miraculously free of ambivalence and have a luminosity in no need of darkness for contrast. I don't know what I'd be doing without my friend Scott Newstok. As soon as he found out I was writing a new book, he was on the job. Beside my desk, under my desk, and all over my shelves are piles of books, hundreds, that's he's sent me through the magic of Amazon Prime. My email has a folder of over a thousand forwarded articles from him; sometimes I was getting five or six a day. Many of these books and essays on suffering, I'm embarrassed to admit, have gone unread. But I've looked at a few (I live by the rule that primary sources should be the primary source of one's attention, and secondary sources should be the secondary source), and they've enhanced my thinking and writing. Also, Scott invited me to give a talk at Rhodes College in which I first worked out the big ideas of this book for public consumption. Scott's enthusiasm and conversations are like regular gusts of wind: they keep me from burning out.

I thank Emiliano Battista, whose conversations always elevate my thinking and, when they're not over the Skype, do so over lovingly grilled pork and the finest wine we can afford. He read this book in manuscript with the kind of care given by great critics to great texts. I thank Michael Judge, whose "Wino Wednesday" sessions with me about love, suicide, jazz, and Japan are fundamental to who I am. I thank Rick Zollo for giving his learned, improvisational, blues-soaked mind to my chapter on Sidney Bechet. I thank John Rapson, the splendid composer and musician, whose soft-spoken insights into jazz, punctuated with teacherly demonstrations at the piano, encouraged me to write about music. I thank Jerry Partridge for his generosity in talking to me about restorative justice. I thank my oenological-ontological Friday-evening Bread Garden crew—David Depew (now, alas, clinking his glass in absentia from Bend, Oregon), David Hingstman, Bob Sessions, Rob Ketterer, and Jim Throgmorton—for our unfailingly illuminating chats that were the true first draft of this book. I thank Sarah Kyle, who listened to my grief, talked to me of hers, and then fell in love with me, as I with her, in the Mithraeum buried deep below the Church of San Clemente in Rome. She likes to remind me that the great paradox of being alive can also be approached through joy.

An editor is often an agent of pointless suffering. How extremely lucky I am to have Elizabeth Branch Dyson as mine! She keeps my goals in mind and inflicts pain only when she knows it's for the greatest good of my manuscript. In the margins she writes comments like "Rewrite this passage imagining that you are suffering from the malady." An agent of unalloyed good, she makes me know myself better.

I also want to thank the primary shapers of my sensibility: my parents, my sisters, my grandparents, and my children. They've cultivated the private world out of which my public persona blossoms. It's a testament to my family that I'm able to write a book about suffering and emerge with gratitude for existing.

Thanks to Kirkwood Community College, for giving me release from two classes (friends at more prestigious institutions, take note: that semester I had to teach only three classes rather than my usual five). A big thanks also to Kim Hiett Jordan and the Dallas Institute of Humanities and Culture for awarding me the Hiett Prize in the Humanities, that most ingenious gift to people at the beginning of the careers (when they need the money and honor) rather than at the end (when they usually don't). Without their generosity and encouragement, I don't know if I could have finished this book.

Finally, let me give thanks to the great music of America. When I was sixteen, I was disdainful of my generation's music. The tunes on the 1980s radio stations struck me, in a Holden Caufieldish way, as the quintessence of a phony culture, either a homogenized celebration of crass materialism or a twangy nostalgia for values that never existed. I was determined to find better. In the pretentious, adventurous way of an overly judgmental teen, I checked out from the library Igor Stravinsky and Pierre Boulez, the Band and the Velvet Underground, Thelonious Monk and Eric Dolphy. I still have a taste for all that jazz—well, most of it.

In that wondrous pile of albums was *Louis Armstrong and His All Stars: Live at Wintergarden, New York and Blue Note, Chicago*—probably a grandpa-ish sort of record, I reckoned, but I'd read that he was influential. The other records I liked in an almost theoretical way, where one must grow from appreciation into passion. *Live at Wintergarden* I loved immediately and wholeheartedly, and have ever since. One moment on the album particularly floored me. Armstrong sings a song he wrote called "Someday You'll Be Sorry," a ballad about how his lover will eventually regret how she's treating him. As the forlorn song eases into its final bar, Armstrong lets loose a great, life-affirming chuckle. I was wonderstruck. How can something be so sad and so happy? What is this big-souled sensibility that can sympathetically embody grief and yet still laugh at itself with abandon? Here, I felt, is the ability to be present to the great contradiction that is human life. Here at last is something real—something big-hearted and broadminded, something not hung up on rebellion but on finding the hum of one's own voice, something that doesn't abase others but solicits the expression of their own voices. Several years later, when I first read Plato's *Symposium*, in which Socrates argues that the true poet should be able to compose both tragedy and comedy, I immediately thought of Pops's booming "huzzah!" The next album in the pile was *The Quintessential Billie Holiday, Volume Four*, which features her collaborations with Lester Young, not that his name meant anything to me at the time. Stand back! This stuff isn't just for grandpa!

In my chapter on Sidney Bechet I've tried to pay homage to an art form that has plugged me into the fullness of being alive and has shown me that such aliveness is possible in the wide-open craziness of America. In acknowledging the shapers of this book, I tip my hat to jazz. And to the music that sent me to it hungry.

NOTES

INTRODUCTION

1. Robert Burton, *The Anatomy of Melancholy* (New York: New York Review Books Classics, 2001), 278–79.

2. Arthur Schopenhauer, *Suffering, Suicide, and Immortality*, trans. T. Bailey Saunders (Mineola: Dover, 2006), 2.

3. Charles Darwin, *Evolution: Selected Letters of Charles Darwin, 1860–1870*, ed. Frederick Burkhardt, Samantha Evans, and Alison M. Pearn (Cambridge: Cambridge University Press, 2008), 11.

4. Richard Dawkins, *River out of Eden: A Darwinian View of Life* (New York: Basic Books, 1995), 131.

5. C. S. Lewis, *The Problem of Pain* (New York: HarperCollins, 1996), 135.

6. Blaise Pascal, *Pensées*, trans. A. J. Krailsheimer (New York: Penguin, 1995), 37.

7. *Mahabharata*, vol. 2, ed. and trans. J. A. B. van Buitenen (Chicago: University of Chicago Press, 1975), 803.

8. "Louis C.K. Hates Cell Phones," https://www.youtube.com/watch?v=5HbYScltf1c, published September 20, 2013; quotations lightly edited to remove repetition and interjections.

9. Pascal, *Pensées*, 13.

10. Hannah Arendt, *Between Past and Future* (New York: Penguin, 2006), 58.

11. Deuteronomy 15:11.

12. Michel de Montaigne, "Of Physiognomy," in *The Complete Essays of Mi-*

chel de Montaigne, trans. Donald M. Frame (Stanford: Stanford University Press, 1957), 796.

13. James Baldwin, *Collected Essays* (New York: Library of America, 1998), 311. The quotation is from "Down at the Cross" in *The Fire Next Time*.

14. "If an Emerson were forced to be a Wesley, or a Moody forced to be a Whitman, the total human consciousness of the divine would suffer. The divine can mean no single quality, it must mean a group of qualities, by being champions of which in alternation, different men may all find worthy missions. Each attitude being a syllable in human nature's total message, it takes the whole of us to spell the meaning out completely." William James, *Writings: 1902–1910* (New York: Library of America, 1987), 437.

PART I

1. The translation is by W. B. Yeats, "Oedipus at Colonus," in *The Collected Plays of W. B. Yeats* (New York: Macmillan, 1952), 353.

2. Thomas Nagel, "A Philosopher Defends Religion," *New York Review of Books*, November 8, 2012.

3. Galen Strawson, "What Can Be Proved about God?" *New York Review of Books*, December 6, 2012.

4. Martin Luther King Jr., "Suffering and Faith," *Christian Century* 77 (April 27, 1960), 510. The remarks may be found online at http://king encyclopedia.stanford.edu/encyclopedia/documentsentry/suffering _and_faith.1.html.

5. Charles Taylor, *A Secular Age* (Cambridge: Harvard University Press, 2007), 25.

6. Thomas Merton, *Seeking Paradise: The Spirit of the Shaker* (New York: Orbis Books, 2003), 85.

7. "I suspect music is auditory cheesecake, an exquisite confection crafted to tickle the sensitive spots of . . . our mental faculties." Steven Pinker, *How the Mind Works* (New York: Norton, 1997), 534.

8. Susan Neiman, *Evil in Modern Thought: An Alternative History of Philosophy* (Princeton: Princeton University Press, 2002), 23.

9. Alexis de Tocqueville, *The Old Regime and the Revolution*, trans. John Bonner (New York: Harper & Brothers, 1856), 214.

10. Friedrich Nietzsche, *On the Genealogy of Morals/Ecce Homo*, trans. Walter Kaufmann (New York: Vintage, 1969), 68; essay 2, section 7. For my Nietzsche citations I give the page number of the translation, then after the semicolon a more universal citation.

11. Peter Singer, *Practical Ethics* (Cambridge: Cambridge University Press, 2011), 163.

12. Friedrich Nietzsche, *The Gay Science*, trans. Walter Kaufmann (New York: Vintage, 1974), 129; section 73.

13. Michel de Montaigne, "Of Cripples," in *The Complete Essays of Michel de Montaigne*, 958.

CHAPTER 1

1. William Carlos Williams, "To Elsie," in *Selected Poems* (New York: New Directions, 1976), 53.

2. Isaiah Berlin, "John Stuart Mill and the Ends of Life," in *Liberty*, ed. Henry Hardy (Oxford: Oxford University Press, 2013), 220.

3. John Stuart Mill, *Autobiography* (New York: Penguin, 1989), 112.

4. Ibid., 117.

5. Mill, *Autobiography*, 50–51.

6. Ibid., 67.

7. John Stuart Mill, "Nature," in *Collected Works of John Stuart Mill: Essays on Ethics, Religion and Society* (Indianapolis: Liberty Fund, 2006), 374.

8. Ibid., 385.

9. John Stuart Mill, *Basic Writings of John Stuart Mill* (New York: Modern Library, 2002), 11.

10. Ibid., 18.

11. Ibid., 27.

12. The quotation comes from Bentham's *The Rationale of Reward*. The statement is popularized by J. S. Mill in *Utilitarianism*. See Ross Harrison, *Bentham* (London: Routledge, 1983), 5.

13. Mill, *Basic Writings*, 241.

14. Michael Sandel, *Justice: What's the Right Thing to Do?* (New York: Farrar, Straus & Giroux, 2009), 56.

15. William Shakespeare, *Hamlet*, act 2, scene 2.

16. Jeremy Bentham, "The Utilitarian Theory of Punishment," in *An Introduction to Principles of Morals and Legislation* (London: Athlone, 1970), 158.

17. Isaiah Berlin, *Liberty*, 222

18. Mill, *Basic Writings*, 247.

19. Ibid., 248.

20. Mill, *Autobiography*, 184.

21. Ibid., 147.

22. Ibid., 187–88.

CHAPTER 2

1. Nietzsche, *On the Genealogy of Morals/Ecce Homo*, 16–17; *Genealogy*, "Preface," section 3.

2. Bertrand Russell, *History of Western Philosophy* (New York: Simon & Schuster, 1967), 767.

3. Friedrich Nietzsche, *The Gay Science*, trans. Walter Kaufmann (New York: Vintage, 1974), 255; section 325.

4. Ibid., 211; section 225.

5. Nietzsche, *On the Genealogy of Morals/Ecce Homo*, 326; *Ecce Homo*, "Why I Am a Destiny," section 1.

6. Friedrich Nietzsche, *Human, All-Too-Human: A Book for Free Spirits*, trans. R. J. Hollingdale (Cambridge: Cambridge University Press, 1986), 66; section 113.

7. Nietzsche, *The Gay Science*, 181; section 125.

8. Friedrich Nietzsche, *Thus Spoke Zarathustra: A Book for None and All*, trans. Walter Kaufmann (New York: Viking, 1966), 18; "Zarathustra's Prologue," section 5.

9. Friedrich Nietzsche, *Beyond Good and Evil: Prelude to a Philosophy of the Future*, trans. Walter Kaufmann (New York: Vintage, 1989), 153–54; section 225.

10. Nietzsche, *Thus Spoke Zarathustra*, 17; "Prologue," section 5.

11. Nietzsche, *On the Genealogy of Morals*, 17; "Preface," section 3.

12. Ibid., 85; essay 2, section 16.

13. Nietzsche, *The Gay Science*, 216; section 250.

14. Ibid., 185; section 129.

15. Nietzsche, *On the Genealogy of Morals*, 65; essay 2, section 6.

16. Ibid., 67; essay 2, section 7.

17. Ibid., 81; essay 2, section 14.

18. Friedrich Nietzsche, *The Will to Power*, trans. Walter Kaufmann and R. J. Hollingdale (New York: Vintage, 1968), 403–4; section 769.

19. Friedrich Nietzsche, *Daybreak: Thoughts on the Prejudices of Morality*, ed. Maudemarie Clark and Brian Leiter (Cambridge: Cambridge University Press, 1997), 224; section 556.

20. Nietzsche, *Thus Spoke Zarathustra*, 99; Second Part, "On the Tarantulas."

21. Nietzsche, *Daybreak*, 121; section 202.

22. "For just as the popular mind separates the lightning from its flash and takes the latter for an *action*, for the operation of a subject called lightning, so popular morality also separates strength from expressions of strength, as if there were a substratum behind the strong man, which was *free* to express strength or not to do so." Nietzsche, *On the Genealogy of Morals*, 45; essay 1, section 13.

23. Rüdiger Safranski, *Nietzsche: A Philosophical Biography*, trans. Shelley Frisch (New York: Norton, 2002), 233.

24. Nietzsche, *On the Genealogy of Morals/Ecce Homo*, 309; *Ecce Homo*, "Thus Spoke Zarathustra," section 3.

25. Nietzsche, *The Gay Science*, 272; section 341.

26. Gottfried Wilhelm Leibniz, *Theodicy*, trans. E. M. Huggard (LaSalle, IL: Open Court, 1985), 130.

27. Nietzsche, *The Gay Science*, 113; section 48.

28. Nietzsche, *Twilight of the Idols*, 87; "Expeditions of an Untimely Man," section 17.

29. Nietzsche, *The Will to Power*, 532–33; section 1032.

30. Nietzsche, *On the Genealogy of Morals/Ecce Homo*, 222; *Ecce Homo*, section 1.

31. Nietzsche, *Twilight of the Idols*, 33; "Maxims and Arrows."

32. "The secret for harvesting from existence the greatest fruitfulness and the greatest enjoyment is—to live dangerously. Build your cities on the

slopes of Vesuvius! Send your ships into uncharted seas! Live at war with your peers and yourselves!" Nietzsche, *The Gay Science*, 228; section 283.

33. Nietzsche, *Twilight of the Idols*, 36; "Maxims and Arrows," section 33.

34. Nietzsche, *The Gay Science*, 268–69; section 337.

35. Giorgio Agamben, *Remnants of Auschwitz: The Witness and the Archive*, trans. Daniel Heller-Roazen (Brooklyn: Zone Books, 1999), 99.

36. Nietzsche, *The Gay Science*, 220; section 271.

37. Friedrich Nietzsche, *Twilight of the Idols/The Anti-Christ*, trans. R. J. Hollingdale (New York: Penguin, 1990), 128; *The Anti-Christ*, section 7.

38. "The overcoming of pity I count among the noble virtues: as 'Zarathustra's temptation' I invented a situation in which a great cry of distress reaches him, as pity tries to attack him like a final sin that would entice him away from himself." Nietzsche, *On the Genealogy of Morals/ Ecce Homo*, 228; *Ecce Homo*, section 4. Cf. *Thus Spoke Zarathustra*, part 4, "The Cry of Distress."

39. James, *Writings: 1902–1910*, 149–50.

CHAPTER 3

1. Quoted in Hannah Arendt, *Between Past and Future* (New York: Penguin, 2006), 7.

2. Ibid., 58.

3. John Stuart Mill, "Nature," in *Collected Works of John Stuart Mill: Essays on Ethics, Religion and Society* (Indianapolis: Liberty Fund, 2006, 386.

4. Hannah Arendt, *The Last Interview and Other Conversations* (Brooklyn: Melville House, 2013), 34–35.

5. Hannah Arendt, *The Origins of Totalitarianism* (Orlando: Harcourt, 1976), vii.

6. Arendt, *The Last Interview*, 21.

7. Ibid., 15.

8. Ibid., 23.

9. Hannah Arendt, *Essays in Understanding: 1930–1954* (New York: Schocken, 1994), 198.

10. Arendt, *The Origins of Totalitarianism*, 459.

11. Hannah Arendt, *The Portable Hannah Arendt*, ed. Peter Baehr (New York: Penguin, 2000), 396.

12. Hannah Arendt, *The Human Condition* (Chicago: University of Chicago Press, 1958), 247.

13. Ibid., 322.

14. Hannah Arendt, *Eichmann in Jerusalem: A Report on the Banality of Evil* (New York: Penguin, 2006) 152.

15. Richard Wolin, "The Banality of Evil: The Demise of a Legend," *Jewish Review of Books*, Fall 2014. An online version is at https://jewish reviewofbooks.com/articles/1106/the-banality-of-evil-the-demise-of-a -legend/?print.

16. Quoted in Telford Taylor, *Anatomy of the Nuremberg Trials: A Personal Memoir* (New York: Knopf, 1992), 363.

17. *Eichmann in Jerusalem*, 279.

18. Matthew Crawford, *Shop Class as Soulcraft: An Inquiry into the Value of Work* (New York: Penguin, 2009), 134.

19. Ibid., 67.

20. Arendt, *The Human Condition*, 133.

21. Hannah Arendt, *On Violence* (Orlando: Harcourt, 1970), 56.

22. Philip Larkin, "Aubade," in *Collected Poems* (London: Noonday Press, 1989), 209.

23. Arendt, *On Violence*, 76.

24. Ibid., 81.

25. Ibid., 80.

26. Milan Kundera, *The Curtain: An Essay in Seven Parts*, trans. Linda Asher (New York: Harper Perennial, 2006), 136

27. Quoted in Elisabeth Young-Bruehl, *Hannah Arendt: For Love of the World* (New Haven: Yale University Press, 1982), 57.

28. John Berger, "Fellow Prisoners," *Guernica*, July 15, 2011, https://www .guernicamag.com/john_berger_7_15_11/

29. Arendt, *The Portable Hannah Arendt*, 26.

30. Hannah Arendt, *Men in Dark Times* (San Diego: Harcourt Brace Jovanovich, 1968), ix.

31. Zbigniew Herbert, "Report from a Besieged City," in *The Collected Poems: 1956-1998*, trans. Alissa Valles (New York: Ecco, 2007), 417.

INTERLUDE ON THE PROBLEM OF EVIL

1. Powerful arguments about how immortality would render human life meaningless have been made by philosophers like Bernard Williams in "The Makropulos Case," Hans Jonas in *Morality and Mortality*, and recently Samuel Scheffler in *Death and the Afterlife*.
2. David Hume, *Dialogues concerning Natural Religion* (Indianapolis: Hackett, 1998), 37.
3. Matthew 5:45.
4. Immanuel Kant, *Critique of Pure Reason*, trans. Norman Kemp Smith (New York: St. Martin's Press, 1929), 7.
5. Michael Wolff, "A Life Worth Ending," *New York Magazine*, May 20, 2012.
6. Immanuel Kant, *Lectures on Philosophical Theology*, trans. A. W. Ward and G. M. Clark (Ithaca: Cornell University Press, 1978), 2.2.
7. Gabriel Marcel, *The Philosophy of Existence*, trans. Manya Harari (London: Harvill Press, 1948), 8.

PART II

1. Pliny the Elder, *Natural History: A Selection*, trans. John F. Healey (New York: Penguin, 1991), 347.
2. Virgil, *Aeneid*, book 2, lines 109 et seq. My translation.
3. Confucius, *The Analects of Confucius: A Philosophical Translation*, trans. Roger T. Ames and Henry Rosemont Jr. (New York: Ballantine, 1998), 78; 2.11. After the semicolon I give the standard citation of book and section number.
4. W. H. Auden, *The Complete Works of W. H. Auden: Prose: Volume VI* (Princeton: Princeton University Press, 2015), 579.
5. Zbigniew Herbert, *The Collected Prose: 1948–1998*, ed. Alissa Valles (New York: Ecco Press, 2010), 13.
6. Ibid., 649.

CHAPTER 4

1. Job 38:28–31.
2. Job 14:7–10.
3. Harold Cushner, *The Book of Job: When Bad Things Happened to a Good Person* (New York: Schocken, 2012), 36.
4. Sigmund Freud, *The Basic Writings of Sigmund Freud*, trans. A. A. Brill (New York: Modern Library, 1995), 174.
5. G. K. Chesterton, "The Book of Job," in *In Defense of Sanity* (San Francisco: Ignatius Press, 2011), 100.
6. Ibid., 98.
7. Plato, *The Last Days of Socrates*, trans. Hugh Tredennick (New York: Penguin, 2003), 44–45.
8. Robert Frost, *Collected Poems, Prose, and Plays* (New York: Library of America, 1995), 381, 383.
9. Ibid., 374.
10. Proverbs 12:21.
11. Anthony Griffith, "The Best of Times, the Worst of Times," *The Moth*, recorded February 28, 2003, http://themoth.org/posts/stories/the-best -of-times-the-worst-of-times.
12. Clifford Geertz, *The Interpretation of Cultures* (New York: Basic Books, 1973), 104.
13. *The Book of Job*, translated with an introduction by Stephen Mitchell (New York: Harper Perennial, 1992), 88.
14. Ibid., xxx.
15. Job 2:13.
16. Quoted in Alexander Altmann, *Moses Mendelssohn: A Biographical Study*, (Oxford: Littman Library of Jewish Civilization, 1998), 137.
17. John 20:25–28.

CHAPTER 5

1. Epictetus, *Discourses and Selected Writings*, trans. Robert Dobbin (New York: Penguin, 2008), 42; *Discourses* 1.16.20. After the quotations by Epictetus I give a generic citation. Translation slightly altered.
2. Pierre Hadot, *The Inner Citadel: The "Meditations" of Marcus Aurelius*, 310.

3. Tacitus, *The Annals of Imperial Rome* 6.22.

4. The quotation from Epicurus comes from the Christian theologian Lactantius's *The Wrath of God*. Mark Joseph Larrimore has some doubts that Epicurus is its source. See Mark Joseph Larrimore, ed., *The Problem of Evil: A Reader* (Malden: Blackwell, 2001), xx.

5. Hadot, *The Inner Citadel*, 75.

6. Epictetus, *Discourses and Selected Writings*, 232; *Handbook*, chapter 27.

7. Walt Whitman, "Then Last of All," in *Leaves of Grass: Comprehensive Reader's Edition*, ed. Harold W. Blodgett and Sculley Bradley (New York: New York University Press, 1965), 516

8. Quoted in Luc Ferry, *A Brief History of Thought: A Philosophical Guide to Living*, trans. Theo Cuffe (New York: Harper Perennial, 2010), 36; *Discourses* 3.24.

9. Mark Medina, "Magic Johnson on Larry Bird: 'We're mirrors of each other,'" *Los Angeles Times*, April 12, 2012, http://articles.latimes.com /2012/apr/12/sports/la-sp-ln-la-magic-johnson-on-larry-bird-were -mirrors-of-each-other-20120412.

10. Aleksandr Solzhenitsyn, *The Gulag Archipelago: 1918–1956*, vol. 2 (New York: Harper Perennial Modern Classics, 2007), 617.

11. Katja Maria Vogt, "Taking the Same Things Seriously and Not Seriously: A Stoic Proposal on Value and the Good," *Epictetus: His Continuing Influence and Contemporary Relevance*, ed. Dane R. Gordon and David B. Suits (Rochester: RIT Press, 2014), 55–75.

12. Voltaire, *Candide*, ed. Cynthia Brantley Johnson (New York: Pocket Books, 2005), 45.

13. William James, "On a Certain Blindness," *Writings: 1878–1899* (New York: Library of America, 1992), 854.

14. Epictetus, *Discourses and Selected Writings*, 58.

15. Ferry, *A Brief History of Thought*, 22.

16. Epictetus, *Discourses and Selected Writings*, 152; *Discourses* 3.8.5. Translation slightly altered.

17. Ibid., 19; *Discourses* 1.6.30–32.

18. Quoted in John W. McDonald, *Walt Whitman, Philosopher Poet* (Jefferson, NC: McFarland, 2007), 127.

19. Epictetus, *Discourses and Selected Writings*, 66; *Discourses* 1.28.3–5.

20. Ibid., 162; *Discourses* 3.22.54.

21. Ibid., 37; *Discourses* 1.13.3–4.

22. Robert Warshow, *The Immediate Experience: Movies, Comics, Theatre, and Other Aspects of Popular Culture* (Cambridge: Harvard University Press, 2001), 208.

23. Ibid., 208–9.

24. Epictetus, *Discourses and Selected Writings*, xi.

25. Quoted in McDonald, *Walt Whitman, Philosopher Poet*, 63.

26. Horace Traubel, *With Walt Whitman in Camden*, vol. 3, ed. Gertrude Traubel and William White (Carbondale: Southern Illinois University Press, 1982), 253.

27. Quoted in Alfred Kazin, *God and the American Writer* (New York: Vintage, 1998), 119.

INTERLUDE ON HEAVEN AND HELL

1. Quoted in *Polish Writers on Writing*, ed. Adam Zagajewski (San Antonio: Trinity University Press, 2007), 112.

2. Pindar, "Pythian X," in *Pindar: The Odes*, trans. C. M. Bowra (New York: Penguin, 1969), 22–23.

3. Leszek Kołakowski, *Modernity on Endless Trial* (Chicago: University of Chicago Press, 1990), 81.

4. Robert Frost, "Birches," in *Frost: Collected Poems, Prose, and Plays* (New York: Library of America, 1995), 118.

5. *Paradiso* 12.34–36. My translation.

6. Luke 17:21.

7. Friedrich Nietzsche, *Twilight of the Idols/The Anti-Christ*, trans. R. J. Hollingdale (New York: Penguin, 1990), 77.

8. C. S. Lewis, *Letters to Malcolm: Chiefly on Prayer* (New York: Harcourt Brace Jovanovich, 1964), 107.

9. I'm paraphrasing the dialogue here and in what follows. A fine version of the story can be found in Carole Satyamurti, *Mahabharata: A Modern Retelling* (New York: Norton, 2015).

CHAPTER 6

1. Franklin Perkins, *Heaven and Earth Are Not Humane* (Bloomington: Indiana University Press, 2014), 18–19.

2. Roger T. Ames and Henry Rosemont Jr., *The Analects of Confucius: A Philosophical Translation* (New York: Ballantine, 1999), 123; 8.13. After the semicolon I cite the book and section.

3. Ames and Rosemont, *Analects*, 189; 15.24.

4. Alan Watts, *The Way of Zen* (New York: Vintage, 1985), 29.

5. Herbert Fingarette, "The Music of Humanity in the Conversations of Confucius," *Journal of Chinese Philosophy* 10 (1983): 217.

6. Ames and Rosemont, *Analects*, 109; 6.23.

7. Ibid., 76; 2.3.

8. Ibid., 157; 12.13.

9. Ibid., 51. For help with the Chinese terms I've leaned heavily on Ames and Rosemont's superb introduction to their translation, where they provide a detailed commentary on the Confucian lexicon.

10. Kongzi, "The Analects," trans. Edward Gilman Slingerhand, in *Readings in Chinese Philosophy*, ed. Philip J. Ivanhoe and Bryan W. Van Norden (Indianapolis: Hackett, 2001), 11.

11. Ames and Rosemont, *Analects*, 189; 15.24.

12. Ibid., 158; 12.19.

13. Ibid., 154–55; 12.7

14. Ezra Pound, *Confucius: The Great Digest/The Unwobbling Pivot/The Analects* (New York: New Directions, 1951), 29.

15. Kenneth Burke, *The Philosophy of Literary Form* (Berkeley: University of California Press, 1973), 293.

16. "Zhuangzi," trans. Paul Kjellberg, in Ivanhoe and Van Norden, *Readings in Classical Chinese Philosophy*, 240.

17. Simon Leys, *The Analects of Confucius* (New York: Norton, 1997), xix–xx.

18. Probably Leys is thinking about the essay's opening words: "Confucius' distaste for oratory: the weight of chosen words. He fears their being weakened by glib and easy usage. The hesitation, the reflection, the time before the word is everything, but so is the time after it." Elias Canetti, *The Conscience of Words*, trans. Joachim Neugroschel (New York: Seabury Press, 1979), 171.

19. Ames and Rosemont, *Analects*, 144; 11.12.

20. Max Weber, *The Religion of China: Confucianism and Taoism*, trans. Hans Gerth (New York: Macmillan, 1964), 235-36.

21. Ames and Rosemont, *Analects*, 147; 11.23.

22. Ames and Rosemont, "Introduction," *Analects*, 47.

23. See, for instance, 6.28.

24. See, for instance, 14.36.

25. Ames and Rosemont, *Analects*, 150; 11.26.

CHAPTER 7

1. Sidney Bechet, *Treat It Gentle* (New York: Da Capo, 1978), 4.

2. Ibid, 6.

3. Ibid, 7.

4. Ibid, 19.

5. Ibid, 21.

6. Ibid, 29.

7. Ibid, 41.

8. Philip Larkin, "For Sidney Bechet," in *Collected Poems* (London: Noonday Press, 1989), 83.

9. Quoted in Ted Gioia, *The History of Jazz* (Oxford: Oxford University Press, 2011), 50.

10. Bechet, *Treat It Gentle*, 104.

11. Ibid, 107.

12. Albert Murray, *Stomping the Blues*, 2nd ed. (New York: Da Capo, 2000), 51.

13. André Comte-Sponville, *A Small Treatise on the Great Virtues: The Uses of Philosophy in Everyday Life* (New York: Metropolitan Books, 1996), 112

14. W. E. B. DuBois, *Writings* (New York: Library of America, 1987), 539.

15. Simone Weil, "The Iliad, or the Poem of Force," trans. Mary McCarthy, in Simone Weil and Rachel Bespaloff, *War and the Iliad* (New York: New York Review of Books Press, 2005), 36.

16. Simone Weil, *On Science, Necessity, and the Love of God* (London: Oxford University Press, 1968), 172.

17. Weil, "The Iliad, or the Poem of Force," 37.

18. Bechet, *Treat It Gentle*, 46.

19. Martha Nussbaum, *Political Emotions: Why Love Matters for Justice* (Cambridge: Harvard University Press, 2013), 266.

20. Bechet, *Treat It Gentle*, 201.

21. Homer, *The Odyssey*, trans. Samuel Butler, book 8.

22. Augustine, *The City of God against the Pagans*, trans. R. W. Dyson (Cambridge: Cambridge University Press, 1998), 471–72 (11.18).

23. Leszek Kołakowski, *Modernity on Endless Trial* (Chicago: University of Chicago Press, 1990), 191.

24. Ralph Ellison, *Living with Music*, ed. Robert G. O'Meally (New York: Modern Library, 2001), 128.

25. Brendan Gill says, "Not a shred of evidence exists in favor of the argument that life is serious, though it is often hard and often terrible. And saying that, I'm prompted to add what follows out of it: that since everything ends badly for us, in the inescapable catastrophe of death, it seems obvious that the first rule of life is to have a good time." Quoted in Charles Simic, *The Life of Images: Selected Prose* (New York: Ecco Press, 2015), 264.

CONCLUSION

1. John Berger, *Hold Everything Dear: Dispatches on Survival and Resistance* (New York: Pantheon Books, 2007), 51.

2. Paul Kalanithi, *When Breath Becomes Air* (New York: Random House, 2016), 143.

3. Ibid., 199.

4. Ibid., 143.

5. Elizabeth Hinton, *From the War on Poverty to the War on Crime: The Making of Mass Incarceration in America* (Cambridge: Harvard University Press, 2016), 6.

6. Ibid., 5.

7. Hafiz, *The Gift*, trans. Daniel Ladinsky (New York: Penguin, 1999), 39.

8. Brentin Mock, "Life after 'The New Jim Crow,'" *Citylab*, September 30, 2016, http://www.citylab.com/crime/2016/09/life-after-the-new-jim-crow/502472/.

9. William Wordsworth, *The Prelude*, book 11, lines 143–44.

10. John Keats, *Selected Letters of John Keats*, ed. Grant F. Scott (Cambridge: Harvard University Press, 2002), 290–91.

11. John Hick, *Evil and the God of Love* (New York: Palgrave Macmillan, 2010), 385.

12. Ibid., 334.

13. Ibid., 386.

14. Quoted in Greil Marcus, *The Old, Weird America: The World of Bob Dylan's Basement Tapes* (New York: Picador, 2011), 4.

15. For instance, Seneca in his letter to Polybius says, "Nature requires from us some sorrow. . . . Never will I demand of you that you should not grieve at all."

16. George Herbert, *The Laurel Poetry Series: Herbert*, ed. Dudley Fitts (New York: Dell, 1962), 159.

17. Michel de Montaigne, *Travel Journal*, trans. Donald M. Frame (San Francisco: North Point Press, 1983), 154.

18. Ibid., 130.

19. Ibid., 154.

20. Michel de Montaigne, "Of the Useful and the Honorable," in *The Complete Essays of Michel de Montaigne*, trans. Donald M. Frame (Stanford: Stanford University Press, 1957), 599–600.

POSTLUDE

1. W. H. Auden, "The Shield of Achilles," in *Collected Poems* (New York: Vintage International, 1991), 598.

2. Michel Foucault, *Discipline and Punish*, trans. Alan Sheridan (New York: Vintage, 1995), 228.

ACKNOWLEDGMENTS

1. John Milton, *Complete Poems and Major Prose*, ed. Merrit Y. Hughes (Indianapolis: Hackett, 2003), 462.

INDEX